SIGNAL-7

SIGNAL-7

The Deadly Rampage of Hank Earl Carr

By Sam Nall

SIGNAL-7

Limited Edition
ISBN 0-941072-73-8

CHARYBDIS PUBLISHING
St. Petersburg, Florida

Southern Heritage Press
St. Petersburg, FL
1-800-282-2823

Foreword

On March 26, 2004, I had the privilege of attending a retirement luncheon for a bona fide hero. Not someone who won a Super Bowl or an Oscar, but an officer of the law; a man who devoted nearly thirty years to making the state of Florida a safer place. From inside his unprotected helicopter, the man dodged bullets while in pursuit of a heavily-armed killer who endangered every citizen within sight of the stolen vehicle he was driving over 100 miles an hour.

Although this book is primarily about the deadly rampage of Hank Carr, it is a tribute to all law enforcement officers, specifically those who made the ultimate sacrifice in the line of duty.

This story was emotionally difficult to write. I considered discontinuing the project several times, but I believe strongly that we need constant reminders of the dangers the men and women of law enforcement encounter daily. Along with their families, law officers are fully aware that the badges they proudly wear make them targets, not only for hardened criminals, but also for those who seek scapegoats for societal woes. Yet with their hands often bound by regulations, public opinion, slick attorneys and political correctness, we expect them to selflessly and flawlessly protect and serve at a moment's notice.

The information is presented as accurately as possible, but to facilitate readability and minimize repetition, much of the radio traffic, police reports, court records, videos and interrogations have been edited or omitted. Hostage negotiations alone lasted over four hours; the trial filled four videos and the interrogations consisted of over 100 pages. Events and dialogue are presented in chronological order except where I felt the story developed and read more clearly when presented at the time they were relevant, known to be true and/or revealed in court.

I feel privileged to have written this story solely because of the wonderful people interviewed and befriended in the process. Never have I worked with such caring, dedicated and talented individuals, nor will I likely in the future.

Dedicated to the men and
women in law enforcement.

Acknowledgments

To anyone who contributed to *Signal-7* but was overlooked in the acknowledgments or not mentioned in the story, please forgive me. It was not intentional.

Thanks first to my wife Marie. Without her faith, patience and understanding, there would be no *Signal-7*.

To my editors Harold Britt, Joe and Linda Burda.

To the following for providing information and granting access to their respective agencies and personnel:

Tampa Police Department; Chief Steve Hogue and Joe Durkin
Hernando County SO; Sheriff Richard Nugent and Lt. Joe Paez
Hillsborough County SO; Sheriff Henderson and Lt. Rod Reder
FHP; Captain Greg LaMont and Lieutenant Jackie Freeman
Pinellas County SO; Sheriff Everett Rice and Lt. Tim Ingold
Pasco County SO; Sheriff Bob White and Kevin Doll
Pasco County Fire Rescue; Captain Cindy O'Neal

For providing videos, audio tapes, police records and transcripts, thanks to Joe Durkin, Joe Paez, Deputy Marisabel Kelly, Detective Henry Duran, Lieutenant Scott Bierwiler, Deanna Dammer.

To others who provided information and assistance: Stella Canty, Denise Martinez, Chris Kempton, Scott Matthews, Phyllis Payne, Bob Hite, Curt Allen, Deputy Bert Stockton, Deputy Kim Porter, Lt. Wayne Morris, Lt. Mike Rickie, Terry Oliver, Carlos Garcia, and Tom and Kathy in the research department of the Tampa Tribune.

A heartfelt *thank you* to everyone who shared with me the painful and personal details of that horrific day in May.

Photos courtesy of:

Detectives Henry Duran and Julie Massucci; TPD
Lieutenant Scott Bierwiler; Hernando County SO
Captain George Crotta; Florida Highway Patrol
Gary Kimble; HCSO Crime Scene Supervisor
Tampa Tribune; front, rear and spine
Sergeant Jim Diamond III, Retired

"It is not how these officers
died that made them heroes;
it is how they lived."

Let them never be forgotten

PART I

HERNANDO COUNTY

1

Hernando County Airport
Brooksville, Florida
May 14, 1977; 1730 hours

Lonnie Coburn loved to fly airplanes nearly as much as he loved law enforcement. With illegal drug activity increasing in his hometown of Brooksville, where he and his wife were raising their four-year-old son, Chris, the 25-year-old Hernando County Sheriff's Deputy often talked about the creation of an Aviation Unit to patrol the shoreline and forests from overhead. He and his friends urged the department, specifically Sheriff Melvin Kelly, to purchase a fixed-wing aircraft and a helicopter. Optimistic over future success with the project, the determined deputy drove to St. Petersburg to purchase an instruction manual for helicopter pilots. If the HCSO ever went airborne, he planned to be ready for the job.

"We're a perfect match," Coburn said to his wife Nona. "I know Hernando County as well as anyone. And like the mighty eagle, I was born to fly."

His wife Nona, not unlike most people, had a fear of flying. But being a supportive wife, she went along with the plan. If that's what Lonnie wanted, so be it. Never mind the fact that she already worried about him whenever he left home wearing his badge and uniform. Add to that the intrinsic risks involved with flying and the possibility of ambush from the ground. The harsh realities, she concluded, of being married to a law enforcement officer.

"We could certainly use an airplane," Sheriff Kelly agreed. "No doubt about that. The problem is financial. An Aviation Unit would cost a chunk of money, and as you know, taxpayers are reluctant to let go of it. They want topnotch protection, but balk when confronted with a price tag."

"And when I talk Mike into joining the department," Lonnie told his wife, "we can fly together. With Mike, me and Jerry in the sky, the drug pushers won't have a chance."

His cousin, 22-year-old Mike Coburn, also loved to fly. But at that point in his life, Mike was content working for Sims Furniture Outlet rather than strap on a weapon and patrol the streets at night. The Coburn's grandfather had moved to the area over forty years earlier, in 1933, so Lonnie and Mike were both born and raised in Brooksville and were constant companions since childhood. With Lonnie being three years older, he bought Mike his first bottle of beer—his *Right of Passage* into adulthood, so to speak.

The cousins frequently played golf and softball together, and nearly every Thursday evening they met up with their friends Alan and Sammy for beer, burgers and low-stakes poker, affectionately referring to themselves as the *Rat Pack.*

"I always kept my winnings inside a cigar box," Mike recalled. "Lonnie's goal was to empty my box, but he never could get the job done." After a pause, Mike said, "Well, except one night when he talked us into playing Acey Deucy. That was his game. I was up 300 bucks, but ended the night owing him thirty."

Mike got even with his cousin on the golf course. Although Lonnie was a better golfer, Mike used psychological means to take advantage of Lonnie's competitive nature. He patiently waited for Lonnie to make an errant shot, then with some subtle comments and playful razzing, he tormented Lonnie until the competitive pressure got the best of him.

"His ball landed in three inches of water," Mike said. "He wanted to take a drop, but I convinced him he was strong enough to chip it out, so he went for it. All he got was a shower, and he got so upset that his club ended up in a tree. I beat him that day."

Lonnie occasional took Mike along on patrol and often pleaded with him to apply with the HCSO for a deputy position.

"I will," Mike promised. "After I sow my wild oats."

In 1976, the Coburn boys were issued their fixed-wing licenses. Then in 1977, they pooled their resources and bought a tandem-seat, single-engine Bellanca Champ.

"Lonnie just had to have that Champ," Mike Coburn said. "He loved the sound of the 65-horsepower engine. To me, it sounded like a John Deere tractor."

Mike and Lonnie Coburn competed in the air as well. When they took the Champ out for a workout, they invented games to challenge each other. He tried to keep it secret from Nona; she worried enough as it was.

"One test," Mike explained, "was to see who could fly farthest with only one wheel touching the runway. Another, we would see who could land and bring it to a stop in the shortest distance."

In their touchdown-and-quick-stop competition, Lonnie declared victory, accomplishing the feat in under thirty yards.

They never thought of themselves as daredevils or risk-takers, but simply as adventurous men with confidence in their abilities. Now, if only the department could finance an airplane.

Lonnie began studying for his commercial pilot's license. He planned to take the test in February of '78, then to get his rating in a helicopter. "He was a good pilot," Nona admitted. "After some arm twisting, I would fly with him, but it wasn't often. And I never would allow Chris to go along."

On the job, Deputy Coburn and Deputy Jerry Jennings were the Brooksville version of Starsky and Hutch. Jennings had a fixed-wing license as well, and he went along with Lonnie to Destin, Florida to pick up the Champ and help him fly it back to Brooksville.

The two friends often settled their arguments on the golf course, with the loser assigned to chef duties at the next cookout. "Lonnie usually kicked my rear end at golf," Jennings confessed. "But on the grill, I was king."

Brooksville was still a sleepy little community in 1977. The HCSO consisted of a couple dozen men and no chain of command, with everyone answering directly to the Sheriff. Most of the officers grew up in the area; they were Southern boys, family men, proud of their heritage and proud of their profession.

In addition to Lonnie Coburn, several other officers at the HCSO flew fixed-wing aircraft, including Thomas Mylander and Deputy Tom Nowlin.

Deputy Mylander had joined the Pinellas County Sheriff's Office in 1970. He and Lieutenant George McNally created an Aviation Unit and flew the Bell G5A Helicopter. But Mylander and his wife Sandy tired of all those big city traffic jams, and in October of 1977, the former Marine moved his family to Hernando County and joined the Sheriff's Office as a detective. Along with Tom Nowlin and Lonnie Coburn, the young pilots constantly badgered Sheriff Kelly to create the Aviation Unit, but he always had the same answer: "We don't have the funding."

Not at that time, anyway.

*

Earlier that year, on the afternoon of May 14, Lonnie Coburn drove home in his patrol car. He, Nona and Chris lived in a mobile home near the east end of the Hernando County Airport, about six miles southwest of Brooksville. In exchange for free rent, Lonnie provided airport security whenever he was home or off duty. Nona, who worked as a substitute mail carrier for the US Post Office, prepared an early dinner while Chris helped his father wash the car.

"Over here, son," Lonnie said to Chris, after scrubbing a front door. "Rinse it off for me."

Chris obliged, squirting most of the spray on the door, but also included a playful shot at his father.

When time to dry off the vehicle, impatient Chris had already worked up an appetite, so he went inside the mobile home to see if his mother had dinner ready. While Lonnie wiped down the car, he observed a DC-3 drop down for a landing, from east to west. With Lonnie being a pilot himself, the landing aroused his interest. Not that is was unusual to see a DC-3 arriving on the 7,000-foot runway, but because of the direction it landed. The wind came from east. A brisk wind at that. Under normal procedure, the plane should come in west to east, directly into the headwind.

Lonnie leaned against the patrol car, stroked his thick moustache and watched it taxi all the way to the west end, far from the hangars, into a deserted area with nothing but trees and brush. At first, Lonnie wondered if they had a problem with the aircraft. Then instinct took over, sensing something was amiss.

Three years earlier, in 1974, a heinous crime touched the lives of Lonnie and the Coburn family. Another cousin, a long-haul truck driver, had pulled into a rest stop along the freeway. While in the bathroom, three lowlife thugs slipped into the building after him. One man entered an adjacent stall and stood on the metal toilet. From that position, he fired a round into the unsuspecting man's head.

The cold-blooded trio then stole $300 from his wallet and walked out while the truck driver died in a pool of blood. He left behind a loving wife and four young children.

Lonnie Coburn would never forget that day, nor would he forget the day law enforcement brought the killers to justice. Although a small consolation, the courts promptly convicted.

Lonnie stuck his head inside the mobile home and hollered for his wife. "Honey!"

Nona left the kitchen and stepped into the room. "I'm right here. Are you ready to eat?"

"Not right now. There's something going on west of us. I have to go over and check it out."

"Well, okay. Be careful."

"Hey, I'm always careful."

Again, Nona worried.

Lonnie hopped into the patrol car. He stopped at the hangar first, where he found Charles Chase, the airport manager.

"What's up?" Chase asked him.

"A DC-3 came in from the east."

"From the east? That's strange."

"Yeah, then it disappeared at the end of the runway."

"Oh yeah?"

"Let's check it out."

Chase jumped inside the car with Coburn.

Lonnie gave him a gun and they drove west on the runway, but before reaching the aircraft, they spotted a small U-haul truck tucked in behind the trees.

"You're right," said Chase. "Something ain't right."

Lonnie eased the patrol car in behind the DC-3, squeezed his mic and called for backup. At the Sheriff's Office six miles away, his friend Jerry Jennings heard the call and took off for the airport. When he arrived, Lonnie had already arrested two men who were unloading 80 bales of marijuana into the U-haul truck, but the pilot and co-pilot escaped into the woods.

After ordering the smugglers to unload the remaining marijuana, Deputy John Whitman arrived and hauled them to jail. Charles Chase taxied the DC-3 back to the airport.

The arrest and confiscation of 4,000 pounds of pot didn't satisfy Deputy Coburn that evening. "Two of them shook us," he told Nona when he arrived back home "But if they're still in the county, I'll find the rodents."

"Just be careful," said Nona.

"Hey, I'm always careful."

He went out later that evening and drove the populated area north of the airport. The smugglers weren't likely to stay in the woods overnight, Coburn assumed, so they'd have to surface somewhere and seek transportation back to south Florida where they came from.

When driving past a convenience store, Coburn spotted a stranger standing at a pay phone, so he parked the patrol car and walked past with his eyes searching for anything that might connect the man to the smuggling team. The odor of aviation fuel got his attention first, then he noticed the man's aviator's watch.

"Nice watch," Lonnie said to the man.

"Yeah," he answered nervously. "Thanks." The man turned away.

"Do you fly?" Lonnie asked.

"Huh?"

"Your aviator's watch. I was wondering, do you fly?"

"Uh, yeah, I do."

The smuggler couldn't avoid Lonnie's intense eyes.

"What do you fly?" the deputy asked.

"What? Uh, well—"

He pressed the worried man a little farther. "Have you ever flown a DC-3?"

"Huh? Uh, well—"

The poker player from the Rat Pack bluffed until the man folded. Lonnie arrested him on the spot, and by the following morning, they had all four bad guys in custody.

"We took every one of those bales of marijuana to jail," Deputy Jerry Jennings remembered proudly. "We made 'em unload all of it in the jail cells."

That's where it remained until the trial.

When the court date arrived, the prosecutor and judge allowed the entire 80 bales in the courtroom, delivered and stacked with inmate labor. When the trial ended in late October, the jury found all four men guilty of pot smuggling.

Jennings and Coburn witnessed the destruction of the marijuana at an abandoned mine, where authorities doused it with diesel fuel and lit the torch. The controlled burn left nothing but ashes and a "well done," but the best reward was yet to come.

After the convictions, the confiscated DC-3 became property of the Hernando County Sheriff's Office, and several months later, the valuable aircraft went to auction.

"We sold it for over 40 grand," Deputy Nowlin said. "Enough for the Sheriff to purchase a used helicopter and a fixed-wing airplane."

Thanks to the work of Lonnie Coburn, they made the purchase without tapping the taxpayers.

Sheriff Kelly congratulated Lonnie personally. He also told him the Tampa Police Department was in the process of upgrading their equipment and planned to unload a Hughes 300B helicopter that had been in service since 1970.

"It looks like we're ready for that Aviation Unit," the Sheriff told his small cadre of pilots.

"That's great," Deputy Coburn said. "When?"

"We should have her by summer."

"Great."

"Will you be ready to fly it?"

"You bet I will, Sheriff. You bet I will."

When Nona arrived home from work that evening, Lonnie took her out to dinner and surprised her with the great news.

"Honey," he exclaimed, "We did it. Hernando County is finally goin' airborne."

Nona didn't share the same level of excitement.

The ambitious deputy studied hard and looked forward to testing for a commercial license, which he scheduled for the first day of March 1978.

"He marked the date on his calendar in big letters," said his friend Jerry Jennings. "He wanted it bad."

2

Hernando Sheriff's Substation
Ridge Manor, Florida
February 21, 1978; 1930 hours

When Deputy Nick Mills suffered a heart attack late in his career, the Sheriff moved him from a patrol car to light duty, and on the evening of February 21, he was dispatching from the Sheriff's substation in Ridge Manor on the east side of the County. The small substation was located on U.S. Highway 301 at the intersection of State Road 50, approximately four miles east of Interstate 75. Several miles east of the substation on 301 reached Sumter County and two miles south crossed into Pasco County. Mills, a gregarious man with a gift of gab, knew most of the law enforcement officers from all three counties.

Directly across the street from the substation on U.S. Highway 301, Charlotte Best operated the Stop and Go convenience store and made friends with nearly everyone who stopped in.

Mills' wife prepared dinner for him that evening, and on her way to the substation, she went by the Stop and Go to pick up some soft drinks for herself and Nick.

"When she came out," said Mills, "she noticed two men loitering in a two-tone Plymouth Fury."

What Mrs. Mills didn't know, however, was that only an hour earlier the Sheriff's Office had received a BOLO—Be On the Look Out—for two black men driving a vehicle matching the description of the Plymouth.

On a normal shift, only one deputy patrolled the tiny community of Ridge Manor, with one officer working the substation. "Lonnie had recently injured an ankle on a parachute jump," his friend Tom Mylander recalled. "So he was assigned light duty in Ridge Manor that evening."

Using Unit-16 as his radio ID, Coburn dropped by the substation shortly after receiving the BOLO from Sumter County.

"It's a stolen car and possible kidnapping out of Leesburg," Mills said. "They could be coming this way."

"With the time lapse," answered Lonnie, "they could already be here. It's only forty miles to Leesburg."

The updated BOLO had interrupted their conversation, mostly Lonnie talking about his upcoming examination for a commercial pilot's license on Tuesday, only one week away.

At that point in his career, Lonnie served double duty. In addition to his aviation skills, he excelled in photography, as did fellow deputy and friend, Joe Paez.

"When Sheriff Kelly got wind of it," Paez said, "he issued us a wide-angle Nikon camera, a used Dodge van, and assigned us to photo forensics."

The deputies purchased a metal case with personal funds and kept the camera inside. They alternated photo technician duty, and every Tuesday, the *Football*, as they called it, exchanged hands. Earlier that afternoon, Paez took the football from Lonnie, and when the initial BOLO hit the airways, he was home with his family, with the Crime Scene Investigations (CSI) van parked in the driveway.

The BOLO originated with a worried husband in Leesburg calling police to report that his wife, Karol Lee Hurst, was missing. He said his wife always picked him up from work at 4:00 p.m., always on time, but she never showed up that day, and at seven o'clock that evening, the young woman still hadn't been located.

Mister Hurst's description of the family car: a brown-and-white Plymouth Fury. Description of the woman: twenty-one years old, very pretty and seven months pregnant.

Mrs. Mills entered the substation with dinner and drinks just as Lonnie prepared to leave.

"There are two suspicious looking men hanging around outside the Stop and Go," she said, and handed dinner to her husband.

"What are they doing?" asked Lonnie.

"They were driving around the store like they're casing the place. They parked in back."

"Get a description?" Lonnie asked.

"Well, both of the men are black. The car is a Plymouth, I think. A two-tone Plymouth."

The two officers exchanged a quick glance.

"I'm on it," Lonnie said, and ran out the door.

No sooner had he left when the phone rang at the substation and Mills took the call.

"Hernando County Sheriff, Ridge Manor. Deputy Mills."

"Nick, this is Charlotte across the street. There are a couple guys in the store that have me a little concerned."

"We're on the way, Charlotte."

"Thanks."

"Just keep away from 'em."

About the same time Lonnie drove away, Deputy Tom Nowlin pulled over a speeder near Lake Neff, about six miles southwest of Ridge Manor. He also heard the BOLO.

"As I left my patrol car and walked toward the stopped vehicle," Nowlin said, "I heard the call from Unit-16."

"I may need some backup," Coburn said over the radio. "It's that BOLO out of Leesburg."

"What's your Ten-20?" asked Nowlin.

"I'm at the Stop and Go on 301 and 50."

"Okay, I'm Ten-51."

Ten-51: the Ten-code for *en route*.

The Lake Neff speeder got lucky that evening. Deputy Nowlin leaped inside the 1971 Nova and took off toward State Road 50.

Like many Hernando deputies, Nowlin grew up in Florida. His great-grandfather, a Civil War veteran from Indiana, fought with General Sherman and ended up in Brooksville after the war.

Nowlin began his law enforcement career with the Marine Patrol in Key West. Since the area was awash with narcotics, keeping him constantly active, he loved the assignment. But in 1977, he moved back home to Brooksville and went to work for the Hernando County Sheriff's Office.

"It was tough to leave Key West," Nowlin admitted. "We had very little crime in Brooksville at that time. It was boring duty."

Unfortunately, on a night in February of 1978, Brooksville would be anything but boring.

The two suspicious men—Ulysses Mack Ruffin and Freddie Lee Hall—saw Deputy Coburn pull up in the patrol car. The presence of law enforcement quickly changed whatever they had in mind at that moment. Instead, they bought a stuffed Teddy bear from Charlotte.

Coburn drove behind the store and parked with his headlights on the rear of the Plymouth, illuminating the license plate. He noted the number and radioed the station for information on the vehicle, who owned it and if it had been stolen. As the response came back, he watched Hall and Ruffin return to the Plymouth, acting as if they hadn't seen the Deputy.

Coburn got out with his 12-gauge pump shotgun.

"Stop right there!" he demanded.

The men took a few more steps before turning toward the officer. The larger man said, "Hey, what's up?"

"Put your hands on the back of the car!"

"We ain't done nuttin."

"Put your hands on the car! Now!"

With a witness observing from a distance, the men reluctantly did as the officer said. Lonnie first patted down the larger man but found no weapons. When he patted down the smaller man, with his shotgun aimed in the air, the larger man swung around and grabbed him in a bear hug. The officer struggled to break free, but the muscular man clung tighter than a straight jacket.

When the shotgun discharged harmlessly into a layer of low-hanging clouds, the smaller man reached into Lonnie's cross-draw holster, pulled out the .357 handgun, and shoved it into the deputy's ribcage. Two shots went off in rapid succession.

Lonnie never worked without his bulletproof vest. At that time, however, the two panels only covered the front and back, leaving the sides open and exposed. As the officer slumped helplessly to the ground, the thugs scrambled into the Plymouth, spun around the store and fled south on 301.

Bleeding profusely, Lonnie crawled to the open door of his patrol car and reached for the radio.

"Unit-16, I've been shot," he moaned into the microphone. While desperately gasping for air, he said, "Shooters southbound on 301in the two-tone Plymouth."

Deputy Mills heard the call and sprinted out the door, leaving his wife to handle the radio. Charlotte Best heard the gunshots and saw the Plymouth barrel past the store southbound.

She ran out to help.

Still a few miles away on State Road 50, Deputy Nowlin heard the distress call on his radio. With lights flashing and siren wailing, he floored the Nova all the way from Interstate 75 to 301.

Deputy Mills arrived first and found Coburn on the ground next to the cruiser. He carefully turned the deputy to his side and saw the blood-soaked shirt.

Lonnie was still alive, losing blood fast.

"We'll get the bastards who did this, Lonnie. We'll get 'em."

When Deputy Nowlin arrived, he found Mills on the radio and Charlotte leaning over the fallen officer.

He heard an ambulance approaching from 301.

"I went from officer to friend," Nowlin reflected sadly, his eyes growing moist. "The only thing I could think of was that he was my friend, just lying there, dying."

Nowlin grabbed a blanket from the trunk and ran back to Coburn. Pushing Charlotte aside, he wrapped the blanket around the deputy and offered comfort.

"You'll be okay," he said hopefully. "The ambulance is here."

"I'm going to die," the deputy whispered, trying to get up from the pavement.

"No way, Lonnie. Stay down. The ambulance is here."

The emergency crew promptly took over. They removed his shirt and vest and found the bullets had entered under Lonnie's armpit before traveling to the front of his chest and lodging between the vest and his breastbone.

While preventing further loss of blood, the rescue paramedics rushed him to the emergency room at Lykes Memorial Hospital in downtown Brooksville.

Every officer who heard the next broadcast shuddered.

"We have an officer down! Suspects southbound in a brown-and-white Plymouth Fury. One black male in his thirties, six feet tall, 200 pounds. Second black male slightly taller, heavier, approximately 30 years old. Both men wearing dark jeans. One with a dark shirt, the other a white shirt."

Profoundly affected, Nowlin stumbled around the crime scene, detached from his surroundings. In any other situation, he would have left everything untouched for the investigation team, but when he saw Lonnie's gun belt, empty holster and the Teddy bear, he absently tossed them in the back of his Nova.

For a fleeting moment, he wished he had never left Key West.

Several miles south on Highway 301, Deputy Mike Jane of the Pasco County Sheriff's Office heard the BOLO. He hadn't seen a vehicle matching the description, so he pulled off the road, doused his lights and waited. Within minutes, the Plymouth sped past.

"I'm in pursuit of the vehicle," he said over the radio, after giving dispatch his location.

Jane followed with headlights extinguished. The Fury turned off at State Road 575 near the town of Lacoochee, on the outskirts of the Withlacoochee National Forrest.

Deputy Jane made the same turn.

When the fleeing driver spotted the cruiser, he swerved into an orange grove, abandoned the car and took off running. Deputy Jane continued the pursuit of foot, but realized he was an easy target in the darkness wearing his light-colored uniform. Once again, he radioed his position, and while awaiting backup, he aimed a flashlight into the Plymouth. On the back seat, he saw a handgun, a woman's purse, and a grocery bag from a Pantry Pride in the town of Leesburg.

Jane radioed the pertinent information, and within minutes, the officers concluded that the car belonged to Karol Hurst of Leesburg, the woman kidnapped after leaving the Pantry Pride Supermarket.

But no sign of Karol.

Deputy Nowlin hit the siren and raced toward Lacoochee to assist in the search.

Sheriff Kelly organized a massive search team comprised of over 200 officers, most of them off duty. With bloodhounds taking the lead, they met up with Deputy Jane and sent the dogs into action. The elusive suspects nearly made it to Dade City, but deputies caught up with Hall at a cemetery; Deputy Rick Peters caught Ruffin trying to scale a security fence at a packinghouse.

"They were lucky to come out alive," Deputy Nowlin observed, and quietly wondered if the outcome would have been different had he been the one who found the men who shot his friend. Many of the officers no doubt wondered the same thing.

While in custody, and after intense questioning, the two suspects eventually admitted their crimes and led officers back to the body of Karol Lee Hurst. The heartless killers also confessed to raping the pregnant woman even after she wrote them a 20-thousand-dollar check so they wouldn't harm her baby.

"Instead," Detective Bernie Bishop said, "the dirtbags shot her in the head at zero range and left her to die alone in the woods."

Deputy Wade Hudson left the Sheriff's Office and drove to the mobile home at the Hernando County Airport.

Nona greeted him at the door and knew immediately.

"Lonnie?"

"He's been shot, Nona," Wade told her. "Come on, I'll take you to the hospital."

After dropping Chris at her mother's home, Nona rode with the deputy to Lykes Memorial Hospital, where a doctor met her in the waiting room and informed her that Lonnie had passed away.

While playing pool with his friends, Mike Coburn heard about the shooting. He drove directly to the hospital, where the first person he encountered was Sheriff Kelly's wife.

"Lonnie has died," she tearfully informed him.

"I just went numb," Mike Coburn said.

Enraged, he stepped outside and aimlessly punched his fists into the parking sign. In tears, he promised he would one day become a deputy, just as Lonnie always hoped he would.

"I'll fly that chopper for you, Lonnie," he sobbed. "I'll do it. You'll see. That's a promise."

Deputy Nowlin called dispatch to ask about Lonnie.

"Unit-16 is Signal-7" came the emotional reply.

In police radio jargon, Signal-7 means *dead.*

Deputy Joe Paez got the call at home. "We need the CSI van at the Stop and Go store on 301 and State Road 50."

"What do we have?" Paez asked.

"It's a shooting, Joe. It's Lonnie Coburn."

Paez jumped inside the CSI van and rushed to the Stop and Go store, where he and Detective Tom Mylander solemnly worked the crime scene. As the two men dusted for prints, Mylander received a phone call from the hospital.

"When he came back," Joe Paez said, "I could read his face. He looked at me and I said, 'Lonnie?'"

Mylander nodded. "Yeah. Signal-7."

"We finished up without saying a word."

Once he completed work at the convenience store, Deputy Paez set out for the most difficult assignment of his career: he drove to the County Morgue to take pictures of the deceased officer. He removed Lonnie's clothes, from bottom to top. When eventually focusing on his friend's blood-encrusted HCSO insignia and black, trademark mustache, Paez broke into tears.

The Rat Pack assembled one final time; Mike drove the hearse while Sammy and Alan rode in front along with him. Although only a week away, Lonnie Coburn never had the opportunity to take the test for his commercial license.

"Hall received the death sentence, but he should never have been on the street," Detective Mylander pointed out, shaking his head incredulously. "He had already served time for raping another woman and gouging out her eyes so she couldn't testify... Ruffin received life in prison, whatever that means."

*

Nona Coburn recovered about as well as any young wife and mother could be expected under the circumstances. Raising an active four-year-old son and a promotion to a regular, fulltime letter carrier filled her days. Eventually she remarried, and she often prayed that her son would never become a police officer.

Late in July of 1978, Sheriff Kelly authorized the purchase of a Hughes 300B from the Tampa Police Department and assigned Tom Mylander to head the Aviation Unit. With a promotion to sergeant, Nowlin also joined the unit, and they soon added a turbine-driven helicopter called a NOTAR—no tail-operated rotor—which they picked up from a defunct organization in Arizona.

Nowlin eventually took over the unit, and in 1985, Hernando County elected Tom Mylander as Sheriff.

Under Sergeant Nowlin's direction in 1997, the Sheriff traded the Hughes 300B to the Citrus County Sheriff's Office. In exchange for the 300B and mechanical assistance from the Director of Aircraft Maintenance, Bill Borcherding, the HCSO wound up with an LOH-6 Scout, one that had a patriotic history. Howard Hughes had built the Light Observation Helicopter for surveillance in Viet Nam. Enemy fire brought it down on more than one occasion, but because of its incredible stability and crash survivability, the pilots walked away from the resilient craft unharmed.

Mike Coburn made true his promise to cousin Lonnie. Not only did he eventually join the Sheriff's Department, but he also learned to fly helicopters and became a member of the Aviation Unit with his friend Tom Nowlin. He flew the LOH-6, and in deference to his slain cousin, he named it the *Lonnie-6*.

On that ill-fated night in February 1978, Deputy Jerry Jennings and his wife Elizabeth celebrated an anniversary over dinner in New Port Richey. Upon returning home, they heard the devastating news about Lonnie. Jennings rushed directly to the hospital, but like Mike Coburn, he arrived too late.

"Elizabeth got pregnant shortly after that," Jennings said. "We decided to name him Lonnie Charles if he's a boy. Lonnie Charlene if she's a girl."

In early December, Elizabeth Jennings gave birth to a beautiful daughter named Lonnie Charlene. As a young girl, Lonnie learned the story behind her namesake. As a young adult, she moved to nearby Orlando, and whenever she visited her hometown of Brooksville, she placed flowers on Lonnie Coburn's gravesite.

In a tribute to the slain officer, the Florida Legislature designated a stretch of State Road 50—from Highway 301 to the Sumter County line—as the "Deputy Lonnie Coburn Memorial Highway."

3

Hernando County Sheriff's Office
Brooksville, Florida
May 19, 1998; 1429 hours

From the primary dispatch station at the Hernando County Sheriff's Office Communication Center, Peggy Brooks handled dispatching duty while her husband, Deputy Tom Brooks, worked patrol on night shift. An uneventful day for both up to that point, and Peggy eagerly awaited Sheila Gunter to take over at 1500 hours. In their respective professions, however, boredom can end in a heartbeat. At times, in the *absence* of a heartbeat.

At the station adjacent to Peggy Brooks, Jessica Vore pulled a fax from the teletype, perused it and promptly handed it to Peggy. "It's a BOLO from the Tampa Police Department."

Peggy read the faxed report then keyed the mic and broadcast on Patrol-1, the default radio channel for Hernando County patrol units. The first word from her mouth was *Hernando*—the radio identifier for the Sheriff's Office, the calling party.

"Hernando, all units, a BOLO in reference to two officers being shot in Tampa."

The announcement of a cop shooting demanded attention, and to most of the veteran officers at the HCSO, Deputy Lonnie Coburn always came to mind. And for the younger officers who never knew Deputy Coburn, his photo and memorial hung on a wall next to the reception desk, where they effectively served as a reminder of the dangers inherent in their profession.

"The shooting occurred at Interstate 275 and Floribraska," Peggy Brooks continued. "Two homicide detectives were shot. First suspect is a white male, five-ten, one-seventy-five, shoulder-length blonde hair. Last seen wearing a white shirt and blue shorts. Armed with unknown type of revolver. Suspect has handcuffs on the right wrist. Last seen eastbound on Floribraska in a black Ford Ranger. Delivery truck with initials APD on the side. Florida tags W-whiskey, Z-zulu, M-Mike, 22 Quebec. Time lapse nineteen minutes. Hernando clear, fourteen-30 hours."

The time lapse indicated the Tampa Police Department had issued the lookout nineteen minutes earlier, meaning the shooting occurred prior to 2:10. With a 19-minute time lapse, Tampa officers or FHP may have already apprehended the suspect, but maybe not. He could also be forty miles from the crime scene by this time, and possibly even in Hernando County.

Several minutes later, Peggy came back on the radio with updated information regarding the bulletin, but in that short period of time, she thought about her husband Tom, a six-year veteran and a member of the SWAT team. With Tom being on the night shift, she correctly assumed he was home sleeping. They lived with their soccer-playing son, Gage, in a mobile home on the property of Moton Elementary School near Cortez Boulevard, just a few miles from the Sheriff's Office. Deputy Brooks provided security for the school in exchange for residence in the mobile home.

"Hernando, all units," said Peggy. "Ten-33, copy and update."

Ten-33: the Ten-code for *Emergency Traffic*. The possibility of a life or death situation.

Peggy continued with the update, changing the license number from 22 to 72 and the truck color from black to white. Apparently, the witnesses had given conflicting information back in Hillsborough County or somewhere during the chase.

"Reference to the shooting out of Tampa. Suspect vehicle is going to be a white Ford truck. Florida tag W-Whiskey, Z-Zulu, M-Mike, seven, two, Quebec. Initials APD on the doors. It comes back to a 1997 Ford pickup registered to Pep Boys out of Tampa."

After a moment, she repeated some of the information.

"Suspect is a white male, five-ten, one-seventy-five, shoulder-length hair. Vehicle last seen eastbound from this location, I-275 and Floribraska. Hernando clear, fourteen-38 hours."

Patrol units stationed throughout the county listened intently for each subsequent update.

In the interim, Peggy again thought of her family. She worried about her husband, as all spouses in law enforcement do. Her son Gage would still be in school at that time of day, probably thinking about soccer instead of studies. Tom, a top-notch soccer player in high school, now played on the Bay Area Indoor Soccer League in Tampa. He drove long distance to play the game he loved, and in fact had competed in a league game a day earlier. The Brooks family took their soccer seriously, with Peggy the quintessential Soccer Mom and fundraiser for the teams. And with Peggy being pregnant at the time, a soccer-playing son named Zane was on the way.

Concerned over the growing threat regarding the BOLO out of Tampa, Peggy grabbed a phone and called home. Her husband awoke from a nap. "Hello?"

"Tom, turn on the radio."

"The radio?"

"Yes. Turn it on. Something big is going on. I gotta go."

With respect to his wife's experience and instinct, Deputy Brooks turned on the bedside radio and grabbed his uniform.

From the communication station directly in front of Peggy, Mary Booth took incoming calls on a landline, coordinated input from other law enforcement agencies, and fed information to the dispatchers.

Mary took the next call on a landlinc. "Hello, Hernando County Sheriff's Department."

"Hey, Hernando," the Florida Highway Patrol dispatcher said to Mary, "can you get your chopper up, please?"

"We already have our chopper up."

"Okay, we got our trooper stopped behind that vehicle at 54 and the interstate. The one that shot the two Tampa troopers."

"Oh, my God. Okay. All right, thanks. Bye."

A Florida Trooper had pulled over the shooting suspect in Pasco County, a few miles north of the Hillsborough County line, and over twenty miles from Floribraska and Interstate 275 in Tampa.

The Communication Center supervisor, Steve Porter, relayed all pertinent information to the patrol supervisor for evaluation.

With activity currently at State Road 54 and possibly continuing north, proper procedure for Hernando was to garner resources north of that location. Considering information as received, the supervisor determined his helicopter would best be deployed to State Road 52 if needed for intercept.

He passed instructions back to dispatch.

Peggy then broadcast the update to all units in Hernando County, informing them that the suspect who shot the two law enforcement officers was still on the loose, only now he had fled north. Everyone listening on the Hernando frequency realized it meant the suspect and accompanying dangers were moving toward Hernando County.

Following the supervisor's instructions, Peggy keyed the mic and contacted the helicopter pilot on utility channel. "Hernando, Air-1."

The radio ID *Air-1* referenced the Sheriff's airborne chopper, with the backup helicopter assigned *Air-2*.

When the call came, Sergeant Tom Nowlin was flying reconnaissance west of Brooksville in the LOH-6—the same chopper Deputy Mike Coburn called the Lonnie-6.

Deputy Phil Johnson remained at the hangar on standby with the NOTAR, Air-2; Mike Coburn had worked the night shift and wasn't scheduled back at the hangar until 1700 hours.

Nowlin heard the call and squeezed the broadcast trigger on the LOH-6 cyclic. "Air-1, go ahead."

"We need you to be en route to 52," the dispatcher said.

Nowlin hesitated momentarily. He wondered if Peggy had made a mistake. After all, State Road 52 was below the county line, well into Pasco County.

"Arc you advising State Road 52?" the copter pilot asked, sensing something out of the ordinary.

"At State Road 52 and I-75. Trooper is with the shooting suspect from Tampa at this time."

"Ten-4. I'm Ten-51 from the Boy Scout Reservation."

Mary answered another landline call. "Hello, Hernando County Sheriff's Office."

"Yeah," said Chris, the Highway Patrol dispatcher, "we need your helicopter."

"He's Ten-51." Then Mary verified previous information. "The suspect is at 54, right?"

"Yeah, at 54 and the interstate."

"Okay."

Chris then received a call from a Highway Patrol unit. "I gotta go," he told Mary. "Bye."

Currently flying over western Hernando near the village of Weeki Wachee, Nowlin had at least 25 miles between himself and State Road 52. He banked the LOH-6 to the southeast and headed directly toward the interstate as fast as the chopper could fly, about 110 knots.

Nowlin enjoyed flying the compact little chopper, and although not the fastest bird in the sky, he liked the way it handled.

Business had picked up considerably in the 20 years since Lonnie Coburn died. Hernando County had tripled in population, dragging the crime rate right along with it. Nowlin no longer had any reason to pine about leaving Key West, especially after he met and married his wife Barbara in 1979.

"From that point on," he said, matter-of-factly, "I knew it was the best decision I ever made."

For nearly 20 years, Nowlin enjoyed the family life, with a lovely wife and two children—Laura and Justin—and he earned a fair wage doing what he loved, flying helicopters for law enforcement. When the God-fearing man said, "It can't get any better than this," he meant exactly what he said.

"Four-05, Air-1."

The radio call to Air-1 came from Lieutenant Marc Rivenbark, the patrol supervisor.

"Go ahead, oh-5," Nowlin answered.

"You have the fuel to make it to 52?"

"I have the fuel, but it's gonna take 15 to 20 minutes."

"Ten-4."

The 35-year-old lieutenant spoke in a gruff, Southern drawl, but his subordinates unanimously agreed that Rivenbark was one of the kindest and most intelligent officers they ever met: high praise indeed from fellow officers. The fact that Rivenbark questioned the fuel situation in an airborne helicopter within moments of emergency communication seemed to speak for itself.

Lieutenant Rivenbark began his career with HCSO in 1982 and grabbed regional attention in '93. As a sergeant in CID—Criminal Investigations Division—he led the investigation of a serial killer named Edwin Kaprat III, a handyman who sexually assaulted and murdered five of his elderly clients over a three-month period. He then concealed evidence by torching their homes.

"He always used rubbing alcohol as the accelerant," Rivenbark explained. "Rubbing alcohol is water soluble, and when fire fighters doused the flames, the accelerant was either dispersed or consumed by the fire. Effectively, neither the arson dogs nor the fire technicians could detect any accelerant."

Although the fire burned the evidence, according to Rivenbark, Kaprat made a mistake. Since everyone has rubbing alcohol in their vanities, the killer let his victims provide the accelerant, but each time he carelessly left the vanity doors open.

"It worked for a while," Rivenbark said, "but my crew eventually cracked the case."

After an intense interview by Deputies Scott Bierwiler and Carlos Douglas, Kaprat confessed and received a free pass to death row, exactly where the victims' families and the law enforcement officers wanted him. Case closed.

The Highway Patrol dispatcher called back to Mary, this time with greater urgency. "Y'all got the chopper up?"

"Yes. Fifteen minutes."

"Fifteen minutes?"

"Yeah, Chris," Mary said, fully aware of the emotions welling in his voice. "Fifteen minutes."

"Okay, thanks." Then he gave the bad news. "We got a trooper shot."

"You have a trooper shot?"

"Yeah."

Mary hung up the phone and communicated the information to Peggy Brooks, but before broadcasting the update, unit Alpha-11 radioed dispatch. "Alpha-11, Hernando."

"Go ahead, Alpha-11."

"Does he have the subject stopped, or is he in pursuit?"

"Hernando, Alpha-11, be en route to Interstate 75. The trooper has been shot."

Stunned now by the announcement of yet another officer being shot, only this time in the neighboring county, unit Alpha-11 didn't immediately respond.

". . .Uh, Ten-4, Hernando."

Deputy Alan Jernigan heard the broadcast and radioed dispatch from Cobb Road, where he was running a radar check from a location receiving complaints about speeders.

"Sierra-90, Ten-51 also," said the married father of three, who then proceeded to close down the radar unit and swung his car east toward Interstate 75.

Deputy Scott Bierwiler keyed his mic next. "Alpha-10, Four-05, on Utility."

"Ten-4, Alpha-10."

With that call, Bierwiler had requested unit Four-05, Lieutenant Rivenbark, to switch his radio to the utility channel so they could leave the primary frequency open for dispatch.

While Peggy Brooks monitored radio traffic from the primary control panel at the dispatch station, lights and numbers lit up on all the active frequencies, including primary, Patrol-2, SWAT, Tactical, Tach-2 and the Utility channels.

After switching to utility channel, Lieutenant Rivenbark came back to Bierwiler. "Go ahead, Alpha-10."

"I'm out by Lake Lindsey," the deputy reported. "I'll head out 476 to the interstate if that's Ten-4 with you."

"That's Ten-4."

The deputy roared away from Lake Lindsey, several miles north of Brooksville, then headed east toward I-75 on Road 476.

Only minutes earlier, Bierwiler and Lieutenant Rivenbark had crossed paths in the vicinity of Lake Lindsey and stopped for a brief chat. The two men had been good friends ever since Bierwiler joined the HCSO in 1986.

In 1976, after being diagnosed with multiple sclerosis, Sergeant Frank Bierwiler, Scott's father, resigned from the police force in Corning, New York. He moved to Florida and accepted the position of Public Information Officer (PIO) with the Sheriff's Office. Scott was only nine years old at that time, and in 1986 when he joined the Sheriff's Office, he still felt misplaced as a 20-year-old New Yorker surrounded by all those Southern boys.

Lieutenant Rivenbark sensed the young deputy's discomfort and invited him to the family ranch north of Brooksville.

"I was excited about hanging out with real cowboys," Bierwiler said of the experience. "Marc introduced me to his father and his wife Dayna. Before long, they had me herding cattle into holding pens, where I quickly learned that it's not only bulls that have horns. Then they brought me into a pen with the calves and told me to hold 'em down while Marc and his father castrated them…

"Those calves are a lot stronger than they look," Bierwiler said, flashing a boyish smile. "They tossed me in the mud more than once. I was being shown up by Dayna, which was pretty humbling for a macho New Yorker like me."

Although a rude introduction to the rough-and-tumble lifestyle of a Southern cowboy, city-boy Bierwiler also found the positive side of being a ranch hand: Southern cookin'.

"Marc's mother made homemade biscuits, potatoes, cornbread,

roasts, dumplings, and iced tea so sweet you could pour it on your pancakes," he said, no longer sounding like a New Yorker.

The best reward, Bierwiler admitted, came at the end of the day when Rivenbark's father slapped him on the back and said, "You know, son, you didn't do bad for a Yankee."

That adventurous weekend gave Bierwiler stories to tell for the rest of his life, and it solidified a lasting friendship with Rivenbark.

Further cultivating his Southern lifestyle, the Hernando County deputy married a Southern Belle who worked in the Communication Center. The Tennessee Miss instantly swept him off his feet, agreed to marry him in 1988, and together they added three children to the law enforcement family.

With emergency lights flashing and sirens screaming, Deputy Bierwiler took the northern route to the freeway in his cruiser, while Rivenbark took the direct route through Brooksville in an unmarked Crown Victoria.

Sergeant Lanny Corlew called dispatch on Patrol-1. "Four-11, Hernando, I'm Ten-51 from the office with a Stinger."

Lieutenant Rivenbark radioed dispatch. "Four-05, Hernando. I've got a Stinger, too. I'm en route 50 east."

"Ten-4."

Selected officers, usually supervisors, carried *Stingers*—a heavy device comprised of expandable spikes—in the trunk of their cars, folded up inside hard, durable casing. When involved in a pursuit, at the supervisor's discretion and determined by the situation and traffic conditions, officers manually toss Stingers across the road in front of fleeing vehicles, leaving the metal spikes exposed like daggers.

"A Stinger is normally the best means of terminating a dangerous pursuit," Rivenbark explained. "But it can also be hazardous when not handled properly and in a timely manner."

Rivenbark hit nearly 100 MPH en route to I-75, but Deputy Tom Brooks somehow came up behind him in a marked Ford Victoria with lights and siren. Although off duty, as a member of the SWAT Quick Response Team, Brooks had scrambled to assist his fellow officers immediately after hearing the emergency call. Off duty or not, Quick Response meant just that: "Quick."

With additional information coming out of Tampa, Peggy Brooks broadcast another update. "Hernando, all units responding. Vehicle last seen on Interstate 75. Last seen northbound on 75."

Deputy Bierwiler radioed his location on Patrol-1. "Alpha-10, Hernando, I'm now en route via 476. Lake Lindsey area. I'll cut over from the north."

"Ten-4, Alpha-10."

"Hernando, all units responding to the interstate, be Ten-18."

Ten-18; the Ten-code to *complete assignment quickly*. In other words, *emergency* status.

Mary Booth took another call on the landline. "Hello?"

As expected, it came from the Highway Patrol dispatcher. "Hey, Hernando, Brooksville."

"Yeah, go ahead Brooksville," Mary said, acknowledging the emergency now affected both agencies.

"I need to keep the line open with you."

"Okay."

Detective Curtis Turney worked several years for the Zephyrhills Police Department prior to joining the HCSO. The muscle-bound SWAT member worked the Property Crime Unit, where he had just completed paperwork from an arrest in a stolen property case. While still in the Sheriff's Office, Turney took a minute to phone his wife. They were in the process of finalizing plans to spend their seventh wedding anniversary at Jensen Beach, and hadn't yet decided where to leave their daughters Kristen and Jazmin.

After terminating the phone call, Turney picked up the emergency traffic, and a moment later found himself racing toward the interstate in a blue, unmarked Crown Victoria.

As the cop shooter headed north, the Hernando SWAT team had already begun to assemble.

Sergeant Rick Kramer called dispatch from a location in Weeki Wachee on the west edge of the county. "Four-86, Hernando."

"Go ahead, Four-86."

"I'm at Elgin and Powell. They gonna need more units out at the interstate?"

"Ten-4."

"Four-86, I'm Ten-51."

Kramer took off toward I-75 via Cortez Boulevard, which crossed the county and eventually became State Road 50. Fresh off his annual golfing trip to Myrtle Beach, Sergeant Kramer came in rested and ready for action, and if the cop shooter out of Tampa made it into his territory, he intended to be there to greet him.

With plenty of quality golf courses in Hernando County, except for his golfing vacations to South Carolina, Kramer was never far from home in case of a police emergency. Playing to a 14 handicap, by his own admission, his life consisted primarily of law enforcement and golf, not necessarily in that order.

"The highlight of my golf career," Kramer reminisced, "occurred at the Silverthorn Country Club. The club scheduled a promotion and invited Arnold Palmer."

Kramer hoped to be one of the three members selected to play a round with Palmer, but that never eventuated. Although he admitted disappointment, he soon learned that the club must provide security for the celebrity golfer.

"I got the assignment," said Kramer. "I had to walk the entire course in full uniform, but I was able to have several conversations with Mister Palmer."

They talked about golf.

"The most memorable moment came on the par five sixth hole," the young sergeant recalled. "He was taking practice swings near his ball and told me something wasn't right about his swing. I had been studying his strokes all day, trying to pick up a few pointers, and I had already noticed something.

"I said, 'I'm not a pro, Mister Palmer, but it looks like you're dropping your head during the swing.'"

Palmer glanced curiously at the officer.

"He took a couple more practice swings, then looked at me again, smiled, and said, 'Thanks.'"

On the afternoon of May 19, however, golf never entered the young sergeant's mind. Certainly not after hearing the BOLO and subsequent traffic regarding officers being shot.

And the updates only worsened.

While on a landline with Mary Booth, the FHP dispatcher took a radio call from one of his patrol units. "Fifteen-03, Brooksville, on traffic."

"Fifteen-03, go ahead."

Mary wasn't able to discern what the calling trooper said, but she heard the dispatcher expel a mournful whimper followed by three words: "…Oh, my God."

"What?" Mary asked quickly.

"Signal-7."

"Signal-7?"

"Yeah. A Pasco trooper."

This time, the gasp came from Mary. "Is he still northbound?"

"We don't know."

Once she relayed the update to Peggy, Mary came back on the phone. "Okay, Chris, I'll take any information you can give me."

"It looks like it's gonna be that BOLO out of Tampa. The Ford Ranger."

"The white Ford Ranger?"

"Yeah. Tag number is Whiskey, Zulu, Mike, 72 Quebec."

"A delivery truck, right?"

"Some kind of a delivery truck. Initials APD on the side. Alpha, Papa, Delta."

"And it was last headed north?"

"We don't know."

"You don't know which way it's headed?"

"It happened on State Road 54, but we don't know for sure which way they went from 54."

"All right, hold on a second, okay?"

Mary conveyed the information to Peggy, who then keyed the foot-operated microphone and issued an emotional update to the area supervisor, Lieutenant Rivenbark.

"Hernando, Four-05."

"Four-05."

Her voice breaking, she said, "We're now receiving calls that the trooper is Signal-7."

A poignant pause followed. "He is?" Rivenbark asked. "Or he is not?"

"He is."

"Is he still headed north?"

"They don't know."

Other deputies radioed in on Patrol-1.

"Tango-2, Hernando."

"Go, Tango-2."

"I'm Ten-51 to the interstate."

"Ten-4, Tango-2."

"Sierra-20, Hernando."

"Sierra-20."

"I'm not far from 75. I'll be 51 also."

The Sierra-20 call came from Deputy Gary Mason, a member of the neighborhood COPPS unit—Community Oriented Police Problem Solvers—also known as the Bike Patrol.

After three years with the Port Richey Police Department, Mason had been with the Hernando County Sheriff for the past nine years. A Florida native, born in Miami and raised in Brooksville, the deputy spent his off-duty time coaching Little League Baseball in Ridge Manor. Prior to May 19, 1998, his most dramatic day on the force came in '93 when an escaped convict from California slithered into Spring Hill in a stolen car.

"Deputy Scott Brockew attempted a traffic stop," Mason said in reference to that night, speaking with a slow, Southern drawl. "The vehicle came up behind me, then turned off the main road. After I made a U-turn, I arrived to find Scott on the ground outside his patrol car. He had a wound to his gun hand and a bruise where his vest stopped a bullet, but he said he was okay."

"He's on the ground!" Brockew warned Mason, pointing toward the gunman. "He's still armed!"

With Brockew hidden safely behind the patrol unit, Mason circled the shooter, and while taking deadly aim, he observed the assailant's weapon had jammed, rendering it useless. Although procedures and policy permitted Mason to shoot an armed felon aiming a weapon—a clear and present danger—he determined the man no longer posed a threat. Rather than take the easy shot, therefore terminating the life of a criminal who wounded a fellow officer, Mason pounced on the man and restrained him until backup arrived.

Two years later, Deputy Mason earned the 1995 Deputy of the Year award.

While working COPPS patrol in the Hill and Dale housing area north of State Road 50 on Spring Hill Road, he stopped his bike to visit with some neighborhood kids.

"The kids joked about my easy job," Mason said. "To them, all I ever did was ride my bike around the neighborhood. All the sudden a woman came running from her house screaming 'My baby isn't breathing! My baby isn't breathing!'"

With no hesitation, Mason ran inside the house and found a child lying motionless on the sofa—her face had turned a deathly shade of blue and her breathing stopped. By the book, Mason checked her airway, performed the Heimlich routine and began CPR.

The child recovered, and along with a Deputy of the Year award, Mason earned lasting respect and admiration from the community.

While assigned to the West Hernando Middle School system, Deputy Bert Stockton piloted the Resource Officer Program, where for over four years he donated numerous hours of off-duty time to work with students on after-school programs such as weightlifting and basketball.

"My goal," Stockton said, "was to hand pick the good kids and assist them in working with what we considered the *bad kids*. In the end, I learned that they weren't so bad after all. Like everyone else, they just wanted to be understood and respected, but at the same time, they wanted direction and guidance. It was an education for me."

Stockton eventually missed the hard core "cop work." He wanted more excitement in his career, so in April of '98, he requested patrol duty and returned to the COPPS unit and the SWAT team.

On May 19, one month after returning to patrol, Deputy Stockton found himself in the middle of the action he missed, perhaps even more than he wanted.

Moments before the BOLO hit, Stockton was riding his bike through the Whispering Oaks area of Ridge Manor. With a regimen of biking, canoeing, weightlifting and off-road Jeep climbing, the strapping, 36-year-old deputy stayed fit, and at six-foot-three, he towered over the Mongoose bicycle.

Always dressed sharply in his department-issued attire—a white polo shirt, green shorts and black, low-quarter shoes—Stockton had attracted the attention of an elderly, gray-haired woman. She often greeted him with a wave and a smile, then signaled him to pull over and socialize. When time permitted, he chatted with the ever-smiling woman and the conversation usually came around to the deputy's teenage son, 11-year-old daughter and his wife Cindy. Although the woman expressed interest in Stockton's family, her intent was to engage in playful flirting, and talking about his family was her way of keeping the deputy around for a longer visit.

Stockton shrugged and said, "It's all part of the territory."

On May 19, the woman went outside to flirt.

"Since we don't have a donut shop nearby," she said, holding up a bag of cookies, "I baked these for you."

"I appreciate that," he chuckled. "As you know, we can't survive long without donuts or cookies."

The deputy didn't have time to eat any cookies; upon hearing the Signal-7, he called dispatch.

"Tango-8, Hernando."

"Go ahead, Tango-8."

"I'm Ten-98," Stockton said, indicating his current assignment was completed. "Bike Patrol, 51 to that area."

Stockton jumped on the Mongoose and pedaled full speed to his patrol car, where he secured the bike on the rack, leaped inside the car and tore away from the curb. With lights and siren, he took the shortest route to Interstate 75.

"What else can you tell me?" Mary said to the Highway Patrol dispatcher on the landline.

"Pasco says they are now behind the vehicle," he answered.

"Pasco is behind the vehicle?"

"Yes. Northbound."

"Pasco is behind the vehicle," Mary repeated loudly to the Comm Center crew, which now included Sergeant Blackman and Lieutenant Hensley.

Back to the dispatcher, she said, "Anything else?"

"Just be very careful," he warned.

"Be very careful!" Mary yelled to Peggy Brooks and everyone else handling communications.

"Be very careful," Chris repeated. "I mean, he's already shot two Tampa."

"He's already shot the two Tampa PD?"

"Yeah…And he killed our guy."

4

Hernando County Sheriff's Office
Brooksville, Florida
May 19, 1998; 1448 hours

Twenty years and three months after the death of Lonnie Coburn, Deputy Joe Paez still worked for Hernando County. Along with a promotion to lieutenant, he took on dual assignments as Operations Support Commander and the backup Public Information Officer. Paez kept his walkie-talkie turned on while working at his desk, where he often received calls from the media whenever an emergency arose, sometimes before the department had heard about it. There had not been an officer killed in Hernando since Lonnie Coburn, but Paez knew firsthand how fast that could change. When the BOLO out of Tampa hit the airway, he sat up straight, his eyes fixed on the radio.

"Where are they now?" Mary Booth asked FHP dispatch.

The answer came back with urgency. "He's northbound on I-75 at State Road 52. I-75 and 52."

Peggy took the information from Mary. "Units responding, now advising at State Road 52. Northbound on 75."

"K-9 unit will arrive at the interstate in two minutes," Deputy Stephen Kelly radioed in, his sirens audible in the background.

Deputy Danny Hart responded. "Alpha-9, I'm near the interstate."

"All units advised to use extreme caution. It's going to be the white Ford truck. Florida tags Whiskey, Zulu, Mike, seventy-two Quebec. Suspect is a white male with shoulder-length hair. Pasco is behind the vehicle at this time."

"He's now approaching 41 northbound," FHP said to Mary a few moments later.

After a rapid exchange of information, Peggy broadcast to all units on Patrol-1. "He's now approaching 41. Suspect northbound, approaching Highway 41 on the interstate."

"Where's your chopper?" the dispatcher asked.

"Air-1, Ten-20?'

Sergeant Nowlin came back. "Air-1, I'm about a minute from the interstate and Florida 41."

Dispatch confirmed with a Ten-4.

Lieutenant Paez realized that his long-time friend was flying headfirst into the danger zone. Only on rare occasions had he heard "Use extreme caution" when monitoring Patrol-1. Paez glanced over at the pictures on his wall cabinet. On the left, a family photo of his wife Betty and their six children; on the right, a 27-foot sailboat that he and Betty would sail to the Bahamas immediately after retirement. It brought a chill when he suddenly realized that his wife could very possibly be on the interstate at that precise moment. As the senior Medical Case Manager for a major insurance company, she went into Tampa on business that morning, and would then be driving to Ocala for an appointment regarding a worker's comp case.

Ironically, while Paez listened to the radio traffic, his cell phone rang. "Hello?"

"Hi, Joe. It's me."

"Where are you?" he asked his wife.

"I'm home in bed," she joked. "Surely you must—"

"Betty!" he shouted, interrupting her in mid-sentence. "We have an emergency! What's your Ten-20? Where are you?"

"I'm north on 75."

Joe heard a police siren coming from the background of Betty's cell phone. He jumped to his feet. "Where on 75?"

"What's going on, Joe?"

"Where are you?" he demanded.

"Well, let's see, I'm at, uh, 41."

"You gotta get out of there now! There's a pursuit coming north, right behind you!"

Her husband rarely panicked at anything, so Betty understood the situation must be serious. "Oh, nuts. I just missed the exit. I have no where to go."

"You gotta get out of there! You gotta go now! Step on it, get off at the next exit!"

"Okay, I'll go to 50," she said.

"Make it fast!"

"I will. You be careful, dear."

"Betty, I'm sitting at my desk! You're the one in harm's way! Now put the phone down and get out of there!"

"Bye."

Lieutenant Paez now had another reason for concern. He ran out the door and went inside the Communication Center where he could monitor the activity from all sources.

The FHP dispatcher picked up transmission from the Pasco units in pursuit. "Two-62, Two-35, we're Ten-97 at I-75."

In Ten-code, the Pasco units had arrived at the scene on I-75 and were in pursuit of the Ford Ranger.

Within moments, Peggy relayed another update from the FHP dispatcher. "All units, there are shots being fired at the two-90 mile marker. Two-90 mile marker. Shots fired. Shots fired."

Mary said, "They're now at the two-90 marker. It's coming into Hernando County."

Paez gasped, thinking to himself, *Betty just passed that marker.*

A chase that began on the border of Pasco and Hillsborough Counties had nearly reached Hernando County, with the next exit at State Road 50.

As the pursuers closed in, the driver of the Ford Ranger stuck a handgun out the window and fired at the first patrol car, a Pasco County Sheriff's unit; a bullet shattered the windshield, with glass spraying the officer like pellets.

"Brooksville, deputy being shot at! Unit has been hit!"

A moment later, Peggy keyed the mic for Patrol-1. "All units, now advising that a deputy's car has been shot. Unit has been hit."

The Pasco deputy nearly became another victim of the rampaging killer. Although forced to terminate the 90 MPH pursuit, he managed to avoid other vehicles and prevent a crash that likely would have taken lives, perhaps even his own.

Lieutenant Rivenbark called dispatch. "Four-05, Hernando, trying to inquire, does he have anything more than handguns?"

"We're trying to get more information," Peggy told him.

"We need units to go in on 41," Rivenbark said. "Spring Lake Highway."

Sergeant Tom Nowlin, with eyes from above, reached the chase scene and responded. "Air-1, Hernando, you have five units in pursuit at Florida Highway 41 and the interstate. One trooper and four Pasco deputies."

"Ten-4."

"I'm Ten-97," another deputy said on Patrol-1 frequency. "At 41 and the interstate."

"Units approaching there now."

Rivenbark called for the chopper. "Four-05, Air-1."

"Go ahead."

"Can you advise where to deploy the Stinger? I'm now at 50 and the interstate. Do I still have time to get to that overpass to deploy the Stinger?"

"Ten-54," Nowlin answered with the Ten-code for *negative*.

Deputy Stockton called in. "Tango-8, I'm on the Interstate."

Then another update from dispatch. "All units, they're coming into Hernando County at this time."

"Tango-8 to Hernando."

"Go ahead, 8."

"Are they coming in 41 or 75?"

"I-75."

"Air-1, Hernando. It is a white pickup. They're north on 75, about half a mile north of 41. North of 41."

"A white pickup," dispatch repeated. " North on 75. A half mile north of 41."

"Go to the first overpass south of 50," Lieutenant Rivenbark told the officers. "Lockhart Road. We'll try to deploy the Stinger at that location. We got some cover there."

Hernando Deputies Mason, Stockton, Hart, and Jernigan, along with Sergeant Lanny Corlew and Lieutenant Rivenbark, all rushed toward the overpass at Lockhart and Hickory Hill Road.

On the landline, Mary Booth continued dialogue with FHP. "Who is behind the truck now?"

"We got troopers behind him and Pasco SO. Still northbound on 75. They're coming into Hernando County."

Barreling recklessly toward State Road 50, the pickup hit speeds in excess of 90 miles per hour, weaving through traffic, cutting off vehicles and occasionally firing shots out the window at pursuing officers.

"Brooksville, all units northbound from 41, shots fired."

"Hernando, shots fired. Northbound from 41. Shots fired."

A trooper called dispatch with information regarding a Signal-4, an *accident* or *crash,* but the pickup continued north.

"Christ," the FHP dispatcher groaned. "Now we have a Signal-4."

The trooper came right back. "Suspect won't be going for long, Brooksville. He's got a flat tire."

Mary heard the message. "Who's got a flat tire?" she asked the FHP dispatcher.

"The truck has a flat tire."

"The bad guy?"

"Yeah."

"The bad guy has a flat tire, right?"

"Yeah. And he just wrecked one of our units."

"He just wrecked one of their units," Mary echoed.

"Does your helicopter have him?" asked FHP.

"Yes. Our helicopter has a visual on him."

Sergeant Nowlin dropped as low as possible with the Lonnie-6. He had a bird's-eye view when the driver stuck a gun out the window and fired at the officers behind him.

"I'm right on top of him," Nowlin said. "He's still shooting. I'll try to see if he's alone."

The initial BOLO mentioned two suspects, but Nowlin couldn't see anyone on the passenger's side. With the pilot's seat being on the right side of the helicopter, he had to drop down on the driver's side of the pickup for a closer look.

With the driver doing all the shooting, Nowlin risked his own life by descending within fifty feet of the truck. In his words, "I was close enough to make eye contact with the driver."

Just as Nowlin confirmed the driver was alone, a rifle appeared from the window of the pickup. But rather than being pointed toward the patrol cars, the barrel lifted upward, directly at Air-1.

Fortunately, the light, maneuverable aircraft and the skilled pilot reacted in an instant. As Nowlin banked to the left, the driver fired several shots. One shot nicked the rotor blade, but the second bullet ripped a hole in the floorboard about an inch from the sergeant's right foot, then whizzed past his face and crashed through the top of the compartment directly above his head.

"I heard the impact even with my helmet on," Nowlin recounted later. "It missed my head, but I felt the concussion." With a knowing smile, he added, "I wasn't alone in the sky that day. The Lord was my co-pilot."

Given the trajectory of the slug, no one could challenge Nowlin's conclusion. Upon later examination, it seemed to be the only logical explanation for how he avoided being hit or how neither of the bullets brought down the chopper.

"They're shooting," the FHP dispatcher announced, referring to the officers and the assailant. "They're still shooting."

"Oh, my God," Mary uttered.

"Yeah, oh my God," the dispatcher agreed. "He must be a pretty good shot, too. He's shootin' out windows in our patrol car."

"He's shooting out windows on the patrol car," Mary told Peggy. To FHP, she said, "Where are they now?"

"At the 296 mile marker, northbound."

"Two 96?"

"Ten-4. Shots fired. Shots fired."

"More shots fired?"

"Yeah, shots fired at mile marker 296. They're in your county now. Mile marker 296 northbound."

Nowlin squeezed the microphone trigger on the cyclic. "Air-1, Hernando, I've just been shot at. Our unit has been hit."

The dispatcher echoed the call. "Hernando, air unit has been hit. Shots fired. Air unit has been hit."

The FHP dispatcher called the trooper in unit One-80 and asked his location.

"Mile marker 298," the trooper responded. "Shots still being fired. More shots fired."

"More shots fired?" Mary asked, overhearing the trooper's call.

"Yeah, more shots fired."

"My, God."

Tom Nowlin maintained vigil from directly above the Ranger so the driver couldn't get a visual on him.

"He's slowing down," Nowlin said. "…Now he's wrecked. He's wrecked. Wait, he's back on the road again. He's back on the road. He's still northbound on 75."

"Ten-4."

"The pickup truck has big letters," Nowlin continued. "Alpha, Papa, Delta, written on the side of the truck."

"Alpha, Papa, Delta written on the side of the truck."

"It's gonna be a white truck. Be advised, a white pickup, still northbound on 75." After a tense moment, Nowlin came back with another update. "Air-1, he's got a tire out."

"Ten-9?"

"He's got a right rear tire out on the truck."

"Hernando, all units, the truck has a right rear tire out. The truck has a rear tire out."

Nowlin corrected himself. "Left rear, left rear. He's got a left rear tire out. He's firing at the deputies and he's firing at me."

"Hernando, all units, use extreme caution. Suspect is firing at the deputies."

"Air-1, Hernando, he's just going under Church Road overpass at this time."

"Hernando, all units, he's going under the Church Road overpass at this time."

"You don't need to repeat, Hernando," Nowlin requested of the dispatcher. "I'll just advise, okay?"

No response came. None necessary.

The race was on, with Rivenbark and the deputies trying to reach the Lockhart overpass ahead of the Ranger. Even though running on only three tires, the pickup still passed vehicles, mostly those that had slowed and pulled off the road.

Nowlin saw a handgun again pop out from the driver's window, followed by the man's head. Without looking at the road ahead, the driver fired several more rounds at the patrol cars behind him. In a desperate effort to create mass disruption in his wake, and hopefully force officers to discontinue the chase, the assailant fired rounds at a truck driver as he passed on the left; a bullet ripped into the driver's upper arm.

On a landline, Mary connected with Sumter County. "This is Mary with HCSO. We are in pursuit of the vehicle involved in the shooting in Tampa and death of the trooper in Pasco County."

"What road are you on?"

"Interstate 75 northbound, just coming through Hernando County and approaching Highway 50. We have Stingers out, and he has a left rear tire out. He's shooting at everything, including our chopper."

Mary also provided her with the latest information on the suspect and vehicle. The Sumter dispatcher relayed the message to Sumter units, including the Signal-4 near the county line.

Tom Nowlin radioed to Lieutenant Rivenbark. "Air-1, Four-05. Where are you, Four-05?"

"Four-05, we're now setting up at the next overpass. Lockhart and Hickory Hill Road."

"If you're at Hickory Hill Road, you ought to be just right. He's running on three tires and he's slowed down. He's shooting at us."

"Ten-4."

"As soon as you can see me, you'll find him. I'm right over the top of him."

"Hernando, he's shooting at the deputies at this time. He's still shooting at the deputies behind him."

The fleeing pickup swerved nearly out of control, and when shots ceased to come from inside, Nowlin dropped down for another quick look. "It looks like he's reloading his gun."

"Hernando, Air-1, Ten-20?"

"We are approaching Lockhart and Hickory Hill overpass with our units ahead."

"Approaching Hickory Hill, all units."

A half dozen units, later dubbed the *Lockhart Gang*, merged on the median beneath the Hickory Hill and Lockhart Road overpass under the charge of Lieutenant Rivenbark. Several officers took cover behind the concrete pilings, with Deputies Hart and Mason lying on the grass below the sight line. Some of the officers took aim with shotguns; others selected their .40-caliber handguns. The last man in line, Deputy Mason, lay ready with a 17-shot Glock.

Deputy Bierwiler charged down I-75 from the north. "Alpha-10, I'm on the interstate southbound."

"Ten-4, Alpha-10. He's approaching Hickory Hill on 75."

"I'll set up a Stinger at 50."

Behind the first piling at Lockhart, Deputy Jernigan prepared a Stinger. "Stinger is ready!" he yelled out.

"We may not be able to use it!" the lieutenant shouted back. "Be ready to shoot!"

The Lockhart Gang had little time to find cover and assess the hazardous situation. Automobiles and trucks were still approaching northbound, unintentionally providing cover and protection for the white pickup. An open barrage of gunfire would endanger innocent civilians, Rivenbark observed, and with the speed of the chase, the close pursuit, and the proximity of civilians, he assumed the window of opportunity would be narrow and close fast.

With Hernando units on the median at the scene, Nowlin expected the officers to strike the suspect with heavy firepower, so when he approached the overpass, he lifted the chopper to 100 feet.

"There he is!" Deputy Hart shouted.

Rivenbark had only a few seconds to make a decision. Seeing that the truck already had one flat tire and that officers were tucked in extremely close behind, he shouted, "Hold the Stinger! Shoot only when you have a clear shot!"

The gunman displayed no concern for the civilians or anyone else. When he spotted the line of patrol cars and the officers peering from behind concrete pilings, he opened fire. While traveling over fifty miles an hour and ducking below the door, he still had sufficient accuracy to hit the pilings and a patrol unit, forcing the officers to maintain cover.

At the front of the line, a 12-gauge shotgun belched a nine-pellet load that peppered the side of the truck. Then another shotgun blast exploded and police Glocks spit out 9mm and .40-caliber ammo.

"I focused on the door and unloaded my clip," Deputy Mason said. "I was amazed that he kept going."

With the driver's door lined with bullet holes and smashed in by previous contact with a pursuer, the little pickup continued north with smoke streaming from a disintegrating tire.

"I remember the sound of our projectiles striking the cab and the side of the pickup," Rivenbark recalled. "When the angle was no longer safe, I ordered the deputies to stop firing."

The officers ran for their individual patrol cars and sped after the runaway pickup, knowing they had less than two miles before SR 50, where businesses occupied all four corners of the intersection. By any means possible, they wanted to stop the vehicle before it reached a populated point along the freeway.

Cindy Stockton intently followed the chase from her cubicle in the forensics department.

"It was three o'clock," she said, realizing that children would be leaving school. "I grabbed the phone and contacted nearby schools, warning them to halt and reroute bus traffic."

Sergeant Nowlin swooped down and followed the truck north of the overpass.

"He did not stop at Lockhart and Hickory Hill Road," Nowlin continued. "He's still northbound."

Dispatch broadcast the update. "All units, the suspect vehicle is now northbound from Hickory Hill Road."

"Air-1 to all units, he's still firing."

Bierwiler arrived from the north and pulled to the center median on the north side of the 50 overpass. "Alpha-10, I have a Stinger at the overpass on 50 if he comes this way."

"He's coming your way, believe me," Sergeant Nowlin assured Bierwiler. "He's about two miles south of you."

"All units. He's about two miles south of State Road 50 and the interstate."

Deputy Bierwiler sprang from his patrol car, grabbed a shotgun and Stinger, and ran for cover behind the concrete sidings.

Additional backup arrived. "Alpha-23, Hernando."

"Go, Alpha-23."

"I'm coming around that way."

"Twenty-three, standby at this time."

"I'm at 50 and the interstate," radioed Deputy Chris Erickson in a K-9 unit.

Erickson came in behind Bierwiler and took cover next to him, shotgun in hand. With adrenaline flowing, neither officer turned off their sirens, which helped notify nearby civilians and approaching traffic to be aware. If the Ford Ranger made it all the way to 50, they were prepared for intercept.

"Air-1, Hernando, if there are any units at 50, have them guard the exit ramps before he runs off that busy intersection."

"Ten-4."

"Four-05, Air-1, what kind of speed you got now?"

"He's about 50 miles an hour, a mile south of State Road 50 and the interstate. He's approaching 50. He's underneath me if you can see me. Northbound about 50 miles an hour."

Joe Paez anxiously awaited another call from Betty on the cell phone. Fully aware of his wife's tendency to obey the speed limit at all times, he worried that he should've been more emphatic with his warning. Even on the interstate, she rarely drove over sixty-five.

At sixty-five miles an hour, Betty Paez arrived at State Road 50. While slowing to exit, she observed a flurry of police activity. "Oh, my goodness," she uttered. "What is going on?"

When Betty turned off the highway, she checked in her rearview mirror. Approximately half a mile behind, she could see the police helicopter and a white pickup passing an 18-wheeler with a red cab. Directly behind the pickup, she observed the patrol cars and flashing lights, but when she turned away and drove east, she never saw the assailant fire several rounds at the driver of the 18-wheeler.

"Shots fired," Nowlin repeated. "He's still shooting."

Deputies Bierwiler and Erickson observed the chopper coming at them, directly above a white pickup and followed by the convoy of patrol cars. With their sirens still screaming, the deputies could barely hear each other.

"This is it!" Bierwiler shouted.

"Okay, I got him!"

"We gotta knock him down!"

"Ten-4!"

"Air-1, Hernando, if we have anybody that can keep him from getting off the interstate, we'll be safer and so will the public. If they can block that exit ramp off 50."

"Ten-4."

"Four-86, I'm 50 east on the truck route. I'm 51 that way."

Speeding toward the intersection at 50 and I-75, Captain Bob Henning screamed into the microphone. "Four-04, Hernando!"

"Go, oh-4."

"Have all units at the scene go to Tach-2!"

On the main frequency, another unit called with a Ten-20.

"Unit calling?"

"I'm at 50 and the interstate also."

"Ten-4."

Sergeant Nowlin issued another warning. "Units in the area of 50 and the interstate, we need to block the exit ramp. Make sure he doesn't get off."

As officers positioned their cars at the 50 exit ramps, attempting to block all exits and entrances, the pickup bore down on them with more shots being fired. They ducked behind their respective vehicles, positioning themselves to return fire once the opportunity presented itself.

Nowlin breathed a premature sigh of relief, assuming that the deputies had successfully prevented the pickup from taking the 50 exit into the populated area.

"He's staying on the interstate," Nowlin said into the radio. "He's going over the overpass."

The crippled pickup passed the exit ramp and came face to face with the Crown Vic driven by Detective Curt Turney. In an instant, the pickup suddenly veered off the highway onto the grassy shoulder between the interstate and exit ramp, whipped a U-turn, and slipped past the blockade.

Once again, the driver eluded officers, only now he was headed eastbound on 50: exactly what they hoped to avoid.

"Negative!" Nowlin said, correcting his last call. "He's just turned off the interstate. Just turned off the interstate at 50."

"Which direction?" asked the dispatcher.

A ground unit responded. "Eastbound! He's eastbound!"

Air-1 confirmed. "Eastbound! He's headed eastbound!"

Detective Turney gunned the Crown Victoria and picked up the pursuit along with a number of other units from Hernando, Pasco and the Highway Patrol.

A quarter mile east on 50, Betty Paez turned into the Sunrise Plaza and parked near the Wynn Dixie Marketplace. A look back at

State Road 50 revealed nothing but one police car headed westbound with lights and siren. After a sigh of relief, she picked up the cell phone and called her husband.

Inside the Communication Center, with his eyes darting about the dispatch screen and his ears tuned to the radio, Paez answered on the first ring of his cell phone.

"Yeah?" he said, and stepped away from the center of activity.

"Hey, it's me," Betty told him. "Everything's okay here, how about there?"

"Where are you?"

"I'm at the Wynn Dixie on 50. I'm going inside. Do you want anything while I'm here?"

"No! Stay in your car and keep your eyes open. The pursuit is east on 50. It's coming your way."

"Oh, no," she sighed. "Not again."

Betty checked that the doors were locked. With the three o'clock sun pounding overhead, she remained in the car and left the motor running with the air conditioning blowing full blast.

Robin Best worked at the Shell Station/Food Mart on the north side of State Road 50, about 100 yards east of I-75; her brother Sam worked for the HCSO, a member of the SWAT team. On May 19, Robin took the day off and Stephanie Kramer worked the day shift until 4 p.m. By 3 o'clock, Kramer was checking her watch regularly, eager to get home and spend time with her boyfriend Chris.

On a grassy plot of land adjacent to the Shell Station on the west, Mark and Maureen Blanton owned and operated the Indian River Fruit Market, an open-air fruit and vegetable outlet. Maureen had gone to Atlanta that day, and Mark's part-time assistant, 75-year-old Bill Keith, attended the store while Mark ran back home to pick up some tools.

"It was a typical day," Blanton said of May 19. "A little hot, but nothing unusual."

A shallow drainage ditch, scattered trees and shrubs separated the Shell Station from another business on the east end of the parking lot.

A single-level Days Inn Motel occupied the land farther east, and on the south side of 50, across the four divided lanes, stood a Race Trac gas station and a McDonald's. Prior to three o'clock that afternoon, business came mostly from Interstate 75 traffic, with the remainder primarily from residents of Ridge Manor and a mobile-home park located directly behind the station.

Just before the buildup of officers in the area, Ken Greene pulled into the Shell Station in a white pickup with a camper shell on the back. As a delivery driver for All Florida Courier Service out of Spring Hill, Greene was en route to Jacksonville carrying medical supplies for a nursing home. Observing police activity in the vicinity, he called his office from the pickup.

Phyllis Pierce, co-owner of the courier business, took the call and handed the phone to her husband Ron.

"What's up, Ken?"

"Man, there are cops all over the place," Greene said. "They were all along the freeway with their guns pulled."

"Where are you?"

"I'm at the Shell Station on 50."

"Well, you should be safe there, especially if you're surrounded by cops."

Greene noticed another All Florida Courier pickup at the center island of the station. "Looks like one of our trucks beat me here."

"Yeah, that'll be Roger," Pierce said, referring to a driver named Roger Swartz.

"Sure hope those cops aren't after me," Greene quipped as he crawled out of the pickup.

"Should they be?" Pierce asked.

"Not that I know of."

"Well, then, you have nothing to worry about."

"Right. Hey, I see Roger in—"

Greene didn't finish the thought.

About the only thing Pierce heard for the next few moments was the roar of engines, screeching tires and police sirens.

The bullet-riddled Ford Ranger, running on three tires with dark smoke spewing from the left side, careened across State Road 50. It rolled through the center island at the Shell Station, narrowly missing the second All Florida Courier pickup.

The pony-tailed driver grabbed the door latch but the door didn't open; an earlier collision had sealed it closed. With the Ranger still in motion, he crawled out the window carrying a gun in one hand and a second gun tucked inside his cut-off shorts.

"Out of the fuckin way!" he screeched at a startled maintenance man exiting the store. "They're shooting at me!"

Limping noticeably, the injured man fired several shots at fast-approaching patrol cars and hobbled toward the front door of the Shell Station. The Ranger continued rolling forward, coming to rest in the drainage ditch at the east end of the parking lot.

Ron Pierce heard the gunshots over the phone. "What the heck was that?" he asked Greene. "Hey, Ken? Ken? Ken?"

Greene didn't respond. When the phone went dead, Pierce called the FHP to report what happened, only to learn that the telephone lines were all tied up with a higher priority. His drivers, Greene and Swartz, had been caught in the middle of a dangerous pursuit, and were at that moment wisely hugging the ground, right where they stayed until deputies arrived to escort them to safety.

Rivenbark repeated a question for Tom Nowlin. "Four-05, Air-1, please advise."

"At the Shell Station!" Nowlin responded. "He's just wrecked into the Shell Station at 50!"

Patrol cars rushed to the scene from every direction.

Inside the station, Stephanie Kramer heard the screeching tires and wailing sirens. From behind the bulletproof Lexan glass, she looked out toward the gas pumps.

"I saw this truck rolling and a guy fall out," she said. "He was wearing a black T-shirt and shorts."

Clutching a 9mm gun, thc man hustled inside, where frightened customers scattered and raced for the exit. When the armed intruder found Kramer standing wide-eyed inside the cashier's cage, behind the glass, he instinctively dove through the open window and grabbed her around the neck.

"Don't move!" he demanded. "I've already shot two people!"

"Yes, sir," said the terrified woman.

"Do what I tell you and you won't get hurt!"

The man pushed her down, out of sight from the front window.

While on a landline with Sumter County, Mary heard the traffic regarding the wreck at the Shell Station.

"Looks like a signal-4," Mary told Sumter dispatch. "You're out of the woods, he just had a Signal-4 in our county."

"Do you know about where on 50?"

"At 50 and I-75."

Lieutenant Rivenbark called to the chopper. "Four-05, Air-1, is the vehicle stopped?"

"Subject is at bay. Subject is at bay."

"Four-05, Air-1. Ten-9 the last traffic."

The dispatcher responded accordingly. "Last traffic on Patrol-1, the subject is at bay. He is Signal-4 at the Shell Station, I-75 and 50."

"The suspect is in custody?" Rivenbark asked. "Or he is not in custody?"

"Suspect is at bay."

Detective Turney arrived at the station along with the first group of officers, followed closely by Deputy Bert Stockton from the COPPS unit. Turney slid into the station in his blue sedan, coming to a stop on the inside fuel island, not more than ten feet from the store entrance. Stockton rolled in fifteen yards behind Turney, next to the Indian River fruit stand.

"He's inside the store!" a bystander shouted when the officers ran up to the station.

Turney withdrew his Glock and ducked behind the unmarked Ford sedan. Stockton ran behind a concrete pillar supporting the overhead structure. Deputy Bierwiler roared down the northbound on-ramp and slid in behind Stockton's vehicle; he took cover behind a gas pump. Alan Jernigan leaped from his patrol car and helped herd the civilians to safety, away from the building.

Sergeant Rick Kramer screeched to a halt directly in front of the Shell Station. He raced to the first fuel island and took cover.

"Where is he?" he shouted to anyone who would answer.

"He's inside the station!"

Bierwiler aimed his 12-guage at the front window. "I saw the man briefly," the deputy said. "He looked up, smiled at me, waved, and ducked out of sight."

Stockton and Turney rushed to the window with guns raised. When they looked inside, they saw the suspect looking back at them from behind the bulletproof glass. He mouthed the words, "Don't shoot me."

With a foreboding smirk, the assailant held the hostage where the officers could see her, then forcefully pushed the woman down on the floor behind the counter.

Deputy Stockton ducked away from the window and keyed his vest-mounted radio. "Tango-8, Hernando!"

Dispatch didn't respond.

"Tango-8, Hernando!"

"Go ahead, Hernando."

"Suspect has a hostage in the Shell Station! Suspect has a hostage in the Shell Station!"

The dispatcher immediately broadcast the message to all units on Patrol-1. "All units, suspect has a hostage in the Shell Station!"

PART II

HILLSBOROUGH COUNTY

5

Hillsborough County
Tampa, Florida
May 19, 1998; 0830 hours

In the bedroom of his three-room upstairs apartment on 709 ½ East Crenshaw Street, 30-year-old Henry "Hank" Earl Carr slipped into blue cut-off shorts, a white T-shirt and high-top basketball shoes. He swished a comb through his long, thinning, blondish hair and secured it in a ponytail that reached to his shoulder blades. Without steady employment, the day laborer had no work scheduled that Tuesday morning. Instead, his plans included buying some toys for the kids and a wallet for himself, and then dropping his girlfriend's Hitachi video recorder off at a repair shop. After a fast-food lunch, he and the family would spend the day at an inexpensive motel where they could swim and lounge at poolside.

Two blocks south of 709 East Crenshaw Street stood Cleveland Elementary School, an aging brick building between Hamilton and Crawford Streets. Little Joey and Kayla Bennett looked forward to attending the school along with their friends and the other children in the neighborhood. As things looked on the morning of May 19, that day might one day come.

"Daddy, I had a dream!" four-year-old Joey excitedly told Carr when he first saw him that morning. "I dreamed I could swim!"

Although the youngster called Carr "Daddy," it wasn't true. They didn't even have the same surname.

For Carr, it all began in Riverdale, Georgia, a suburb of Atlanta, where on the last day of January 1968, Korean War veteran Harold

Lee Carr and his wife Gail had a son and named him Henry Earl Carr. The baby had difficulty breathing. Doctors quickly diagnosed the infirmity as hyaline membrane syndrome, a lung disease known to be fatal in children when mucus hardens in the lungs and exhausts the muscles during the breathing process.

Television cartoons mesmerized little Hank. The boy squealed in delight at Yogi Bear and Boo-Boo, and soon everyone called him *Boo*. The nickname stuck. The child walked as soon as he crawled, and he learned to read at an early age. He also learned how to handle guns, how to break them down and clean them. The youngster loved reading cartoon magazines. With an IQ bordering that of a genius, he became bored easily, and after doctors diagnosed him with Attention Deficit Disorder at the age of seven, they prescribed Ritalin, a drug used to suppress hyperactivity.

Gail Carr eventually left Harold and married a truck driver by the name of Don Cox, who moved the family to Bradenton, Florida in 1975. Hank created a challenge even in the second grade, where he interrupted other students, started fights, and expressed no interest in academics. As he grew more restless, his mother tried various ways to keep the boy active. She enrolled him in karate classes. He seemed to show improvement, but at the age of 10, his stepfather took a job at a factory 50 miles north of Atlanta.

To gain attention as the new kid it town, Hank bullied the other kids. He'd fight anyone, even much larger boys. A football coach noticed the aggressive behavior and tried to direct him into football. It helped, but only temporarily. With his toughness and attitude, he performed well, but he constantly got into fights.

In 1983, with Hank at the age of 15, Don Cox moved the family back to Florida, this time to the beach town of Englewood. Restless and no longer on Ritalin, the teenage boy dropped from high school and took an interest in booze and cocaine.

The bright, fast-talking Carr rarely had difficulty finding loyal and subservient women. There always seemed to be plenty around who were attracted to his cockiness and enamored by his disregard for authority. But short on funds, his mischief turned to crime when he broke into his first vending machine.

At the age of 17, Carr and a friend robbed a laundry and got away with the crime, but when they broke into a man's home and beat him severely with a pipe, they landed in jail for fifteen months. Carr went to a juvenile detention center, but created so much havoc they sent him to the adult ward.

The incidents didn't end there. He continued defying authority, and on one occasion, he repeatedly beat another inmate. By the time authorities released Carr from jail—with muscles and attitude equally hardened—his mother and stepfather had moved to Tampa.

Hank followed.

He found work hanging siding, but even on probation, he refused to obey authority. When he came home drunk and overly obnoxious to his mother, she tossed him back on the street.

The fights continued; so did robberies, arrests and incarceration.

The seriousness of his crimes jumped to a higher level when he assaulted an officer, sold crack cocaine and threatened to kill a man, but with cells overflowing and an early-release program, he served only six months in prison.

At a party, while on parole and living with his sister, Carr met a young woman named Kathy Stevens. Although the impressionable 17-year-old knew he had served time in prison, he lavished her with charm until she accepted his proposal for marriage and agreed to move to Georgia with him.

There, Stevens saw the dark side.

"We didn't work anywhere," she mentioned during an interview. "I don't know where he got money, but I knew enough not to ask him about it."

Stevens described his violent temper and horrible abuse, which included being dragged by the hair and slapped so hard her eyes were swollen closed. Men also suffered the rage of Carr.

"I saw him hit a man outside a theatre in St. Petersburg so hard it knocked him unconscious."

In defense of her boyfriend, Stevens told of his softer side, saying that sometimes after he beat her, he would prepare a nice breakfast and let her eat in bed. When Stevens informed her parents of the abuse, they dutifully drove to Georgia and hauled her back to Florida where she gave birth to Carr's son.

But Carr refused to let go; he followed the girl back to Florida and made threats on her life. After another encounter with the law, the Hillsborough County Sheriff issued a warrant for his arrest for parole violation, but it only covered the state of Florida.

Meanwhile, he had already met another unsuspecting woman and took off for Marietta, Ohio.

Unfortunately, when Carr left Florida, he never abandoned his propensity for violence and crime. While drinking in a roughneck bar in November 1992, Carr met Evelyn Sacks, a woman who overlooked his violent and criminal tendencies long enough to get pregnant and deliver his daughter—a redheaded cutie they named Tamara Lace Carr, who he nicknamed *Little.*

"He loved her very much," Gail Cox said of her son's feelings for Tamara. "He told me it was the happiest day of his life."

Fatherhood had no notable positive effect on Carr. He got bored fast, just as he did as a teenager. He continued fighting and defying societal decorum. Before the relationship ended in late 1994, Sacks became pregnant a second time and eventually gave birth to a son, but nothing else seemed to change; Carr had already begun seeking thrills elsewhere.

The fights continued.

So frequent, in fact, that several bar owners banned Carr from their bars. In one fight, he bit off a man's ear. He became notorious for attacking from behind, sucker punching his victims, and folks in Ohio thought that was the real reason for the nickname: *Boo!*

*

Joey Bennett's real father lived in Marietta, Ohio.

Joey's mother, Bernice Alane Bowen, was born in Marietta on January 27, 1974, to Connie Rose Bowen and Anthony Parker.

"Bernice and her sister Rosemary endured physical and mental abuse from their father," Connie Bowen confessed. "He beat her and slapped her a lot."

While attending high school at age 15, Bernice met Joseph Lee Bennett, a non-professional laborer in his mid-20's. By age 16, she quit school, and while working at a fast-food restaurant, she became pregnant and married Bennett. They lived with Bowen's parents.

In August 1992, Bernice gave birth to a daughter they named Kaitland Nicole Bennett, but called her Kayla. The following year, she delivered a handsome son with blond hair and an infectious smile. They named him Joseph Anthony Bennett.

Before Bowen's father died from a heart attack, the doctors misdiagnosed his medical condition, and after a legal battle, both Bernice and Rose received a substantial settlement. Bernice and Joe Bennett bought a home and vehicles with the proceeds, but they couldn't buy happiness. In 1994, Joe caught Bernice in an adulterous relationship and walked out the door, leaving Kayla and Joey to stay with their grandmother, Connie Bowen.

Earlier that year, Valentine's Day, Bernice had met Hank Carr, an acquaintance of her husband. When a relationship developed between the two, Carr dropped his pregnant girlfriend, Evelyn Sacks, and by 1995 lived with Bowen.

In February, the local newspaper ran a column of neighborhood indictments, which included Hank Carr for trafficking in marijuana. Once Carr learned about the article and felt the heat, Bowen put the house on the market, assigned custody of Joey and Kayla to Connie Bowen and took off for the south.

Joe Bennett wanted his kids, but as an unemployed man living with friends at the time, he was unable to put up a fight. However, with the new situation as it was, at least he could now see his children without fear of Carr's reckless and violent intimidation.

"We thought it would be a lot better for the children," Connie Bowen admitted. "This way they could still see their father and all the grandparents."

Joseph Bennett's mother agreed. "Carr had threatened my son and told him to stay away from Bernice and the kids. We were afraid of him, and very happy to see him go."

Hank Carr left Ohio with a string of arrests behind him, including several trips to jail, but he committed one more crime before leaving town; he stole Connie Bowen's car. She reported the car stolen and told the Marietta police that Carr might be going to Georgia, where he called home. Around that same time, Officer Michael Brewster informed Connie Bowen that Carr was wanted for selling drugs to an undercover cop at a high school.

Approximately 8 p.m. on July 4, 1995, Spaulding County Deputy Allen Lanier stopped Connie Bowen's Camaro while passing through Griffin, Georgia. He checked Carr's identification.

"You mind stepping out while I run some information?" Deputy Lanier said to Carr and Bowen.

They both obliged, and stood next to the Camaro while the deputy entered pertinent data into a computer. As Carr and Bowen walked around whispering to each other, Lanier picked up information on an outstanding warrant.

"I advised Mister Carr that he needed to stand by," said Lanier, "while I confirmed a hit on drug trafficking charges out of Ohio."

The deputy then told Carr he would have to go downtown to get the problem resolved.

Carr felt otherwise.

"Sorry, baby!" he yelled to Bowen, and took off running across a busy 4-lane highway.

He disappeared on the opposite side of the highway, leaving his girlfriend and Camaro with officers on the roadside. The deputies took Bowen downtown for questioning, and after filing a report, they allowed her to return to the mobile home park where she and Carr lived at that time.

The couple reunited several days later.

With the proceeds from the sale of her Ohio home, they headed west to Arizona, where Bowen bought Carr a new Harley Davidson motorcycle. After riding north to Sturgis, South Dakota for the annual Harley Davidson rally, Bowen took a job at a convenience store and talked about opening a motorcycle business.

Carr had assumed the alias "Eric Weaver" in South Dakota, but reverted to his real name when he pawned some property. He dodged the law until November when police arrested him for beating a man unconscious. He was sitting on the counter one afternoon visiting with Bowen at the convenience store when Bowen noticed a woman was checking out Carr's motorcycle in the parking lot. Bowen ran out, accused her of bumping it and told her to leave the area. When the woman refused, Bowen slugged her.

Carr got involved in the incident and sucker punched a friend of the injured woman's brother. Booked under the alias, he was in jail when South Dakota authorities discovered the Ohio warrant. But with a stroke of good fortune, he managed to bond out, disappearing one step ahead of a long-term sentence.

Early in 1996, Carr and Bowen traveled throughout West Virginia and other points east. While keeping Bowen in the background, Carr invited former girlfriend Evelyn Sacks to visit him in Belle Vernon, Pennsylvania with his daughter and infant son.

"He said he was with his brother," Sacks said.

She soon learned that he lied. Instead, she found him with Bowen, who told her they were conspiring on false identity for Carr.

Carr and Bowen ended up in Tampa, Florida, where they rented an upstairs apartment at 709 ½ East Crenshaw Street. Under the name James Earl Reid—which he had borrowed in part from his mother's brother—Carr managed the apartment complex, worked for Tampa Tent and sporadically loaded and unloaded furniture.

He called himself Joe or Boo, and sometimes Eric, and he opened a bank account in the names of Joseph and Bernice Bennett.

Bowen took a menial job at Kmart. Whenever Carr permitted, she danced at the Starlite Lounge on nearby Nebraska Avenue, where her promotional photos included one of her holding an assault weapon, another clinging to the skeleton of a human skull.

"Sometimes she came to work with bruises all over her body," the manger told an interviewer. "She covered the marks with makeup. She was terrified of the man."

When Bowen missed her children, she contacted her mother and pleaded for the return of custody. The woman prudently refused. But Bowen persisted, saying she was a changed woman and maintaining a respectable job at Kmart.

Bowen eventually convinced her mother that she was capable of raising her children properly. She promised her mother that the days with violent men had ended forever; in fact, she had met a nice man at the Kmart store. "His name is J.T.," she told her mother. "I want my kids back. I miss them. I love them."

But when Carr and Bowen visited Ohio on Thanksgiving Day 1997, Mrs. Bowen learned that J.T. was actually Hank Carr, the man everyone called Boo—the man with a criminal record.

"He took me out to the kitchen table," Connie Bowen said. "He showed me papers that he was getting government benefits for drug addiction. He also showed me papers that he was going to a place to get mental help, and he was going to AA."

When later asked if she had warned Bernice that Boo was wanted by police, Mrs. Bowen said, "Yes, I did. I continually told her."

Connie Bowen's husband Michael confirmed that Bernice knew the circumstances regarding the warrants against Boo, and in fact had known it for several years. But Bowen wanted to believe her daughter had changed. She acquiesced, and after the Thanksgiving visit, Kayla and Joey moved to Florida to live with their mother.

"If I had known the truth," Bowen lamented, "I would never have let them go."

Joseph Bennett never had a chance to say goodbye to his kids.

In thirteen years and four states, Carr had been imprisoned no less than four times. His charges and convictions included burglary with assault, forgery, grand theft, possession of cocaine, resisting arrest, battery on a law enforcement officer, domestic violence, felonious assault, drug trafficking and more.

The state of Ohio still held the outstanding warrant for marijuana trafficking charges.

In that regard, Detective Jeff Seevers of the Washington County Sheriff's Office in Ohio said, "We were surprised we hadn't heard something about that guy in a while. Something violent."

Seevers stated Carr constantly started fights and was capable of doing about anything. He said the career criminal reportedly had stomped puppies to death in front of children, bit off a man's ear, and had been questioned regarding the stabbing death of a teenage girl named Rhonda Manley.

Flanked by pawnshops, liquor stores, used automobile dealers, auto-repair shops, run-down motels, and used-furniture outlets, the neighborhood around Crenshaw and Nebraska struggled to survive the creeping influence of illegal drugs, strip joints and sex for hire. Crenshaw itself offered a natural beauty, with a myriad of sprawling tree limbs shading the homes, but crack houses weren't hard to find if you knew where to look. Hank Carr contributed to the neighborhood decline, dealing in drugs and weapons. He attended gun shows to buy handguns and assault rifles, then traded or sold them.

Neighbors often complained about noise emanating from Carr's apartment. They frequently heard gunfire and observed police activity in the area. Carr openly carried and displayed weapons, fired shots at animals, and once put a bullet through the apartment floor.

As in the past, Carr eluded police by successfully using one of his many aliases. He carried a false identification card with the name of Joseph Lee Bennett, and when police were looking for a felon by the name of Hank Earl Carr, he assumed another identity.

Bowen went along with the ploy, partially from fear of Carr, but also because she loved him and appreciated the attention he gave her children, even though various reports indicated has attention was at times quite painful and humiliating.

"Bernice said he beat the children a lot," testified Iris Adams, a friend who provided Bowen a place to stay for several days. When asked if he particularly targeted one child, she flatly said, "Joey."

Another incident involved complaints about aggressive spanking, and when investigators from the Department of Children and Family Services—formerly called HRS—visited, Carr gave them a different alias in each case.

The department uncovered no evidence of child abuse or neglect during the investigation.

"I got in a fight with a next-door neighbor," Carr explained. "So they called HRS on me. They didn't need to be here but the people called and tried to get me in trouble. I told them if they had a problem with me, they should just jump on me and beat me with a stick or somethin. Don't have my kids snatched away from their mother."

Carr said the investigators eventually apologized.

"They said HRS was wrong, but anyway HRS was up our ass for about a month. And they finally found out that the kids aren't being abused. The kids are fine. They got food. They know we love 'em."

Results of the interview would likely have been different had the investigators known his real name, his felony record, the outstanding warrant, or that he possessed numerous firearms, including more than one assault rifle.

Neighbors of the couple said Carr regularly carried a pistol and had a variety of guns.

"He dealt in a lot of guns," one woman testified. "Bernice carried a gun tucked in her waistband. It didn't matter if she was headed to the store or just getting on the bus, she always had a gun."

Bernice also knew Carr owned a universal handcuff key and that he always carried it with him.

"I saw him practice getting out of them on several occasions," the neighbor told investigators. "He was good at getting the handcuffs from the back to the front by pulling his legs between his arms, over the handcuffs. He said he could get away from any cops. I never saw Bernice with the handcuffs, but she was standing there watching when Boo did it."

For only a couple dollars and a visit to an Army Surplus store, anyone could own a standard handcuff key. They could be picked up off the Internet, the same as police badges and uniforms, since no law prevented the purchase or ownership of law enforcement accessories. Habitual Criminals like Carr knew all about that, and he bragged of having a key. He carried it with him at all times, either in his hip pocket or around his neck, and he often practiced using it.

"I knew he owned a handcuff key," Carr's mother said. "I didn't know he wore it around his neck, but I knew he had one. Bernice knew it, too."

People feared Hank Earl Carr for good reasons. He played hard, hit hard, loathed authority, took no prisoners, and vowed he would never again be one. Always armed, he blamed the police for his legal woes and he made it clear to everyone he *hated* cops.

"There was always gunfire over there," Charles Campbell told a reporter. "He'd go outside and pop off a few rounds. I don't believe he was playing with a full deck. One time he threw a television down the stairs. He was always verbally attacking the kids and Bernice. You could hear it from downstairs."

Curiously, Carr and Bowen frequently spoke in code. "It sounded like gibberish," said the neighbor.

Carr swore to his friends and girlfriend that he would kill himself before ever going back to prison. "He said it often," Carr's mother confirmed. "And he meant what he said."

*

Detectives Bert Batista, Brenda Santiago and Mike Howard stopped at headquarters Tuesday morning before going to the east side of Tampa to work a drug trafficking case. Batista mentioned to Santiago about sore legs from running the Armed Forces 5K race over the weekend, but she offered little sympathy. After all, the pain was self-induced, she told him. Besides, Santiago knew the detective probably placed high in his age division, as he often did.

As a dedicated runner, Batista helped organize the Tampa Police Memorial 5K four years earlier. The popular race had since become an annual event in October, with the proceeds going to the non-profit Tampa Police Memorial Fund.

"How can you be sore from a 5K?" Santiago asked, remembering that Batista had run the prestigious Gasparilla 15K in an impressive 59 minutes. "Three miles is a piece of cake for you, isn't it?"

"It used to be," he responded semi-seriously, patting his stomach. "Guess that's the problem. Too much cake."

Batista decided at that moment to run five or six miles after work, regardless of the temperature. Excuses had come too easily lately, he acknowledged. Running always made him feel better about himself, and he had nothing else planned that evening, anyway. But that was subject to change, of course.

While the trio of detectives worked at tightening the legal noose on a career felon over in east Tampa, their immediate supervisor, Sergeant Dan Grossi, sat at his desk and prepared the duty roster for the month of June.

"I had to make some changes in the schedule," Grossi said. "The Chief transferred Randy to Internal Affairs."

Just one day earlier, on Monday, Chief Bennie Holder announced that Detective Randy Bell would move from homicide investigations to Internal Affairs on the first day of June. "He earned it," Holder said. "He was an excellent interrogator and investigator."

"He possessed all the skills and talent I needed," Captain Terry Slater agreed.

"Ricky joked with Randy about the promotion," said Grossi. "He said, 'Now we gotta be careful what we say around him.'"

The homicide sergeant marked a few notes on his desk calendar, including one about dropping Bell from the schedule and selecting a replacement detective.

Bell graduated from Robinson High School in Tampa, became a police officer in November 1977, and transferred to homicide after six years as a patrolman. The 44-year-old detective looked forward to new challenges even though he expected it might be a little dull after 10 years in homicide. Like any other cop, he assumed he would miss the action and excitement. But at this point in his life, less danger suited him fine.

"At least with these characters," he joked, talking about his fellow officers, "I know where they keep their guns."

Bell maintained the plants and flowers throughout the homicide department. He prepared morning coffee for everyone and cleaned out the pot, enjoyed NASCAR racing and playing softball, and he spoke often about his children and wife Donna.

"Randy once saved an elderly woman from her fire-engulfed home," Detective Jerry Clark said. "And he won an award risking his own life to save EMS attendants from a burning ambulance."

"He was lead investigator on the case against serial-killer Glen Rogers," Lieutenant George McNamara said. In a service evaluation, McNamara wrote, "You are an important contributor to the success of this bureau. Thank you for this outstanding effort."

Rogers, dubbed the *Cross-country killer*, was sentenced to die for the 1995 murder of a Gibsonton woman named Tina Marie Cribbs.

Homicide Detective Julie Massucci worked together with Bell on the killer's conviction. Not only did Massucci confront death on a regular basis professionally, including delivering death notification to victims' families, but during the previous ten years she had endured the passing of several family members and a husband who died of a brain tumor.

"He was the one who inspired me to become a law enforcement officer," Massucci said of her late husband, who was also a Tampa Police officer.

Several years after the loss of her husband to a brain tumor, the mother of two daughters got the scare of her life when her stunningly beautiful 16-year old suffered a brain aneurysm.

"They're nearly always fatal," Massucci said. "But we got her to the hospital in time. They opened the side of her head for surgery, and it took 68 staples to patch her back together."

The detective remarried, once again to a police officer. She and her husband Chuck—also a Tampa Police detective—bought a new home north of Tampa, in Pasco County near the State Road 54 exit off the interstate; a place to escape and forget the big-city crime.

"I would always confide in Randy," said Massucci. "Since he was a stepfather, I went to him whenever Chuck and I had a disagreement over stepchildren. Although he generally sided with my husband, I respected his advice."

When it came time to return Rogers to Tampa for trial, Detectives Bell and Massucci volunteered to fly the bearded killer down from Kentucky in a small Cessna with room for only one officer.

"Randy insisted on going after him," Detective Massucci said. "And so did I."

"But he's a large man," Bell reminded the slender, blonde-headed Massucci, talking to her like a protective big brother. "If anything happens, I can fight the guy. I couldn't live with myself if anything happened to you."

Massucci remained firm. "We left the decision up to Deputy Chief Jane Siling and she agreed with Randy. In retrospect, I'm sure it was the correct decision."

Detective Bell flew with the killer back to Tampa; by agreement, Massucci took over at the airport.

"I will never forget the first Beanie Baby Randy bought for his youngest daughter," Massucci recalled, smiling fondly. "I though it was terribly homely and he shouldn't give it to her. But he did, and his daughter loved it."

Everyone spoke glowingly and respectfully of Detective Randy Bell. Everyone.

6

709 ½ East Crenshaw Street
Tampa, Florida
May 19, 1998

On May 19, Bernice Bowen started the day with an appointment at the Welfare Department, leaving Kayla and Joey in the apartment with Hank Carr. When she returned home, Bowen dressed and fed the children, and at approximately 0945 hours, she carried the broken video recorder outside and placed it in the rear seat of her gray, 1986 Pontiac Sunbird. With bathing suits and beach toys already packed, the youngsters were eager to get to the motel and frolic in the pool.

All in all, it looked like a great day for a swim, with the morning sun beginning to heat up the city of Tampa.

When Bowen returned to the apartment, according to her own testimony, she stopped to visit with an acquaintance from next door. At that point, the stories varied. One thing for certain, tragedy unfolded inside the apartment.

While walking up the stairs, Bowen claimed she heard a gunshot.

"When I got to the top of the steps, I opened the door and saw my son laying there bleeding. I freaked out. I turned around and I ran back down the steps and asked for help."

But another shooting witness saw it differently. "My mom said she wasn't in the room," 5-year-old Kayla Bennett told investigators later. "But she was."

The truth of what actually occurred and who all was in the room at the time of the shooting may never be known by anyone but Hank Carr and Bernice Bowen.

Joey Bennett was indeed lying on the floor, his T-shirt and brand new shorts soaked with his own blood.

Bowen claimed she didn't hear any yelling or see anyone in the room but her son. "I didn't see my boyfriend at the time," she said. "He was in the house, but I didn't see where at in the house. All I know is I just started screaming at the top of the steps, running down the steps, screaming, freaking. . . My boyfriend brought my son down the steps and put him in the car."

Carr didn't wait for help. He loaded Joey into the back seat of the Pontiac while Bowen yelled for her downstairs neighbor, Alisha Webb, to take care of Kayla. Webb, who was in the yard visiting with her aunt Vivian Macar, ran to help the terrified child.

Bowen jumped into the passenger's seat and Carr took off with the dying child alone in the back. They sped away east on Crenshaw, not exactly sure where to go, but knowing they needed help, and they needed it fast.

When investigators eventually asked Bowen what her boyfriend said about the shooting, she told them, "He just said that my son was shot. I didn't ask how or anything. All I know is I just wanted to get my baby to the doctors somewhere."

A right turn on Nebraska Avenue took them south, where a block later they spotted a police officer outside a Cuban sandwich shop called the O and B Deli. Carr swerved into the tiny strip mall, past a coin-operated laundry and squealed to a stop.

"They said they needed emergency medical assistance for their son," reported Police Officer Michael Peterson. "I asked them to stay put while I called an ambulance."

Carr thought the police officer was moving too slowly. "We can't wait!" he shouted frantically to Officer Peterson. "My son has been shot! I gotta go!"

"Then they took off," Peterson said. "So I yelled for them to go down to the fire station about ten blocks south on Nebraska."

At 0955 hours, the Pontiac skidded through a left turn on Hanna Street and took an immediate right turn into an open bay of Fire and

Rescue Station 7. The Rescue Truck had gone on an emergency call earlier, but Engine 7 remained parked inside the bay.

"I was about to back the engine from the bay," said EMT George Carter. "Roy Burkett and I were preparing to run a routine check of the water hoses."

Carter started the engine, but before moving it backward, the Pontiac screeched to a stop halfway inside the bay.

"I saw two adults leap out of this gray sedan," Carter said after witnessing what happened next. "I could see the panic in their eyes. Then they removed a small child from the back seat."

"Help us!" Carr screamed. "Our son has been shot! Help us!"

Carter left the engine running with the gears in neutral. He locked the emergency brake and went to help. "I took Joey from the man and laid him on the floor," Carter said. "I saw he had been shot in the face. He wasn't breathing and he had no pulse."

EMT Roy Burkett also ran over to the child. After taking a closer look, he grabbed the air bag and mask from the engine, cleared the child's airway and administered oxygen.

"I knew there was no chance of saving him," Burkett said. "Once I saw his wound, it was immediately obvious."

"Save my son!" Carr pleaded, standing over Burkett and Carter. "Please, you gotta save my son!"

The experienced emergency technicians knew their efforts were hopeless, but they dutifully went through the emergency procedures until paramedics arrived.

"The parents were horrified," Burkett observed. "They expected us to do something so we tried everything." Burkett shook his head. "But we knew there was nothing we could do."

"It was extremely difficult for me," Carter admitted. "The boy was the same age as my son and there was a slight resemblance."

As the men performed recovery procedures on Joey, someone at the fire station called 911 and reported the incident. The police were notified and the CAD—Computer Aided Dispatcher—sent a message to Rescue Station 5, the nearest station to Nebraska and Hanna.

Urgent response. CPR on an infant at Station Five, Nebraska and Hanna.

Terry Oliver, a 13-year paramedic, answered the call in Rescue Truck 5 along with M. G. Costello. They ran inside the bay and found Carter and Burkett performing CPR, doing everything possible to resuscitate the boy.

"The kid was DOS," Oliver said, shaking his head in a gesture of helplessness. "I knew it immediately."

With the EKG still attached, Burkett confirmed what they already suspected: Joey was DOS—Dead on Scene.

Officer John Simmons rushed to the fire station on Nebraska, as did numerous members of the media and dozens of curious citizens and bystanders.

"It was like a circus," Roy Burkett recalled in disgust. "We pulled the apparatus door down to keep everyone outside."

"I saw the mother kneeling next to the door," Terry Oliver added. "She was hysterical, in tears."

Burkett covered Joey Bennett with a sheet and waited for the Hillsborough County Medical Examiner.

Before officers separated the parents for the interview process, Carr pulled Bowen away from her son and led her outside the station. It was there, as stated in police records, that Carr said, "Tell everyone my name is Joseph Lee Bennett."

Bowen agreed to do as he said.

Officer Simmons talked to the self-proclaimed father outside the station. "He showed photo identification with his name, Joseph Lee Bennett. He told me the shooting was an accident, that his son was dragging a rifle and it discharged."

Carr, still covered with Joey's blood, suddenly darted from the station. While leaving Bernice Bowen and the officer behind, he sprinted back to the Pontiac.

"The father shoved the police officer out of his way and jumped in the car," Terry Oliver observed. "The officer grabbed the car door, but he yanked it right out his hands."

Carr jammed the Sunbird into reverse and squealed backward onto Hanna Street. He drove west, then turned right on Nebraska and sped out of sight.

"He fled north on Nebraska Avenue," Officer Simmons reported. "We were yelling for him to stop, but he kept going."

When Bowen answered questions, she obediently told them that Carr's name was Joseph Bennett. She told them she had gone outside to place the broken VCR in the Pontiac, and while returning, she heard the gunshot and ran inside the apartment.

When asked about the gun, Bowen told Simmons that a friend had come by the night before and asked her husband to keep it for him. The gun Bowen referred to, officers eventually learned, was a high-powered assault rifle.

"He told me it wasn't loaded," Bowen said, referring to the friend and the gun.

Another tragedy from an *unloaded* gun. This time, it occurred in the home of a weapons expert. A weapons fanatic. Hank Earl Carr.

*

Sergeant Dan Grossi received the emergency call from Station 7 at 1000 hours and rounded up his officers.

"I dispatched detectives to the fire station on Nebraska," Grossi said. "And I sent others to 709 ½ East Crenshaw where the shooting had occurred."

While working a robbery case with Julie Massucci, Detective Jerry Clark got a call from Sergeant Grossi. "He told us a child had been shot, and he was at the fire station on Nebraska and Hanna with his parents."

The priority call sent them speeding in an unmarked car. While in route, they discussed what might be awaiting them. "An accidental shooting of a child is one thing," they agreed. "But if it's intentional, that's even tougher."

An attentive Hillsborough deputy stopped them for speeding.

"I told the officer we were responding to a child being shot," said Clark. "He said, 'Go! Go! Go!' and waved us on."

"Marked cars have one advantage," Massucci quipped. "With lights and sirens, you don't get stopped."

Sergeant Grossi contacted Detective Ricky Childers and asked him to meet at Crenshaw Street to assist in the investigation.

Childers had joined Randy Bell in the homicide division in 1985, where they became close friends. Both officers were avid softball players, and both enjoyed spending time with their families. Ricky's wife, Vickie Childers, worked in the Records Division, just a few floors below her husband's office.

Along with Detective Bert Batista and 30 other recruits, Childers entered the Tampa Police Academy in September of 1979, Class #55. They graduated that same December, and in one more year would complete 20 years on the Force. Throughout those years, Childers helped solve many high-profile cases, and in 1990, he saved the life of a teenage girl whose car careened off a highway and flipped into a creek. The off-duty officer ran to the sinking vehicle, dove into the murky water, broke a window and rescued the girl.

The selfless valor and quick reaction by Childers earned him the Distinguished Service Award and Officer of the Year.

Along with Detective Bell, Ricky "Chilly" Childers collected evidence that led to a death sentence for Newton Slawson, a demonic killer who murdered a family of four and cut an unborn child from the mother's womb with a pair of scissors.

Like his friend Randy Bell, Childers had earned the respect of everyone in the department, if not the entire city.

"He was also a jokester," Jerry Clark said. "He had a great sense of humor. Always fun to be around. Even in the worst situations, he could make you laugh."

Julie Massucci enjoyed the playful teasing from Childers.

"I see Miss Clairol swept away the gray again today," Ricky told her whenever she brightened her hair.

"Whenever I bought a new outfit," Massucci said affectionately of her friend, "Ricky would say, 'I see we've been shopping at the Salvation Army again.'"

"He was a kind and gentle man," Detective Jackie Keene offered. "He liked to take his breaks outside the building so he could feed the birds and the squirrels."

Ricky's sons Chip and Corky frequently stopped by the police station to see their father. Referring to Tuesday, May 19, Detective Massucci poignantly said, "Corky was coming down to have lunch with him that day."

Followed by Victims Advocate Donna Wilson, Detectives Clark and Massucci arrived at Fire Rescue Station 7. "The boy's father had already gone when we arrived," Detective Clark said about Carr. "Once we learned where the shooting occurred, Detective Massucci stayed with the mother and I drove over to Crenshaw Street."

Wilson consoled Bowen in an office while Massucci went inside the bay to look at the child and document the scene.

"Then I interviewed the grief-stricken mother," Massucci said, remaining composed under the horrendous circumstance. "She told me that her husband said Joey shot himself. We needed to have her sign a consent letter so we could search her apartment; she signed it Bernice Bennett."

During the interview at the fire station, Bowen mentioned that her son had tried to play with guns before.

"But I always smacked his hand," Bowen insisted. "My son has a fascination with guns. He'd sit right next to my husband whenever he cleaned the guns."

Perhaps even more alarming, according to the court testimony of friend Steve Adams, Carr and Joey had a unique method of greeting each other.

"They'd draw guns," said Adams, Carr's co-worker at a company called Tampa Tent. "Boo would pull a 9mm Glock out and Joey would pull out a 9mm BB pistol. They'd point them at each other. That's the way they greeted each other."

"It seemed very curious to me," said Massucci, "but the mother continually asked how her husband was doing. She appeared to be more concerned about his condition than that of her son."

"I knew my baby was dead," Bowen professed. "And if he lived, he would have brain damage."

Massucci observed blood on Bowen's clothing.

"When I asked her how it got there, she said, 'I got it when my husband hugged me.' It didn't appear to be from a hug. Splattered was a better description. However, she told me she wasn't in the room when the shooting occurred."

"When I arrived at the station," said Lee Miller, the Hillsborough County Medical Examiner, "the deceased was lying on the floor next to the fire engine covered by a sheet. There was an entrance gunshot wound on the right side of his nose."

Understandably, the traumatic experience at Rescue Station 7 left the paramedics and firefighters devastated. After a visit from the Stress Management team, most of the crew terminated their shifts and went directly home; the Battalion Chief called standby personnel to come in for replacement duty.

"This is not normal to have a young child like this killed," Fire Captain Jim McAlister told reporters. "And it's compounded when the child is brought to the station, which is usually a safe haven for the firefighters. They normally have time to mentally prepare when they have an emergency."

Utilizing his customary bag of tricks to evade law enforcement officers, Carr parked the car on Hamilton Street, a block south of 709 Crenshaw. He ran to the apartment and began moving things out, but Officer Andrew Pedersen arrived at that location at approximately 1020 hours and caught him by surprise.

"I saw him coming out on the stairway landing with a rifle in his hand," Pederson said. "I ordered him to put the rifle down."

"I was bringing it to you," Carr said, gripping the weapon.

"Put it down and stay where you are!"

"I came back for my daughter," Carr went on, still not responding to the officer's demand.

"Put the rifle down! Put it down now!"

Carr reluctantly placed the rifle on the landing.

Corporal Brian O'Connor, who had seen Carr at the fire station, responded to Crenshaw with Officers Simmons, Marvin Keys and Ricardo Delatorre. When Captain Sam Diaz arrived, Pederson briefed him on the shooting.

"I was advised that the scene was an upstairs apartment located at 709 Crenshaw," Diaz said. "Officer Keys was standing guard at the entrance. Seated in a chair next to the door was a white male in his 30's, who had identified himself to the officers as the child's father, Joseph Lee Bennett."

Officer Marilyn Lee taped off the area and opened a crime scene log. When homicide Detective Rick Stanton arrived, Carr maintained a cooperative demeanor, but he appeared jittery and nervous. He had presented a photo ID of himself with an address in Virginia, which included the birth date of Joseph Bennett, July 10, 1964, a man who was three and a half years older than Carr.

The officers received no indication that the man was anything but a remorseful, distraught father.

"It was an accident," Carr adamantly told the detective. "My kid was playing with the gun. We were getting ready to take him to go swimming and buy him some toys. He was dragging the gun and it went off."

If the boy was dragging the gun, officers wondered, how was he shot in the face?

"I noticed the subject acting very nervous," Captain Diaz said. "I told Detective Stanton, 'This guy is spooky.'"

Stanton had the same reaction.

Detective Ricky Childers entered the crime scene during initial investigation, as did Chris Watson and Dick Hurd, representatives from the State Attorney's Office.

Sergeant Grossi arrived to coordinate the investigation. He parked his unmarked vehicle in front of the house at 709 and walked over to the growing contingent of law enforcement officers.

"Am I under arrest?" Carr asked the officers, pacing the area and scratching at the wispy goatee growing on his chin.

"No, sir. Just hold on a minute. We have some questions."

While visiting friends at the house on 709 Crenshaw, Patricia Mercer heard the commotion and went outside. "Boo kept saying 'It was accident, an accident, I didn't mean to do it,'" said Mercer. "He was just walking back and forth, and up and down the stairs, and rambling on. Then he went inside the apartment downstairs, looked around and ran out the back door. Then we told the police officers he ran outside behind the house."

"He's running!" an officer shouted, and took off in pursuit.

"As I was walking up the driveway," Sergeant Grossi said, "the man started running. I asked the officers who he was."

"That's the suspect!"

"Then we gotta get him!"

Half a dozen officers pursued on foot, trailing Carr past Cleveland Elementary School and through the back yards of several homes west of Nebraska Avenue. Carr led the chase for six or seven blocks before crawling under some hedges behind a house on Norfolk Street. When O'Connor rounded the corner, he spotted a pair of sneakers on the ground protruding from beneath the hedges.

He pointed it out to Sergeant Smith, and within moments, Carr jumped up and again took off running, but he came face to face with Corporal O'Conner.

"Get on the ground!" O'Connor ordered.

An altercation ensued and the other officers swarmed in.

"Get on the ground!"

"On the ground!"

Carr put up a feckless struggle, but they quickly wrestled him prone and cuffed him from behind. He got to his feet limping and complaining that he injured his right knee. He apologized for running away, saying that he simply panicked. "I wanted to go be with my wife," he claimed, as they escorted him back to Crenshaw Street. "I wanted to see if my daughter was okay."

The assertion didn't connect. After all, when officers first arrived they found Carr clinging to an assault rifle not his daughter.

Police procedure allowed Carr to be cuffed either in front or back, whichever the officers selected. But since they had subdued him belly down, they left him cuffed from behind even though he wasn't under arrest. At that point, they believed he was a grieving and panicked father whose son had been accidentally killed.

"I never shot him on purpose," Carr insisted, tearfully. "I didn't even know the gun was loaded. It was unloaded the night before. I don't know where the bullets came from."

"But you had the gun?" the detective asked.

"I picked up the gun, and I went to turn it around and put it back on the shelf. The butt hit the wall and it went off."

With each answer and explanation, detectives grew more curious: was the kid dragging it or did the butt hit the wall?

"We're taking you downtown, Mister Bennett," said Stanton. "We need to ask some questions."

"But I'm telling you, it was an accident."

"Okay, I understand."

An EMS team with sanitary gloves cleansed Carr's injured knee and wrapped it with an elastic bandage. The officers then placed him in the back seat of a patrol car driven by Officer Keith Billingsley, a seasoned veteran of the Police Department.

"At that point, we were beginning to wonder about the man," said Detective Clark. "I overheard Stanton tell Billingsley, 'Don't let this guy go.'"

In his unmarked sedan, Detective Childers followed Billingsley and the suspect back to the station.

"Hey, officer, could you stop somewhere for a minute?" Carr asked Billingsley, after they exited the freeway in a populated area. "I gotta take a piss."

"You'll be okay," the soft-spoken officer said. "We'll be there in a few minutes."

"Man, I need to stop."

"You can hold it. You're a big boy."

"I can't. I'll piss in the car."

"Well, pal, I wouldn't recommend that. Like I told you, we'll be there in just a few minutes"

It was already hot at 11 o'clock that morning, and at some point during the transport, while sweating heavily in the back seat of the patrol car, Hank Carr had managed to slip his right hand out from the handcuffs.

"That's not unusual," Detective Clark explained. "Even with dry hands, suspects occasionally get out of the cuffs."

In retrospect, some officers speculated the sweat might have had nothing to do with it. It was quite possible that Officer Billingsley had saved his own life that day by not stopping. With Carr likely free from the cuffs at that time, utilizing a restroom may have been the last thing on his mind.

The media arrived at the Police Department ahead of Childers and Billingsley. Once the officers removed Carr from the back seat, an observant reporter noticed something odd.

"Hey, officer," he called out to Detective Childers. "This guy is out of the cuffs. He's just holding one of 'em."

Childers turned Carr and found that one handcuff had in fact been removed; he was holding it in his fist, still behind his back.

"What the heck are you doing?" Childers scolded the man. "You playing games with the handcuffs?"

"They got wet," Carr mumbled. "They just slipped off."

"Yeah, yeah, okay. But don't be playing any games. I'm not in a game-playing mood today."

Childers reattached the cuff and took the sweaty man inside the 78-degree building.

Once Detective Massucci obtained the search consent, she placed Bowen in the back seat of a four-door Dodge Dynasty and took her back to examine the shooting scene.

Donna Wilson went to locate the abandoned daughter.

7

Tampa Police Department
411 Franklin Street
Tampa, Florida
May 19, 1998; 1100 hours

Detective Greg Stout saw Childers enter the eighth-floor homicide office with Carr. "I was the only person in the office at the time. I was doing some paperwork when he walked in."

"I've been in a foot chase," Childers said when Stout commented on his disheveled look.

"Yeah? Who won?"

"The good guys, of course."

"Carr was talking a mile a minute," Stout remembered. "He said, 'Hi there, how are you?'"

Detective Stout glanced curiously at Childers, thinking that under the circumstances, the suspect seemed surprisingly affable.

When Randy Bell arrived at the office to sort through his files in preparation for transfer to Internal Affairs, he heard the conversation and offered to sit in on the interview.

Corporals Jerry Herren and James "Sandy" Noblitt also showed up. "I heard Ricky in there," Herren said. "He gets very loud."

"Ricky came out for our tape recorder and went back into the room," said Noblitt. "The issue, of course, was the baby dragging the gun when he got shot. The officers already doubted that based on the investigation at the scene."

After switching the handcuffs to the front so Carr could sit more comfortably in the straight-back chair, he told the officers he was ready for their questioning. Childers pressed the record button and began by announcing the date, time and location of the interview, then mentioned that Randy Bell was present and the person being interviewed would be a white male named Joseph Lee Bennett. The questions quickly led to the rifle; Carr repeated what he said earlier, that Joey had been playing with it.

CHILDERS: All right, how was Joey handling the rifle? Is he dragging it or holding it, carrying it, or what?

CARR: He was kinda like letting it go. He had it by the barrel. He said it fell and he was just pickin it up.

CHILDERS: Then you grab it and pick it up?

CARR: Right.

CHILDERS: And is that when the rifle goes off?

CARR: Yes, sir.

CHILDERS: Obviously, it struck your son.

CARR: Yes, sir.

CHILDERS: Okay.

CARR: (Carr sobs, gasping for breath.) Oh, God, oh, God.

CHILDERS: Joe, I know it's hard. It's very hard.

CARR: It's unbelievable.

CHILDERS: Where was your wife when this happened?

CARR: She was in the bathroom. I don't know if she seen it or not. She came in and started screamin, "Oh, my God! Oh, my God!" I was screamin, "Oh, my God! Oh, my God!"

CHILDERS: Joe, tell me again for the record, would you state your name, please?

CARR: Sure. Joseph Lee Bennett.

Back at Crenshaw Street, Sergeant Grossi advised officers to transport Kayla and witnesses Alisha Webb and Patricia Mercer to 411 Franklin Street. During transport, Kayla told Officer Marilyn Lee that she was in the room when Joey got shot.

Massucci took Bowen upstairs so she could point out where Joey was standing when shot. "Then she borrowed clothes from a neighbor and surrendered the bloody dress for evidence," said Massucci. "Then I took her downtown for further questioning."

Captain Robert Price met with Randy Bell and Jackie Keene.

"They sent me to the Child Advocacy Center to interview Kayla along with State Attorney Jay Prunner," recalled Keene, a detective in the Crimes Against Children department. "Mister Prunner provided questions and observed us through the one-way glass."

After about an hour at the police station, with Carr's explanations creating more skepticism than answers, Detectives Childers and Bell decided to haul him back to the Crenshaw apartment to recreate the scene by taking him through everything step by step.

Vickie Childers approached the elevator shortly after her husband and Detective Bell left with Carr.

"You just missed Ricky," an officer told Mrs. Childers. "He was standing here with a suspect, but they just left."

Childers and Bell spent another half hour walking through the apartment with Carr, while Detectives Stanton and Clark searched the area inside and outside.

"It was bad enough they took me back there," Carr whined in a later interview. "My son's blood was all over the floor and walls. I tried to tell them exactly what happened."

Stanton advised him the blood splattered on the entertainment center and telephone book underneath it was not consistent with his story. "Then I opened a closet and found another assault rifle. One with a laser scope mounted."

"That one's my wife's," Carr said evasively.

The detectives also found a number of holes in the walls. "They appeared to be bullet holes," said Stanton. "It looked like someone had taken target practice."

"They were calling me a liar," Carr protested. "They thought me and Bernice got in some kind of fight or something. They thought she shielded herself with the child and I shot him anyway."

Stanton denied calling him a liar. "That's not how we do things. But I don't believe it happened the way Carr described it. I believe he may have accidentally pulled the trigger trying to prove a point. But I also believe he purposely aimed the gun at that little boy."

When finished interrogating Carr at the apartment, Detectives Bell and Childers decided to take him back downtown for additional questioning. Before leaving, Bell opened the trunk of Childers' dark-green, unmarked Ford Taurus and placed a black rifle bag inside—the bag contained a North China Industries SKS 7.62 caliber assault rifle. With Carr still cuffed in front, they placed him in the back seat of the vehicle, which had no cage barrier separating the front and rear seats.

"I personally have transported many confessed murderers in a car with their handcuffs in front," Detective Noblitt acknowledged in that regard. "I've learned that you can get more information with sugar than salt."

Before the officers departed with Carr, Detective Clark opened a vacant apartment and found more weapons, including a shotgun and another assault rifle. The cache also included boxes of ammunition, handguns, Kevlar helmets, vests and protective gear. They found no connection to the grieving father, but Rick Stanton pulled Detective Childers aside to give him a heads up on what they found.

The two detectives hauled Carr away in the green Taurus. They drove south on Nebraska Avenue and turned west at Sligh Avenue, the nearest entrance to Interstate 275.

"Are you gonna take me to prison?" Carr asked the detectives.

"Not if it was an accident," they answered truthfully.

*

Now at the downtown headquarters, Detectives Massucci and Noblitt interviewed Bernice Bowen. She repeated earlier claims that Carr was her boyfriend, Joseph Bennett, and that a friend had brought over the rifle on the preceding evening. She stated that her boyfriend did not explain how Joey got shot, and she never had a chance to ask because she was preoccupied with getting help for the child. Although the officers explored details about her boyfriend and their relationship, she never provided any information about the handcuff key or any previous arrests.

"When we ran the name Joseph Bennett through the data bank," Detective Noblitt said, "he came up clean."

MASSUCCI: Did the kids go with you to the welfare department?

BOWEN: The kids stayed with my boyfriend.

MASSUCCI: What happened when you came back?

BOWEN: When I came back, I told the kids to get dressed. Fed 'em breakfast. I told 'em we were gettin ready to go get our VCR fixed. And like I said, I took my VCR down to the car and then I was walking up the steps. I heard the gunshot and I opened up the door and there laid my son. Bleeding. Shot in the face.

MASSUCCI: When you opened the door, the only thing you saw was your son?

BOWEN: I didn't see nobody else or anything.

MASSUCCI: Did you hear anybody yelling or anything?

BOWEN: I didn't hear anything.

MASSUCCI: You didn't hear anything?

BOWEN: All I know is I just started screaming at the top of the steps, running down the steps, screaming, freaking.

MASSUCCI: And then you saw your boyfriend bringing him down the steps?

BOWEN: He brought the baby down and put him into the car.

MASSUCCI: Where did he put him in the car?

BOWEN: In the back seat.

MASSUCCI: In the back seat? Did you sit with the baby and hold him at all?

BOWEN: No, I sat up front. I was watching him. I didn't even hold him.

MASSUCCI: Did your boyfriend have any other guns in the house anywhere?

BOWEN: None that I know of. Not to my knowledge.

MASSUCCI: Have you ever seen your boyfriend cleaning any guns or doing anything with any guns before?

BOWEN: I've seen him clean 'em. But he's never played with them as a toy. It was never a toy for him. And he was all the time warning my son about, you know, how guns can kill you, you know. My little boy was fascinated with 'em. When somebody were to sit down and clean a gun, my little boy was just right there, you know.

MASSUCCI: Did you allow your boyfriend to discipline the kids if they had to be disciplined?

BOWEN: Huh-uh. I did it.

"I treated her like a grieving mother," Massucci said, explaining why the officers had no reason to doubt Bowen. "I was sympathetic. I can't even imagine how it feels to lose a child."

Detective Noblitt took over the interrogation, beginning with questions regarding Carr's role in disciplining the kids. Early in the interrogation, Bowen had mentioned visits from DCF investigators responding to complaints.

BOWEN: Um, the next door neighbor, we were managing them apartments over there and they got mad cause we had to evict them. The land owner wanted us to evict them. They got mad and called HRS. Both times it was written up as harassment.

NOBLITT: Harassment?

BOWEN: Yeah, harassment. I took all the children's clothes off right in front of 'em, look at 'em from head to toe and they seen that the children were fine.

NOBLITT: When the neighbor made those complaints, were they complaining that you also did that or just Joseph?

BOWEN: No. Not me.

NOBLITT: So they haven't accused you of anything?

BOWEN: No, they haven't accused me of anything. They never accused exactly anybody. They just said the children were supposed to be, ah, being abused, is what it was.

NOBLITT: Well, I was just trying to find out because before we started taping your interview, I wasn't aware there were any other investigations in the last few months.

BOWEN: Uh-huh.

NOBLITT: Okay. Reference this morning's shooting, have you told us every single thing that happened?

BOWEN: Everything I know about, sir, yes. To my knowledge.

NOBLITT: In any of these conversations, Joe never made any statement to you about how your son got shot?

BOWEN: He never had a chance. He took me to the fire department, okay, and all he kept saying, if you'll go with me, I'll show you where it's at. And then, I guess the next thing I know, as far as I know, the cops told me that he had taken off in the car.

NOBLITT: Right, but what I'm asking you, when he first got in the car with you? With your son in the car?

BOWEN: Uh-huh.

NOBLITT: Did you ask him how did this happen?

BOWEN: Yeah, I asked him what happened.

NOBLITT: And what did he say?

BOWEN: He said my son was shot.

NOBLITT: That's all?

BOWEN: I didn't ask how or anything. All I know is I just wanted to get my baby to the doctors.

NOBLITT: But Joe never made a statement to you how your son got shot?

BOWEN: No.

NOBLITT: Okay. (to Massucci) Do you have anything else?

MASSUCCI: (to Bowen) Do you have anything else that you want to add before we close the interview?

BOWEN: No.

MASSUCCI: Why don't you go ahead and say your name one last time.

BOWEN: My name is Bernice Bennett.

When detectives ended their interview at 12:46, Bowen thought they were finished with her. "Not just yet," Massucci said. "We'll be finished when the detectives complete their investigation at the scene with your boyfriend."

Detective Noblitt compared notes with other detectives after his interview with Bernice Bowen.

"I concluded this was not Joseph Lee Bennett," he said. "I went to the sergeant and said, 'Where are Ricky and Randy?'"

"They took Bennett back to the crime scene," Grossi answered.

"I don't think his name is Bennett. We need his fingerprints as soon as they get back here."

Detective Keene returned from the Child Advocacy Center with Kayla and the taped interview. After sharing pertinent information with Detective Massucci, they left Kayla with a secretary and took the tape to the office of Captain Price, who then listened to what the child said about the shooting.

"Boo shot Joey with a rifle," Kayla said innocently. "It was the long, black gun, not the nine millimeter."

"She knew the difference in the guns," Massucci told the captain. "She also said her mother was in the room when the gun went off. She remembered because her mom yelled 'Boo!' when the shooting occurred."

"She told us her mom was right beside her in the room," Keene confirmed. "And I believe her."

Evidence also came from a drawing. When asked to recreate the scene in a diagram using stick figures, Kayla depicted her mother and Bennett side by side with Joey lying on the floor.

"The child was absolutely petrified her father would show up at the Police Department," Massucci added. "We turned her over to DCF so they could take her out of there right away."

During a live broadcast from the apartment on Crenshaw Street, a reporter for Channel 28 in Tampa found neighbors who supported the allegation. "Joe Bennett said it was an accident," Dawn Witt reported from beneath a shade tree, "but witnesses are telling us here that actually the five-year-old stepdaughter said that she saw Daddy put the gun up to her four-year-old brother's head and fire. She apparently was right in the room when it happened and was covered in blood herself..."

Detective Massucci grew more disillusioned that the woman with whom she first sympathized as a grieving mother now seemed less concerned about her dead child than she was for the man that shot him. After all, she asked herself, if the shooting truly was an accident, why was the mother so evasive and inconsistent? Worse yet, if the death of her son was intentional, why would she cover for the killer?

8

Interstate 275 and Floribraska
Tampa, Florida
May 19, 1998; 1338 hours

The direct route to the Police Department on Franklin Street normally went down Ashley Street, but the green Taurus driven by Detective Childers slowed at the Floribraska exit. It was well past lunch hour. The detectives hadn't eaten since early morning, and with Childers' weakness for hamburgers, a nearby Checkers may have been their interim destination. Maybe not.

Whether by hidden handcuff key or by sweaty hands, as alleged earlier, Carr somehow managed to remove a handcuff from one wrist. Subsequently, the green Taurus came off the freeway and stopped in the middle of Elmore Street southbound, a street that ran parallel to the freeway and dead-ended at Floribraska.

A white car owned by Tampa Electric Company and driven by Kerry Mauldin came up behind the unmarked police vehicle. Mauldin noticed a stocky, white male leap from the green Taurus with a pistol in his hand so he kept on moving.

"He came toward me as I drove by," Mauldin later told Detective James O'Nolan. "I accelerated to Floribraska and turned west. I went to a phone to call 911."

Several other vehicles exited the interstate at approximately the same time. A white 1997 Ford Ranger came down the exit ramp next. The small delivery truck displayed large red letters "APD" on the doors, with a telephone number for Pep Boys stenciled across the side of the cargo bed.

"I saw the green sedan stop quickly," said Michael Henderson, a Pep Boys delivery driver who stopped directly behind the Taurus. "I didn't hear any gunshots, but I saw what looked like a scuffle inside. They were bouncing around in the seat. The driver rolled toward the door and tried to get out, then this guy gets out the left rear passenger door with a gun in his right hand. At first I thought he was a police officer in distress."

Carr dashed back to the delivery truck, leaned through the open window and shoved the gun against Henderson's chin. "Get out! I'm taking your truck!"

Momentarily traumatized by the image of a hollow-eyed, pony-tailed man shoving a large weapon to his face, the part-time delivery driver and off-duty Hillsborough County Firefighter froze. Carr then stepped back and pointed the Glock through the windshield.

"Didn't you hear what I said? Get out of the truck!"

"That's when I noticed the handcuff on his wrist," the 47-year-old victim said.

Although a fit, 230-pounder, Henderson wisely complied and jumped out. "I backed away as fast as I could. I saw him go back to the driver's door of the Taurus and get something from inside. When he opened the trunk and took out a black rifle case, I ran to a wooded area across the street."

"I came off the freeway and saw a car stopped in the middle of the road," said Melody Jones, another witness at the scene. "I thought somebody was sick or having a heart attack."

Aaron Czyzewski came down the exit ramp after the delivery truck. Like Henderson, he hadn't seen any gunfire. "I saw this man with a blonde pony tail wearing a white T-shirt and blue shorts. He was holding a gun and taking what appeared to be a rifle case from the trunk of the green car. He was walking with a limp, but I thought he was a cop."

Carrying the assault rifle and the detectives' handguns along with him, Carr took off in the Ranger, turning east under the freeway on Floribraska Avenue.

"Mrs. Melody Jones then drove around the vehicle and saw a white male with blonde hair," Detective Mike Howard wrote in his report. "She looked into her rear view mirror and noticed the driver was slumped over, and the white male was getting a black bag from the trunk of the stopped vehicle. He then got into a white pickup and fled the scene. Mrs. Jones' friend ran back to offer assistance."

"After the suspect had fled," Detective John Yaratch reported, "Mister Henderson went to the vehicle and found two victims inside. He saw the passenger sitting in the right front seat and it appeared that he had attempted to turn to the rear. He said it was obvious the victim was not alive at that time. He then looked at the driver, and it was very apparent that he too was deceased. Other witnesses arrived at that time, and Mister Henderson ran to find a telephone."

Henderson spotted a power company employee reading a meter. "I told him what happened and asked him to call 911."

At approximately 1343 hours, the first call reached the emergency center dispatcher.

"Something terrible has happened!" Aaron Czyzewski shouted into the phone. "If I had to guess, somebody's been shot and killed! This guy was running frantically, getting things out of the car. He carjacked the pickup and took off, and then somebody went up to the car and started screaming to call the police!"

During the next call, the dispatcher heard someone screaming in the background. "We got a man shot on the exit on Floribraska! He's shot in the head! He's going to die!"

Sergeant Bill Rousseau, shift commander at District II, received a call from a patrol unit. "We have a carjacking at 275 and Floribraska. Two men shot."

"My first action was to notify the chiefs," Rousseau said. "Then I garnered resources and coordinated between factions of the Police Department."

"Mister Czyzewski saw the suspect flee in a white truck," Officer Victor Gancedo said. "He turned eastbound on Floribraska, under the overpass on I-275. Mister Czyzewski then looked inside the Ford

Taurus and saw the two victims. Assuming they were deceased, he searched for a phone to contact the police via 911."

"My friend started screaming hysterically," Melody Jones told the first officer to arrive. "They've been shot! They've been shot!"

Joseph Jackson came on the crime scene next. "I saw a black woman flagging me and screaming. She told me that two guys had been shot. I went over there, and this other guy told me his truck was stolen at gunpoint."

"Mister Jackson used his cell phone to call for help," Detective Mike Mitchell stated in his report.

"One witness said the suspects were two white males," Officer David Rochelle reported, "but that turned out to be erroneous."

While visiting a friend on Hugh Street, Salphaad Colon heard screaming. He ran over to Elmore Street and saw the green vehicle.

"According to Mister Colon," Officer Coller said, "the driver was bleeding from the back of the head and the passenger was bleeding from the front of the head. He said he also observed a black female checking for a pulse on the passenger."

Back at 411 Franklin Street, Captain Price asked Corporal Herren if he could go investigate a carjacking.

"I can't go right now. I'm waiting for Chilly and Randy to get back with that suspect who calls himself Bennett."

"Sergeant Grossi entered my office at that time," Price said. "So he and two of our detectives dispatched to the scene."

On patrol near the location of the shooting and carjacking, Officer Juan Ramos and Gil Mercado arrived to find Reserve Officer Harold Jones directing traffic around the Taurus. "We saw Detectives Bell and Childers slumped in the front seats."

Officer Ramos reached for Bell. "He's still warm!"

The officers pulled Bell up and checked his vitals. When he found no heartbeat, Ramos immediately performed CPR, only to find blood squirting with each compression.

Officer Mercado continued: "Once we had obtained the necessary information on the suspect and the carjacked vehicle, Officer Ramos advised Frequency 4 what was needed, while I placed the alert over Frequency 5."

"I went to the scene of a shooting along with several District III units," reported Officer Jeffery Thiel. "I observed the deceased to be our detectives. Staff and other officials were notified with Bolos over radio for the suspect vehicle. There were several witnesses at the scene, and Bolos were updated as needed."

"I grabbed the crime scene tape and roped off the area," Corporal Gary Bradford reported. "We manned the lower crime scene and kept out all unnecessary personnel."

Officer Jennifer Power assisted the Department of Transportation in blocking the exit ramp. "We first placed flares and cones along the emergency lane to keep spectators from stopping cars and gawking at the slain officers."

The emergency calls brought numerous officers to Elmore and Floribraska in support of the operation, which necessitated securing the crime scene, traffic control, crowd control, patrolling all major intersections, witness contact, searching for evidence, and setting a perimeter around the suspect's neighborhood.

Fire Rescue units from three stations arrived at the scene.

"Our unit arrived first," said Marlin Taylor, an EMT from Rescue Station 5. "Paramedic Ramon Rivas checked the victims and found no pulse and there were no vital signs."

Captain Jessie Wright confirmed. "There were no vitals on either victim."

"Both victims suffered what appeared to be gunshot wounds to the head," David Chesser noted in his call report. "Neither victim had any life signs, but we attempted to hook an EKG machine on one of them."

Rescue Trucks from stations 8 and 18 arrived within minutes of Rescue Engine 5.

"There were two victims inside the vehicle," George Lee told the detectives. "It appeared that both victims had been shot in the head. We found no life signs."

Ryan Bradford, a 21-year-old paramedic student, also examined Detective Bell. "I observed a gunshot wound to the right forehead, just above the eye. No vitals."

*

Gail Cox lived at 1913 East Paris Street with her brother, Earl James Reid, who had gone to the Orient Road Jail to pick up some car keys. As the 51-year-old man returned home, he heard the news report about a child being shot. He didn't think much about it at the time, but when he arrived at the Paris Street address, three miles northeast of Elmore and Floribraska, he walked up the driveway and heard his sister screaming.

"When I opened the door," Reid said, "she told me Bernice had called her and Joe was killed. I thought it was my son at first, because his name is also Joe. But it was Joey, her grandson."

Reid sat down and offered comfort to his sister, but while they talked, Hank Carr parked behind the house and ran inside.

"He came in the back door," Cox said. "He was crying and started hugging me."

"Mama, I killed Joey," Carr sobbed. "It was an accident."

"He had blood all over him," Reid said of his nephew. "His mother pushed him away. She didn't want to be close to him with the blood on his shirt. He went to the kitchen and washed himself in the sink," the uncle said, "then he wanted a clean shirt. I told him to go up to my room, the door was open, and there were shirts that had just been laundered laying on the dresser."

Carr scrambled up the stairs and came back wearing a black, Harley-Davidson T-shirt from Sturgis, South Dakota; he tossed the bloody shirt in a trashcan at the rear of the residence.

"He told us he took Joey to the fire station, where police released him after getting all the information. He was here about 10 minutes," Reid said. "Then said goodbye to his mother and told her he'd never see her again. After he ran out the back to the alleyway, I walked out on the back porch and saw he was driving a little white truck. I don't even know the make of the truck, but it had red letters on it."

The telephone lines heated up at Police Headquarters, beginning with the office of the shift commander Lieutenant Mary Rendall. As calls came in and the news media swung into action, phones, beepers and pagers for nearly every officer in Hillsborough County started taking hits. The media all delivered the same message: *Two police officers shot!*

At the scene of the shooting, Officer Dale Frix ran to his marked unit. "I called Lieutenant Rendall on my cell phone," the officer said. "I told her the victims were our detectives. I called Captain Rick Duran, then assisted the other officers and initiated a crime scene contamination list."

Captain Diaz overheard the dispatcher placing an alert: "A white Ford Ranger pickup with red lettering on the side has been carjacked from Elmore and Floribraska."

Sergeants Ron Reynolds and Patrick Minnax entered the Comm Center at that time. "They received information that two homicide detectives had been shot," Captain Diaz said. "But their identities were unknown."

Lieutenant Rendall made a call to Chief Holder. "He wasn't in, so I had them page him. I then contacted Assistant Chief Walter Sawyer and Major Cunningham."

Lieutenant Steven Jarrett opened a log detailing the timeline of events as they were handled through the shift commander's office in Uniform District I.

"I drove to Floribraska and observed an unmarked police unit in the center of the street with both doors open," Captain Diaz said. "I walked up to Lieutenant Robert Guidara and glanced into the vehicle. I observed Detective Ricky Childers behind the wheel and Detective Randy Bell on the passenger side. Both were covered with blood and appeared dead."

Detective John Tindall interviewed Patricia Mercer and Alisha Webb before driving to Floribraska and Elmore. Upon arrival, he recalled seeing Sergeant Michael Smith with tears in his eyes. "I said, 'Sergeant, something is not quite right here. We're supposed to be investigating two dead carjackers, and I know you don't have tears in your eyes because of that."

Corporal Noblitt responded to Interstate 275 and Floribraska to investigate the reported carjacking. "I thought I was leaving the Joey Bennett investigation to go investigate a totally unrelated double homicide carjacking . . . Then I got to the scene."

Lieutenant Mike George and Captain Rick Duran supervised the crime scene. They knew Childers and Bell were transporting the man who earlier in the day shot his son and then ran from officers twice; they knew his name was Joseph Lee Bennett and he lived on East Crenshaw near Cleveland Elementary School.

Officers Keith Billingsley, Veronica Hills, David Weaver-Rogers, and Walter Sams combed the neighborhood interviewing witnesses, including taking the information from Michael Henderson and Aaron Czyzewski. They talked to other witnesses: Thomas Wilson, Cedric Gilchrist, Charlene Montgomery, Josefina Diaz and Narada Burton each offered personal versions of what occurred, but none saw or heard any gunfire.

"Upon arrival of TPD supervisors," Officer Buchanan said, "we were advised to relocate the crime scene tape for a larger perimeter. After relocating the tape, we were advised to respond to the area of Cleveland School in search of the suspect and suspect vehicle."

With information obtained from Michael Henderson, Corporal Charles Blount went to the Pep Boys Auto Parts store on Florida Avenue. "I talked to Lee Munter, the manager," Blount stated. "He advised that one of his drivers had been sent to Ybor City to pick up parts but had not arrived. He also confirmed information regarding the Ford Ranger."

Driving westbound on Martin Luther King Boulevard, Detectives Batista, Howard and Santiago heard on frequency 6 that all available units were being dispatched to Floribraska and I-275.

"We turned southbound on Nebraska, then west on Floribraska," Batista said. "When we arrived, I saw officers sobbing, and someone told me Ricky and Randy were dead. I thought I had misunderstood."

The officer repeated the dreadful words to Batista: "Ricky and Randy are dead."

Public Information Officer Steve Cole sped to the scene. "I was called to a shooting scene on Elmore. It wasn't until I got to the car window and recognized Ricky in the driver's seat that I realized it was two police officers."

After working past the lunch hour on a death investigation in south Tampa, Detectives Henry Duran and Paul Southwick stopped at Victoria's on Dale Mabry for a Cuban sandwich. Duran had worked in homicide for many years before transferring over to the traffic unit, and he often considered moving back to be with his friends. After all, he had known Rick Childers for twenty years, he trained Randy Bell, and he loved Julie Massucci like a sister.

As the detectives prepared to leave the restaurant, Duran got a text page from Sherry Dampier, the radio supervisor: *Call 506 10-18.*

He called. "What's up, Sherry?"

"Go to Floribraska and I-275 right now."

"Oh? What's going on?"

"Go now," she said forcefully.

Duran had received many emergency calls, but they were rarely as urgent as the woman seemed to think this one was. "Sherry, come on, what's up?"

"Henry. . .Ricky and Randy have been killed."

"I went to pieces," Duran said. "I didn't know what to say. I couldn't function."

"What is it?" asked Southwick, assuming it might have something to do with Duran's children or wife Rochelle.

Duran managed to recover and pass along the devastating news. Unable to drive, however, he handed the keys to his unmarked car over to Southwick and they fled to Floribraska and I-275.

Police Chief Bennie Holder and Mayor Dick Greco had arrived on scene; media helicopters moved in overhead.

Local law enforcement agencies rushed to assist their brethren in time of need: Pinellas County deputies set up roadblocks on the west end of the Howard Frankland Bridge; Clearwater Police did likewise from the west end of the Courtney Campbell Causeway.

Public Information Officer Debbie Carter and Captain Richard Cipriano went directly to the shooting scene from their offices with the Hillsborough County Sheriff.

"Chief Holder asked me to fill in at TPD Headquarters while Steve Cole handled media at the scene," Carter said. "I worked there for the rest of the week from 7 a.m. until 11 p.m. Captain Cipriano provided peer support."

"I understood how traumatic it must be to investigate the shooting of your own detectives," Sergeant Rod Reder acknowledged, himself a Criminal Investigator for the Hillsborough County Sheriff. "We volunteered to take over the investigation, but they declined, thanked us, and said, 'It's our job, we'll take care of it.'… In our profession, you frequently have to put on the *mask of non-emotion*."

Fortunately, even with a force growing to nearly 1,000 uniformed officers, the Hillsborough County Sheriff's Office had no officers slain by gunfire since 1966.

"In fact," Reder said, "we haven't lost an officer in the line of duty since 1987, when Deputies Donna Miller and Fred Clark died in a car crash while responding to a shooting call."

Detective Gene Black requested Batista and Santiago obtain all telephone toll information for the address at 709 ½ East Crenshaw with the name Joseph and Bernice Bennett.

Batista returned to the office. "I contacted Karen Doyle of GTE Security and requested the toll information. When she said we would need a subpoena, I contacted the State Attorney's Office and obtained same."

Back at Headquarters on 411 Franklin Street, Victims Advocate Donna Wilson took Bernice Bowen to the break area on the seventh floor for a cigarette. Detective Massucci stopped for a sandwich in the cafeteria next door, and upon returning to the homicide office one floor up, she ran into Donna Wilson. "Donna was visibly shaken, so I asked what happened."

"Ricky and Randy have been shot," Wilson blurted tearfully.

"No, no. I just saw them a while ago, Donna. You're mistaken. I'm sure they're still interviewing the boy's father."

To confirm her belief, Massucci ran to the eighth floor to find her friends Randy and Ricky. Instead, she found chaos. Everyone was running around lost, with a glazed, fearful look in their eyes.

"Then I realized it was true," Massucci said. "I don't remember exactly what I did at that point. I was in a daze. Total blackout."

Massucci hurried to find Bernice Bowen. "She was in the Photo Imaging room with Detective Jerry Keith, who took her there to help find an arrest photograph of her boyfriend."

"Sergeant Long requested a photo and the correct name so we could identify the suspect and disseminate the information to other officers," Keith said. "When I found no photos of Joseph Bennett, I asked Bowen to give me any names which she thought her boyfriend might be using. She told me to try the first name of James or Joseph and the last names of Bennett, Reid, Carr, Cox and Bowen."

While Detective Keith scanned photos archived under the name given by the person at the time of the arrest, Detective Massucci came to the room with tears in her eyes.

"I knew Bowen was the only person that was going to be able to help us. I knelt down and took her by the hand. I said, 'Bernice, you need to help us. He has killed your son and he has killed two police officers who were very good friends of mine. We need to identify him and stop him before he kills someone else.'"

"Sure, I'll help you," Bowen said, without a trace of sincerity. "I'll do what I can."

Massucci slowly shook her head. "Not at that time or at anytime after that did she tell me his true identity."

Detective Keith and Officer Wilcox sat with Bowen at a computer connected to the Hillsborough County Sheriff's Office.

"We accessed a computerized database of arrest photos," Keith explained. "As I pulled up each photo, Bowen looked at it to see if any were of her boyfriend."

Bowen told Keith she had only known Bennett for about a year and did not know his real name or date of birth. She thought he might have been arrested in 1997, possibly in Hillsborough County, but could not recall the charges.

She recognized none of the photos.

"I kept asking her where he might be going," said Keith. "If she knew of any friends or relatives. She replied that she did not. Several times during the interview, Detective Massucci begged Bowen to give her the suspect's real name."

"I met with Officer Ralph Reagan," Sergeant Bouknecht said. "He was very upset and informed me that two of our homicide detectives had been killed. After speaking with detectives, I met with Lieutenant Castor, who was seeking an officer who knew Detective Bell's wife Donna. I knew her, so I volunteered."

The Sergeant drove to Town and Country Hospital and completed the death notification.

Doctor Vincent Skotko rushed to Franklin Street to comfort and console the grieving officers and employees.

Sergeant Douglas Cook and Major Keen Newcomb went to the records department to locate Vickie Childers. "We need you to come with us," they told the slain-officer's wife. "We need to talk to you."

Vickie Childers went along cheerfully, assuming it was nothing more than a computer glitch. But halfway into the lobby, she sensed something horrible had happened and stopped cold.

"I want you to tell me right here," Mrs. Childers insisted. "Tell me now."

As heartbreak spread through the entire Police Department, the officers held the woman compassionately and informed her Ricky had been killed.

9

Tampa, Florida
May 19, 1998; 1359 hours

Less than thirty minutes after the shooting occurred on Elmore Street, Wyatt Bertloff pulled his truck into the 7-11 at 22nd Street and Sligh Avenue, a couple miles northeast of the deadly crime scene and about 10 blocks from 1913 Paris Street. The self-employed painter cut the engine and crawled out from the truck. Along with his co-workers Lawrence and Eric, they started toward the store.

"Then this guy I know only as Boo drove up to the next pump," Bertloff told the investigator. "He got out of a white delivery truck and yelled, 'Hey, where's my forty bucks?'"

Bertloff followed the other men inside the building to pay for gas and pick up some hot dogs. Hank Carr came in right behind him. Bertloff recounted what happened next. "After I paid the cashier, I went outside to my truck. Boo followed me out, and while I pumped the gas I overheard him talking to Lawrence."

"My son got shot accidentally today," Carr said in a somewhat cavalier manner.

"What's that?" Lawrence asked.

"My boy got shot. He died."

"Oh?"

The men didn't know whether to believe him, but the shocking comment caught their attention.

"The cops were going to charge me," Carr continued. "But I got one of their guns and shot both of 'em."

Now he had their full attention.

"Then he pulled up his shirt," Bertloff claimed. "He showed us he was carrying a black handgun. A 9mm handgun."

"This is a cop's gun," Carr boasted.

"While Boo finished pumping gas, I looked inside the delivery truck he was driving and saw a bloody set of handcuffs. Then he said, 'I gotta get the hell outta here.'"

Carr drove west shortly after 1400 hours. He made it to Interstate 275, barely avoiding a growing network of law enforcement officers commencing a citywide manhunt for a white delivery truck with red letters on the doors.

Bertloff reported the disturbing encounter, and moments later, a report went out that the suspect vehicle was seen in north Tampa, in the vicinity of Crenshaw Street, back where the drama first started.

Sergeant Robert Nassief in the Major Crimes Bureau conducted an interview with Bertloff and Detective Kevin Morris obtained the security video from the 7-11 manager.

Nearly thirty minutes into the interview with Bowen, Detective Keith repeated questions about her boyfriend's parents.

KEITH: Okay, where does his mother live here? Does she live here?

BOWEN: Yeah, I think so.

KEITH: Where?

BOWEN: In Tampa.

KEITH: Where in Tampa?

BOWEN: (after a few moments to ponder the question) Um, I think she lives at 1913 Paris Street.

KEITH: What's her name?

BOWEN: Gail Cox. Sonya Gail Cox.

KEITH: Is Cox also your boyfriend's name?

BOWEN: No.

Bowen remained consistent, admitting only knowing Hank Carr as Joseph Bennett, the same name as her first husband, Joey's father, a man who had no known criminal record and no arrests.

Detective Keith passed the information to Sergeant Danny Long, who advised Detectives Scott Wolff, Leon Green and Massucci to dispatch to the residence of Gail Cox on East Paris Street.

With updated information coming in fast, Tampa dispatch issued another BOLO: "The shooting occurred at I-275 and Floribraska. Two homicide detectives were shot. First suspect is a white male, five-ten, one-seventy-five, shoulder-length blonde hair. Light eyes. Last seen wearing a white shirt and blue shorts. Armed with unknown type of revolver. Suspect had handcuffs on the right wrist. Last seen eastbound on Floribraska in a white Ford Ranger. Delivery truck, initials APD on the side. Florida tags W-whiskey, Z-zulu, M-Mike, two-two Quebec. Use extreme caution."

*

After a morning of map training at the northern end of their coverage zone, paramedics Cynthia Holland O'Neal and Wayne Buie returned to Fire-Rescue Station 13 for lunch.

"Cindy, have you picked a name yet?" paramedic Carlos Garcia asked Lieutenant O'Neal when she walked into the break area.

"Not yet."

"You better hurry. It's due any day, isn't it?"

"It's due any minute," O'Neal answered.

O'Neal retrieved her lunch from the refrigerator and sat at a table near the television with Garcia and several other members of the Fire Rescue crew.

Located off Old Pasco Road, only a mile from the intersection of Interstate 75 and State Road 54, Station 13 saw plenty of action, mostly from accidents on the freeway, but often from robberies at gas stations and fast-food restaurants nearby. Law enforcement officers frequently stopped by to complete their reports, have a snack or just socialize with the rescue crews.

Highway Patrol Troopers Eric Bromiley and James Bradford Crooks occasionally visited the station.

"I can come up with more names," Garcia said to O'Neal, and flipped on the television.

"I don't need more, Carlos. I just need to select from those you've already given me."

Lieutenant O'Neal made no secret of her fondness for horses. And now her Paint mare was overdue for delivery of a colt, but she hadn't decided on a name. The only thing she knew for certain was that it had to have a connection to John Wayne, her favorite actor.

Also a huge fan of John Wayne, Carlos helped glean names from the actor's movie titles, his characters, horses, and even trivia from his birthplace in Iowa and his given name of Marion Morrison. Like Wayne himself, Cindy had no desire to name the horse "Marion."

"You should use *Duke*," Garcia offered. "That's my favorite."

"No, that's too common. I'm leaning toward Big Jake."

The discussion ceased abruptly when the TV newscast focused on the shooting of a 4-year-old boy in Tampa.

"I'm glad we didn't get that call," Garcia sighed when he heard a child was shot in the face with a high-powered rifle.

The most distressing aspect of their profession, the paramedics unanimously agreed, was responding to calls involving fatally injured children. After watching the Tampa Police detectives escort the boy's father away in cuffs, they shut off the television and finished lunch in silence, each of them emotionally touched by the story.

O'Neal and Buie went back to Engine 13 and resumed their map training assignment. Garcia responded to an emergency call in the Rescue 13 ambulance that ended at a nearby hospital.

*

Hank Carr took the interstate northbound hoping he could evade law enforcement and make it all the way to Ohio for a visit with his daughter Tamara. He drove at reasonable speeds in order to avoid the FHP tagging him with a radar gun.

Undetected, he made it to Pasco County, where officers heard a Highway Patrol dispatcher update information coming from Tampa.

"Brooksville, all units. Signal-5 BOLO on LEO times two out of Tampa. BOLO for vehicle, it will be a 1997 Ford Ranger, white in color. Florida tags…"

Signal-5: *Homicide.*

LEO: Law Enforcement Officer.

The dispatcher gave the vehicle description first, followed by that of the suspect. "Subject should be a Signal-0, unknown type weapon. He should have handcuffs on his right wrist. Last seen…"

Signal-0: *Armed and dangerous.*

A mile south of State Road 54, Florida Trooper Erik Bromiley hit the overhead lights and tracked down a speeder on Interstate 75. The stop took place on the median, where the trooper got out from the cruiser and approached the vehicle.

"I don't normally drive that fast," an embarrassed woman told the officer.

"I'm sure you don't, ma'am," said Bromiley. "You're just in a hurry today, I suppose."

While Bromiley read the woman's drivers license and jotted the pertinent information, Trooper James Bradford Crooks—radio ID Seventeen-77—eased his patrol unit alongside Bromiley. With a nod, the officer acknowledged Crooks' presence and resumed writing the ticket for 20 miles over the speed limit.

Trooper Crooks patiently observed the northbound traffic, which slowed considerably at the sight of two patrol cars. While waiting to have a chat with his friend Bromiley, he monitored radio traffic and heard shift supervisor Lieutenant Greg LaMont respond to the BOLO from FHP dispatch.

"One-80, Brooksville. Thirteen-44, Seven-08 and DOT One-81 are all Ten-26."

The Ten-26 from LaMont indicated all four units had *received message* regarding the BOLO.

The Brooksville dispatcher, Chris, then queried units Eleven-72, Sixteen-36, Seventeen-15, Seventeen-77, Fifteen-03 and Three-44 to determine if they had all received the message.

"Brooksville, Eleven-72, Ten-4?"

Trooper Michael Zwim confirmed. "Eleven-72, Ten-26."

"Brooksville, Sixteen-36?"

"Ten-26," answered Trooper Eric Schaub.

Then he queried unit Seventeen-15.

Trooper Robert Hinton also confirmed. "Seventeen-15, Ten-26, Brooksville."

"Brooksville, Seventeen-77?"

"Twenty-six," said Trooper Crooks.

"Brooksville, Fifteen-03?"

While preoccupied with writing a citation for the speeder at that moment, Erik Bromiley, Fifteen-03, didn't immediately respond.

"…Brooksville, Fifteen-03?"

"Fifteen-03, Ten-26."

"Ten-4. Brooksville, Three-44?"

Sergeant Patrick Moran heard the query and confirmed he had also received the BOLO information. "Three-44, Ten-26."

Trooper James Crooks joined the Highway Patrol less than one year earlier. Raised in the rural community of Clewiston, near Lake Okeechobee, he grew up determined to become a Florida Trooper. Majoring in criminology at the University of South Florida in Tampa, he hoped completion of an internship at the academy would earn him the job he desired. However, the bespectacled lad encountered one major obstacle; he hit the scale eighty pounds over the weight limit. With unbridled enthusiasm, the young man dropped the poundage necessary to meet his fitness requirements and graduated from the academy with excellent scores on the certification exams.

Francis Vega, Crooks' roommate at the academy, praised his friend. "The instructors rode James constantly, but he was determined to make it, and he did."

"James trusted everyone," said Lonzo Griffith, a high school teacher from Clewiston. "He viewed the world through a lens tinted by small-town innocence."

Twenty-three-year-old Crooks took an assignment at the Land O'Lakes office in Pasco County on August 4, 1977, and moved to north Tampa with his fiancée Nadine LaMonte, a schoolteacher from Spring Hill. They set the marriage date for November.

"When I last saw Brad," fellow Trooper Jeff Johnson said, "the only thing he talked about was his job and his fiancée."

As of Tuesday morning, May 19, Trooper James "Brad" Crooks had the proverbial world by the tail, happily fulfilling his dreams.

Hank Carr passed the troopers at approximately the same speed as other afternoon traffic, with a white, extended cab Silverado driven by Dwight Hopkins following closely behind.

"I left Tampa 20 minutes earlier," said Hopkins, the 53-year-old owner of Cross Construction Company in nearby Wesley Chapel. "I was bidding on a major construction project."

Brock Whetstone came by next. Noticing the two troopers, he eased up accordingly. A part-time college student named Timothy Bain cruised along next in line, headed for the exit at State Road 54, then east a couple miles to his job at the Saddlebrook Golf Resort.

Trooper Crooks spotted the Ford Ranger with red lettering on the side. He flipped on the overhead lights and took off. After easing safely into the flow of traffic, he turned off the overhead lights and flashed his headlights at Bain, forcing him to move to the right lane and allow the cruiser to slip past. Prior to the 54 exit, all four vehicles passed a yellow 18-wheeler driven by Arthur Joiner.

"We were all going about 10 miles over the speed limit," said Tricia Bechtelheimer. "The FHP vehicle began pulling up close to the car in front of it, flashing the headlights only. As vehicles moved to the right lane, the officer approached the next vehicle and again flashed his headlights until there was no one between him and the white pickup."

The pursuit, which was also witnessed by Janet Black and David Anker in a white passenger van, turned off at the State Road 54 exit and found a line of cars backed up from the stop sign.

Meanwhile, the FHP dispatcher relayed the updated information to Hernando County, where the officers were already moving toward Interstate 75.

"Be very careful," the dispatcher cautioned, "He's already killed two people."

Hank Carr sped up when he saw the cruiser on his tail. He still had 900 miles to reach Ohio, and he knew if one officer had him in sight. a dozen others would soon follow. He yanked the steering wheel and veered off the interstate at the 54 exit.

Trooper Crooks followed and contacted dispatch. "Seventeen-77, Brooksville."

"Go ahead, 77."

"Ten-4, Brooksville, I'm behind the vehicle we had that BOLO on at this time."

"Ten-20?"

Trooper Erik Bromiley released the speeder and returned to his patrol unit, where he heard Crooks announce the suspect's location.

"Seventeen-77, at 54 and 93. White Ford Ranger, Florida tags Whiskey, Zulu, Mike, seven, two, Quebec."

LaMont contacted dispatch. "One-80, Brooksville."

"One-80."

"Tell him to stay back from the vehicle. Have him follow it; we're Ten-51 out there to assist."

With lights flashing, Trooper Bromiley worked his way onto the freeway and sped off to assist Trooper Crooks. Before the dispatcher relayed the message, Crooks came back on: "They're actually pulling over at this time."

"Just stay away from him," LaMont warned the rookie. "Do not approach the vehicle by yourself. Stay away from the vehicle and wait for assistance." He got no response from the young trooper. "Seventeen-77, are you Ten-48? Seventeen-77, do not approach the vehicle by yourself. Stay back until you get assistance." And still no response. "Brooksville, go ahead and Ten-49 out there. Also advise Pasco or Hernando to get a helicopter headed out there."

Chris called Hernando County. "Hey, Hernando, can you get your chopper up? We got our trooper stopped behind that vehicle at 54 and 93. That one that shot the two Tampa troopers."

Lieutenant LaMont tried again. "Seventeen-77, are you listening to me?"

While consoling TPD officers at Floribraska Avenue and Elmore Street in Tampa, Highway Patrol spokesman Mike Guzman heard the emergency traffic on the FHP frequency.

"I had a horrible feeling at that moment," the lieutenant said. "I took off immediately, driving over a hundred miles an hour."

With walls closing in, Carr had stopped in the center of the off ramp, forcing the inexperienced Crooks to stop behind him. Coming up from behind, Dwight Hopkins tapped on the brakes and slowed his Silverado. Whetstone, Bain, Joiner and Janet Black did the same. The Ford Ranger unexpectedly darted to the left as though it would cut across the ditch and return to the freeway.

"Then he pulled off to the side and stopped," Hopkins recalled vividly. "I thought he was going to wait for the trooper, but instead he jumped out fast, ran to the front of the cruiser and aimed the gun right at him. Point blank."

"A white male," Whetstone said. "Balding, with a ponytail. Once the cop stopped, the guy just opened up."

"The first blast shattered the rear widow of the cruiser," Hopkins exclaimed. "The way the glass showered my truck, I thought it was a shotgun. I instinctively ducked below the dash for a second, and when I looked up, I saw him walk over to the driver's window and fire another shot directly at the trooper."

"I heard one big boom," said Bain, his vision partially blocked by the Silverado. "I ducked down, then sat back up. Not even a second later, I heard another shot. Louder than pistol shots, probably shotgun or rifle fire. It was totally uncalled for. He didn't have time to draw his gun or anything."

Carr glared ominously toward the man in the white truck behind him: Dwight Hopkins.

"The man looked evil," Hopkins said. "It was like looking into the face of the devil himself."

Instantly incensed at the murderous attack on a law enforcement officer, Hopkins mashed his foot on the accelerator, swung around the patrol car and aimed his Silverado directly at the assailant.

Carr saw him coming and threw himself inside the Ford Ranger, narrowly avoiding the on-charging truck.

"I wasn't trying to be a hero," Hopkins added modestly. "It was purely a reflex action. At that point I thought he might try to shoot me so I went after him."

Hopkins—a solid 185-pound man who played All-City football at King High in Tampa—rammed into the driver's door, knocking the smaller truck onto a berm, but Carr maintained control of the Ranger and spun the wheels toward State Road 54.

Carr struck the trooper with such speed and surprise that Crooks never had time to get the vehicle out of gear and into park. As he lay lifelessly on the front seat, the cruiser began rolling forward, clipping the right side of the Silverado.

"I couldn't just sit there and let him get away," said Hopkins of the assailant.

Hopkins took off after him and a frantic chase ensued. Whetstone followed the lead, and all three vehicles roared down the exit ramp and sailed through traffic on 54.

With the cruiser still creeping forward, Timothy Bain and Arthur Joiner ran after it.

"The young man in the striped shirt tried to reach through the window to stop the trooper's car," Janet Black told the investigators, referring to Bain. "He couldn't reach the gearshift, so he opened the door and hit the brakes."

"I asked the trooper if he was okay," said Bain, who sliced his hand on the broken window. "But there was no motion. Nothing. I'll always remember his face. It was like he was looking back at me. I couldn't believe it. It was like something you see in a movie."

Joiner reached for the trooper's radio mic. "Hey, hello, hello, is anybody there? Hello?"

Lieutenant LaMont answered. "Yeah, go ahead."

"Hey, listen, one of y'all's officers has been hit at the exit to Highway 54."

"Say what?" asked the Brooksville dispatcher.

LaMont responded with the Ten-code to send an ambulance. "Brooksville, Ten-71!"

Joiner keyed the mic again. "Yeah, somebody hit the guy. I don't know which way he went on 54."

"Brooksville, we need to contact Zephyrhills, have them watch for that vehicle."

"That's Ten-4."

Carr swerved the Ranger onto the westbound lane of 54 and went under the freeway with two pursuers closely on his tail. After several hundred yards, he suddenly whipped the Ranger into a sliding U-turn and lifted a gun to window.

"I quit following at that point," Whetstone said. "I went directly to a gas station and called 911."

A damaged fender dug into the front tire of Hopkins' Silverado, making steering extremely difficult, but he managed a U-turn and continued the pursuit bumper to bumper. "When I saw him trying to aim the gun at me, I backed off," Hopkins said, almost apologetically. "I slowed down and yelled at someone to call 911. When I saw the truck turn north on the freeway, I drove back to tell the other troopers what happened."

"Another FHP cruiser arrived on the scene," Janet Black said. "Shortly after that, two more troopers arrived."

Erik Bromiley arrived first. "When I saw the traffic coming to a stop, I headed for the side of the highway to get past. Upon reaching the exit ramp, a number of white males came running toward me and yelling that a trooper had been shot."

Bromiley ran over to Crooks. He observed the blood and picked up the radio. "Officer down! Officer down!"

Sergeant Terry Prescott checked in. "Three-55, Brooksville!"

"Brooksville, Three-55, all units be 51 to 54 and 93!"

"Three-55, I'm westbound on 54 from Zephyrhills. I can't quite reach where they're at."

"They're not sure whether it went east or west on 54," LaMont told Prescott. "Are you Ten-48 on the vehicle description?"

"I heard a white Ford Bronco or Explorer."

"Negative. A white Ford Ranger pickup. White Ford Ranger pickup truck. Alpha, Papa, Delta. Delivery. APD delivery. APD on the side of it. A white male wearing a shirt and blue jeans. Signal-0 and he's already struck Seventeen-77."

"Ten-4."

Trooper Jerry Broxson responded. "Fourteen-46, I'm Ten-51."

With fellow officers rushing to the scene, Erik Bromiley grabbed a medical box from his cruiser and ran back to Trooper Crooks. He observed the glazed eyes, the blood and the bullet-entry wound at the side of his nose; he heard no wheezing, no sound, no response.

From Crooks' radio, Trooper Bromiley heard Lieutenant LaMont call for a helicopter.

"One-80, advise EMS to go ahead and get a Life Flight started out there just in case we need it, that way it's already there."

"Brooksville, One-80, what's your Ten-20?"

"Spring Lake Highway and 50," LaMont responded. "I'm going as fast as I can."

Bromiley concluded that a medical chopper would no longer be necessary. In a voice heavy with emotion, he keyed the microphone. "Fifteen-03, Brooksville."

"Yeah, Fifteen-03, go ahead."

"He's Signal-7."

"What?"

"Signal-7."

*

The fatal shooting occurred only a couple miles from where Cindy O'Neal and Wayne Buie parked Engine 13 to verify that a new street name and location was correct on their zone map. "I can't believe the heat," Buie said, and cranked up the air-conditioning unit.

"Yeah, and it's only May. I suppose this is the downside of living in Florida."

A dispatcher from the Emergency 911 center interrupted their thoughts of the weather.

"Station 13," said the voice on the radio, "respond to a gunshot wound at I-75 and State Road 54. Gunshot wound at Interstate 75 and State Road 54."

O'Neal picked up the microphone. "Engine 13, copy."

There would be no more map training that day for O'Neal and Buie. With their siren and lights warning traffic along the way, they roared toward the freeway.

Likewise, outside the hospital, Carlos Garcia ran to Rescue 13, sent the "Copy" response to dispatch and activated lights and siren. Being considerably closer to the scene of the gunshot wound, Engine 13 arrived first, coming in east of the freeway.

"It's probably at one of the gas stations," O'Neal surmised.

"Yeah, probably another robbery."

O'Neal spotted the patrol cars and congestion. "It's over there on the south side."

"We'll have to go up the off-ramp," said Buie, who steered the big engine across eastbound lanes of 54.

Dwight Hopkins sat alone on the open tailgate of his Silverado. He observed the fire engine approach and stop fifty feet from the first patrol car. Although a trooper had already obtained a description of the suspect and vehicle from Hopkins, he was advised to standby for a more detailed interview.

"I wanted to call my wife," he admitted. "I didn't want her to see it on the news and worry about me."

Joyce Hopkins already worried. At that moment, she was at home nervously watching news coverage as the deadly incident continued to unfold. She knew her punctual husband of 30 years was scheduled to arrive at Interstate 75 and State Road 54 at approximately 2:30, nearly the same time the shooting occurred.

Cindy O'Neal climbed down from the fire engine and trotted over to the nearest officer, a man she recognized instantly. "What's going on, Erik?"

Bromiley could barely speak above a whisper when he looked at O'Neal. "He's gone."

"Gone? Who? Gone where?"

"He's been shot. . ."

"Who?"

Bromiley nodded toward the patrol car and O'Neal then noticed the driver's door wide open with one leg protruding outside from the driver's seat. O'Neal gasped and ran to the wounded trooper, where she saw another face she recognized. She checked for a pulse as tears immediately welled. Trooper Crooks was a man she proudly referred to as her friend, and now she pronounced him dead.

Fighting back tears, O'Neal went back to the engine and called dispatch. "Engine 13 to Dispatch."

"Copy, 13."

"Responding from the gunshot wound at 54 and 75… Confirmed Signal-7. Cancel Rescue 13."

Less than a mile away, Carlos Garcia approached in Rescue 13 and overheard the radio traffic. He knew the next call from dispatch would come to him.

"Rescue 13, Pasco. As per Engine 13, cancel call on the gunshot at 54 and the interstate."

"Copy. Rescue 13 back in service."

Barely an hour later, Garcia learned that the Signal-7 was for his friend James Crooks.

Cindy O'Neal and Wayne Buie covered the deceased trooper with a sheet, secured the area for the shaken officers and set the fire-line tape. While they assisted moving onlookers back from the scene, they observed a growing array of law enforcement vehicles speeding north in pursuit of the killer.

One of the unmarked vehicles with lights flashing belonged to Florida Department of Law Enforcement agent Ray Velboom. By agreement between agencies, whenever an officer-involved shooting occurred, FDLE handled the investigation; therefore, as the on-scene supervisor, Velboom took control of the crime scene; specialists Jon Wierzbowski, Lynn Ernst and Mike Rafferty processed the scene with assistance from the Pasco Crime Scene Unit.

"I removed the sheet to take a look at the officer," Velboom said. "His weapon was still strapped inside the holster, and his seatbelt was still fastened."

O'Neal and Buie remained on scene for several hours, until after the Medical Examiner from Pinellas County arrived to transport the body. She then called dispatch. "Engine 13, back in service."

When Lieutenant O'Neal returned home that evening, her phone rang continuously. The first call came from her mother. Like nearly everyone else in the state of Florida, her mother had followed the newscast all afternoon and evening, and a neighbor had informed her that Cindy was the first paramedic on scene with the Trooper.

"Come over here as soon as you can," her mother said, trying to console Cindy. "You'll be real happy to see this beautiful animal that was born today."

Cindy didn't know of any John Wayne characters called James or Bradley or Crooks or Trooper, so she stuck with her first choice; she named him Big Jake.

Among the first officers to arrive at SR 54 included Sergeant Don Young, Lieutenants Guzman and Nathan Dawson of the FHP. And, ironically, Detective Chuck Massucci. "I was southbound on I-75," Massucci said. "I called Julie and she was crying. As she was telling me about Randy and Ricky, I saw the troopers and stopped to help."

During the crime scene investigation, State Attorney Walter Rice and Pinellas Medical Examiner Marie Hansen concluded that the first bullet entered just below Crooks' glasses and exited the back of his head before blowing out the rear window. The second bullet struck Crooks on the left shoulder by the FHP patch, glanced up and struck the trooper in the head.

Mike Guzman fought back tears as he spoke to media. "As road-blocks were being established to locate Bennett...Trooper Crooks came in contact with him..." A fellow trooper offered a comforting pat on the shoulder, enabling Guzman to continue the gut-wrenching report. "...in the northbound entry ramp at State Road 54...Trooper Crooks was then shot...and killed...by Bennett."

As a memorial to the fallen trooper, his friends erected a cross on the shoulder of the exit ramp, halfway between the freeway and State Road 54. One year later, on the anniversary of the officer's death, Cindy and the crew of Station 13 placed flowers around the base of that memorial.

"It was a bittersweet day for me," O'Neal reflected sorrowfully. "It was by far the hardest day of my career."

"Brad Crooks touched us all," Carlos Garcia added. "I'll always remember what a respectful, friendly man he was. I never saw him without a smile."

As highway deaths increased over the years, roadsides throughout the state became littered with gifts and flowers placed at fatality crosses such as the one erected for Trooper Crooks. In an effort to beautify the roads and memorials, the State of Florida decided—at the written request of the victims' families—to replace each cross with a metal emblem called *Safety Markers*. Each one reads, "Drive Safely," and below those two words "In Memory" appears.

On a Safety Marker located at the side of the State Road 54 off-ramp of Interstate 75, "Trooper James B. Crooks" is printed beneath the words "In Memory."

The Greater Wesley Chapel Chamber of Commerce memorialized the fallen trooper by dedicating a section of State Road 54 as Trooper James "Brad" Crooks Highway. They placed a large, blue memorial near the freeway exit on the north side of State Road 54. It ended with the heartfelt words: "The citizens of Wesley Chapel thank you."

Trooper Crooks had prudently prepared his fiancée and family for the possibility this dreadful day might one day come.

"Brad told me what to expect," Nadine La Monte reflected mournfully. "Just a knock at the door."

"May I come in?" Captain Gary Odom asked.

"I have a question," Nadine said. "Is my Brad dead?"

The trooper hung his head and nodded.

PART III

10

Pasco County
Interstate 75
May 19, 1998; 1445 hours

At speeds exceeding 90 miles an hour, the delusional Carr hoped to make it out of Pasco County and then slip through Hernando County, giving himself the possibility of leaving Florida unimpeded by law enforcement. He had no other option. At a minimum, he needed to stay beneath the radar until he could disappear into a residential area near the freeway. If police caught him on the open highway, he had no place to hide.

While following the BOLO reports out of Tampa, Pasco County Deputy Jim Campbell turned off Bruce B. Downs Highway and came west on 54, unaware that another shooting had occurred just a short distance west of him. "When I saw a truck matching the description, I pursued with lights and siren."

Campbell notified the dispatcher, advising him that the truck and suspect were now heading northbound on Interstate 75. Any hope Carr had of making it to Ohio suddenly faded. The best he could hope for at that point was to make it to the next populated exit, State Road 50 in Hernando County.

Unfortunately for Carr, Deputy Campbell presented an immediate problem.

"The driver opened the sliding rear window and looked directly at me," Campbell said. "With one hand on the steering wheel, he fired a round through my windshield with an assault rifle. We were doing about 100 miles an hour. He squeezed off a second shot and I ducked.

His third shot hit my rearview mirror. Glass fragments pelted my arms, chest and face. A bullet fragment lodged in my neck."

Captain Tom Hennessy and Lieutenant Bruce Schmelter of the Pasco Sheriff's Office picked up the chase along with injured Deputy Campbell.

"Take the shot if you get the opportunity!" Hennessy yelled to his lieutenant after seeing Carr firing at civilians. "We need to stop this guy!"

Schmelter responded, firing 13 rounds at the truck. Carr returned fire at all pursuing officers. As Pasco units continued pursuit, the FHP dispatcher repeated warnings for all units to be very careful.

"...He's already killed two Tampa PD and our guy."

Carr weaved frantically through traffic, forcing vehicles off the road around him. When the Pasco cruisers got close, he fired more rounds. When traffic got tight, he fired at other drivers, including a lady in a station wagon.

Pasco Deputy Bob Cressman requested permission to empty his weapon at the fleeing killer, but could only squeeze one round at the truck without endangering the public.

"Where's your chopper?" FHP asked Hernando.

"He's about a minute from the interstate and 41."

A report came from another Pasco officer. "He's now approaching 41 on the interstate. He's northbound, approaching Highway 41 on the interstate."

As Lieutenant LaMont traveled southbound on I-75 at a high rate of speed, he heard the suspect's location updated and saw a Sheriff's helicopter heading southeast. Anticipating the suspect would reach the overpass at 41 ahead of him, LaMont stopped on the median half a mile north and prepared to intercept.

"Shots fired at the 290 marker," Pasco told the dispatcher. "Unit has been hit."

The dispatcher keyed all units. "Brooksville, there are shots fired at the 290 mile marker. At 290 mile marker. Be advised shots fired. Unit has been hit."

Pasco and FHP pushed hard from behind, while Hernando swept down from the north and maintained vigil from overhead. Sergeant Nowlin zoomed in from the northwest and reported that he saw five units in pursuit at Florida Highway 41 and the interstate: "...One trooper and four Pasco deputies."

FHP troopers fired shots down from the overpass at Highway 41 and Carr fired back.

When Lieutenant LaMont spotted the white pickup, he moved into position. "As he reached my location, I pulled the right wheel of my patrol car onto the pavement, but he immediately swerved and intentionally struck the right front wheel."

Simultaneously with the glancing collision, a bullet shattered the right rear window of LaMont's cruiser. Undaunted, the lieutenant whipped his battered vehicle onto the freeway and joined pursuit, but excessive damage to the steering and suspension forced him to pull off the highway and contact the Pasco County Sheriff's Office.

"Signal-4, Brooksville. I-75 and 41."

The chase entered Hernando County: more shots fired.

"Shots fired at mile marker 296! Mile marker 296, northbound. Shots fired!"

"Four-05, we're now setting up at the next overpass. Lockhart and Hickory Hill Road."

Another barrage of gunfire occurred at Lockhart Road, mostly from the officers, but the pursuit continued northbound.

Christopher Espinosa, a 56-year-old truck driver from nearby Brooksville, slowed down when he saw the chase running up behind his trailer. When the white pickup came alongside the cab, Espinosa saw a handgun aimed directly at him. The hand recoiled and flames exploded from the end of the gun barrel. In an instant, the truck driver felt an excruciating pain in his left arm. The bullet tore through the center of a tattoo, ripped a hole in his arm and splintered the bone. Miraculously, it missed all vital organs. In agony, Espinosa brought the rig to safe stop while observing the crazed shooter firing rounds at pursuing patrol cars.

For Espinosa, the trip scheduled to end in New York City never made it to State Road 50. A passenger in the truck, Mike Arroyo, told a reporter, "I saw the pickup comin too fast for the truck. I told Chris to pull over, but by the time I said it, it was too late."

Carr, while passing a slow-moving 18-wheeler half a mile from State Road 54, next fired at Kevin Luke, a 26-year-old Eagle Carrier driver out of Corbin, Kentucky. The slug ripped through the driver's window of the red cab and lodged in the headrest approximately six inches from Luke's left ear. He received minor glass injuries, but nothing serious.

At State Road 50, Carr observed law enforcement officers and vehicles waiting to unload on him. Although the flat tire had slowed him, with a last gasp of desperation he tried to run straight through the roadblock. But rather than risk direct contact with an unmarked unit or hit more spikes, he suddenly spun off the freeway and cut a path into the nearest potential sanctuary, a Shell Station.

The news media had reported Joey Bennett's death around 1000 hours; reports on the death of Tampa detectives hit the airways closer to 1400 hours; the trooper, about 1435 hours; news outlets throughout the country picked up the story long before Carr snared his hostage in Hernando County. Reporters in helicopters arrived within minutes, and for better or worse, the killer had a national audience. He also had a terrified hostage at gunpoint.

*

The voice of Hernando County Sheriff's Captain Bob Henning boomed over the radio. "Four-04, give me hostage negotiations and call out SWAT!"

"Ten-4."

"Also get us a perimeter around the rear of the station!"

"All units responding, get a perimeter around the rear. We are calling out SWAT and hostage negotiations at this time."

Sergeant Doug Campbell entered the fray with a call to the patrol supervisor, Marc Rivenbark. "Six-10, Four-05."

"Go ahead, Six-10."

"Have Mari Kelly get the hostage negotiation equipment out and be Ten-18 to the area."

"Ten-4."

With the chase devolving into a hostage situation, the front-line deputies backed off behind vehicles and gas pumps, where Sergeant Kramer assumed command of the immediate perimeter.

"Does everyone have a bulletproof vest?" Kramer yelled out to the deputies.

"Not here!" an officer replied.

"If not, go to the outer perimeter!"

Kramer moved his troops back from the gas pumps.

"Four-05, Air-1, can you see if there is anyone in his truck?"

"Negative. I can not see if anyone is in there."

Sergeant Kramer ran to the Ford Ranger, his shotgun pointed at the side window.

"I do not see anyone in the pickup," he informed the lieutenant.

"Ten-4."

"Four-04, Hernando!"

"Four-04, go ahead."

"Give me a unit out here at I-75, on both sides to direct traffic. It's a mess out here."

"Ten-4."

"Four-86, approaching I-75 and 50."

"Ten-4, Four-86."

Deputy Stephen Kelly checked in. "K-2, I'm Ten-51 out there."

"Ten-4, K-2."

"Four-11, Hernando."

"Four-11."

"Get EMS on the accident scene. I-75 south of 50. Marker 298."

"Four-05, what units do we have available for traffic?"

"Alpha-6, Four-05, I'm approaching I-75 and 50. Where do you need me?"

"Get in the eastbound lane of 50 at the light. We need to direct traffic around our current location."

Deputy Bert Stockton ran to the Indian River fruit stand, where he found Bill Keith lying face down beneath a vegetable bin, fearing for his life and seeking cover. With help from the deputy, the man got up, slipped out the south end of the fruit stand and ran to the west, out of harm's way.

Still wearing biking shorts, Stockton then ran to his patrol car to retrieve SWAT accoutrements from the trunk. "I didn't want to take a chance on missing anything while changing clothes," Stockton said, "so I just placed my SWAT vest over my polo shirt, slipped on my knee pads and grabbed my helmet."

Although the deputy made the transition sound easy, it wasn't. His standard SWAT uniform included a weighty Kevlar helmet with a bulletproof face shield and a heavy tactical vest. Each team member also had his own noise/light distraction device called *Flash Bang* and a hand-thrown canister of CS irritant. Making their load even heavier, they carried .40-caliber Glocks and fully automatic 9mm Heckler & Koch MP-5's, 120 rounds of 9mm and 75 rounds of .40 caliber shells, a knife, and a hand-held radio with a headset and a boom mic. They also carried a first-aid kit, gas mask, and at least one pair of handcuffs. In a matter of moments, the SWAT officers transformed from mild-mannered social workers into fully armored warriors.

The Hernando SWAT team also consisted of two designated Snipers—Deputies Scott Card and Jim Walker. Each man carried a Remington 700 and a .308 caliber rifle with magnifying optics. The remaining team members, referred to as *Grenadiers,* carried 37mm chemical deployment launchers.

"Six-10, Four-05."

"Go ahead, Six-10."

"We need to establish a command post for negotiations and SWAT."

"Ten-4."

"Four-04, Hernando, have units at the scene go to Patrol-2."

"Ten-4. All units on scene go to Patrol-2."

"Hernando..."

With officers converging in high numbers, radio traffic filled SWAT, Utility, Tactical and two Patrol channels, with dispatchers skillfully monitoring each of them.

"Four-86, I'm 97 at the interstate blocking traffic."

"Ten-4. That's on the eastbound side."

"Alpha-6, I'm coming off the interstate."

"Four-05, Four-86 is at the eastbound side. Alpha-6 will be at the other side."

"Hernando, we need to turn all vehicles around. We don't need any east-west traffic. We need to reroute them in the other direction."

"Four-86, Alpha-6, did you copy to reroute traffic?"

Unit Four-86 confirmed.

While hovering above the gathering swarm of officers and patrol units, Sergeant Nowlin looked down at the floorboard and saw the entry point from the round that narrowly missed his foot. Then he glanced at the exit hole in the housing inches above his head.

"Air-1, Four-05."

"Go ahead, Air-1."

"Judging by the hole in the floor of the chopper, he's using either a nine millimeter or a forty-five."

"Ten-26."

"Four-05, Four-04. It looks like the best location to set up will be the Race Trac parking lot."

"Ten-4."

"We need a place to set up phone communications."

"Four-04, Hernando."

"Go ahead."

"I need a unit on the east side of this location."

"Four-86 is blocking the eastbound lane, redirecting traffic."

Deputy Stockton squeezed the microphone. "Tango-8, all units on scene. I had the last visual on him... I was up in front... it appeared at. . . that he..."

With the blitz of activity and radio traffic, Deputy Stockton lost transmission.

Rivenbark asked him to repeat. "Ten-9, Tango-8."

"I need to update everyone on the scene," Stockton said. "If you could hold traffic."

Hostage negotiator Marisabel Kelly radioed from unit Four-84, informing the dispatcher she was en route. "Four-84, Ten-51."

Like Sergeant Nowlin a decade earlier, Kelly started her career as a Florida Marine Patrol Officer, worked four years in Key West, and had now been with the Hernando County Sheriff for over ten years. In addition to her COPPS assignments and negotiation duties, the Panamanian-born deputy also served on the Hernando County Crisis Response Team (CRT), where she conducted training sessions and coached the teams.

"When I'm off duty," Kelly joked, "I'm a zookeeper."

Using the term affectionately, Kelly referred to her home as a zoo, where over the years she, her husband Stephen and son Roberto had a penchant for adopting and raising lost animals. It seemed only fitting that her husband worked the K-9 unit.

"I was working on an alarm ordinance in Spring Hill when we got the BOLO regarding a shooting out of Tampa," Kelly said. "When I heard the shooter was northbound, my first thought was, *I sure hope he doesn't make it to Hernando County.*"

Contrary to her wishes, Carr made it, and the following message appeared on Kelly's beeper: *Go to I-75 and State Road 54.*

With lights and siren, she drove to the Sheriff's Office on Cortez Boulevard. After retrieving the proper negotiation equipment from the supply closet, she headed for I-75, where her husband Stephen now anchored the exterior perimeter of the Shell Station with Thor, his trusty canine.

"Four-21, Hernando."

"Go ahead, Four-21."

"Mechanic wants to know, did Four-20 advice that the helicopter had been hit or just been shot at?"

"Standby on that. We're unable to advise at this time. There's too much traffic going on at Patrol-2."

"We'll wait till he heads back to find out."

"Ten-4."

"Four-04, Four-05, what's your 20?"

"At the Race Trac with Six-10."

Brooksville came back to Mary on a landline. "Do you have 300 and a half northbound for EMS?"

"EMS is at 298, at the Signal-4."

"Yeah, but we need them first because we got a gunshot wound."

"You have a gunshot wound?"

"Ten-4. A truck driver."

"Tango-1 and Tango-3, Ten-97 at the scene."

A deputy at the Shell Station talked to a witness and issued a firsthand update. "I've got a witness here who says the suspect has at least two guns."

"Ten-4."

Deputy Stocked tried again. "Tango-8, Four-05."

"Go ahead, Eight."

"Did you copy my last transmission about the last sighting of the suspect?"

"Ten-54," Rivenbark responded, indicating he had not received the transmission.

"Curt and I were right up front," Stockton reported, referring to Curt Turney. "We had a good visual on him. He ducked down, and it appeared that he pushed the clerk into the front south corner. So they may have separated and he went to the east."

"Were they inside of the store?"

"They were in front of the counter. When he ducked down, I lost visual."

"Four-04, Four-05."

"Oh-5."

"Have all units maintain the perimeter. SWAT team and hostage negotiations en route. Everybody maintain positions."

"We're establishing command modes now."

"Hernando, Four-05, can you advise where EMS is needed?"

"Ten-4. At this point, I believe it's gonna be a Pasco Deputy with injuries."

With a flurry of controlled activity taking place outside the Shell Station, Hank Carr settled in for a long afternoon. On the floor behind the cash register, with one gun in his hand and one lying on the floor, he told Stephanie Kramer he would not harm her as long as she did what he said

"Get me some cigarettes," he demanded. "But don't try to run, because I don't want to shoot you."

She obediently provided the cigarettes and sodas.

Although initially terrified, Kramer kept her wits and played along sympathetically. To win his confidence and hopefully save her own life, Kramer asked about his injury and even offered to dress the wound.

He accepted the offer.

"Now I have to make some phone calls," Carr told her. "I have to say goodbye."

*

Officer Reggie James drove to 1913 East Paris Street. He rapped on the front door and Earl Reid answered. After identifying himself, Reid invited the officer inside.

"I met and interviewed Gail Cox," James said. "She informed me that the suspect had been there and had already gone."

While Officer James questioned the sobbing woman, Detectives Green and Wolff arrived at the residence and took over the interview.

"After obtaining information about Carr's visit, I asked Mister Reid's permission to look around the house," Wolff reported. "He agreed, and took us outside to the trashcan containing the bloodied white T-shirt."

The detectives requested a Crime Scene Technician to collect the evidence and take photographs. At approximately 1515 hours, the telephone rang and Mrs. Cox took the call. With a tearful gasp, she acknowledged it was from her son and reluctantly handed the phone to Detective Wolff.

"The suspect advised me he was holding a female hostage," said Wolff. "I asked what his situation was at that point. He said he was bleeding and he had one or two gunshot wounds in his buttocks and back, that police had shot at him from overpasses, helicopters and stationary police cars."

In the conversation with Wolff, Carr confessed to shooting Joey but insisted it was an accident.

"You won't go to prison if it was an accident."

"Look, one way or another, I'm going to die right here. I'm losing an awful lot of blood."

"If it was an accident," the detective repeated, "you won't go to prison. You need to let us help you."

"Maybe not for Joey, but I'll fry for killing cops."

"What cops?" Wolff asked innocently.

"You don't know?"

"No."

"The cops that were bringing me to jail."

"How were they killed?"

"I got out of the cuffs and grabbed the driver's nine millimeter from the holster and shot him in the head. The passenger tried to fight me and I shot him in the face."

"Are you sure they were both killed?"

"Yeah. Oh, yeah, they're both dead. I shot them both right in the face. They're dead."

"And what happened after that?"

"I got out of the car with the keys and told the driver of the truck to get out of the truck. I got the rifle from the trunk and took off."

"Where are the guns now?" the detective asked.

"I have both the nine millimeters with me and I have plenty of bullets. I will not go back to prison."

"Is the lady okay? The hostage okay?"

"Yeah, she's okay. She's being very nice."

"Is it okay if I speak to her?"

"Yeah."

Carr believed he had convinced Kramer the shooting was an accident, and to get what he wanted, he allowed her to take the phone.

"He says it was an accident," Kramer told the detective. "I think it was an accident, too."

The detective prudently went along. "I think it was an accident, too. Now, is there anyone else in the store with you?"

"No."

Kramer told Wolff that Carr had asked her for cigarettes and a Mountain Dew and that she had complied with the requests.

"That's good," the detective said. "Just comply with his wishes and try to be strong, okay?"

"I will."

"She's an innocent bystander," Wolff told Carr when he got back on the phone. "You don't want to harm her. She had nothing to do with any of this."

"Nothing will happen to her," Carr asserted. "No harm will come to her."

"You really need to lay down your guns and come outside after releasing the hostage. We need to help you."

Carr agreed to release the hostage, but only if the police allowed him to see his wife. While waiting for a decision on how to proceed, the Detective kept Carr talking, hoping to keep him on the line and obtain information. Detective Green contacted command, advising that communication be set up between TPD and the Hernando County Sheriff. They also traced the phone number of Carr's call and passed it along to the Hernando negotiation team.

*

Back at State Road 50, the walls closed in on Hank Carr.

"Air-1, Four-05."

"Go ahead, Air-1."

"Put units around behind the station," Nowlin requested, viewing the scene from his lofty vantage point. "It's a mobile home park. There are a couple people in vehicles. Suggest you get some units to go around to the mobile home park."

"Four-05, anybody at the scene copy?"

"Four-11, Four-05. I have the first deputy that was behind him on I-75. He's still not positive that he ran inside, but he thinks he did because somebody fired back at him."

"Ten-4."

"Four-05, I've got the manager who was inside the store. Says there is only one hostage. She's a female. The suspect has at least one gun, maybe two. He had one strapped to his leg. Possibly a Glock or whatever he came in the store with in his hand."

"Okay, just maintain what you have."

"Four-11, Four-05, where you at?"

"Four-11, all traffic is on Patrol-2 at this time. Four-05 is at the Race Trac Station."

Major Richard Nugent, the ranking Hernando officer on scene, took command and called dispatch. "Four-03, Hernando."

"Go ahead, Four-03."

"Do we have an ETA on the SWAT team?"

"SWAT van just left the SO."

"Four-03, contact FHP. I'd like to have their ranking officer meet at my vehicle. I'm right at the intersection at the interstate off-ramp in a blue vehicle."

"Ten-4."

"Four-05 to Air-1. It looks like the Highway Patrol units have the back covered."

"We have two of our deputies, one marked and one unmarked. They're going through the mobile home park trying to get people to move out. They're all on foot. We have no marked units in the back at the mobile home park."

"Six-10, Hernando."

"Six-10, go ahead."

"Have all my hostage negotiators respond to the Days Inn Motel, room one-zero-two."

Hernando confirmed.

"Four-04, Four-05."

"Oh-5."

"I need an accurate idea of who's here, where they're at, and what they can see."

"I'm workin' at it."

"Four-86, I'm on the other side by the Waffle House.

"Four-19, I'm right in front of the store about thirty feet away."

"Six-10, Four-04."

"Go ahead."

"We'll be setting up negotiations in room one-zero-two in the Days Inn."

"Air-1, Hernando."

"Go, Air-1."

"Call out Four-22 or Four-23. Have them go to the hangar and standby with the other helicopter. In approximately 30 minutes I may need them to relieve me for fuel."

"Ten-4."

Lieutenant Paez, the Operations Support Commander, heard the message and called Deputy Phil Johnson at the hangar. With Deputy Mike Coburn working the night shift, Paez called him at home.

"I need to get a hold of Mike," the lieutenant told Suzann Coburn, Mike's wife. "It's urgent."

Deputy Coburn took the phone. "What's goin on, Joe?"

"We need you ASAP. All hell broke loose around here."

"Is Tom okay?"

"Yeah, he's up in the 6."

"Tell Phil I'll be there in fifteen.

"He'll have the NOTAR ready."

Twenty years and three months had passed since the night Mike Coburn promised his cousin Lonnie posthumously that he'd one day fly the Sheriff's helicopter in his absence. Mike fulfilled that promise years earlier, and now as deputy in the Aviation Unit, the father of three would race to another shooting scene, this time to rendezvous with the *Lonnie-6* and hopefully assist in terminating the career of another cop killer.

Anticipating the possibilities and hoping to stay one step ahead of the killer, Lieutenant Paez asked dispatch to contact Citrus County for air support.

"Have them contact Sergeant Nowlin on the VHF frequency."

In the aviation office at the Inverness Airport, Lieutenant Mike Richie took the call from Hernando dispatch and scrambled to the department's turbine powered McDonald Douglas 500 helicopter.

Hernando SWAT leader called dispatch. "Delta-1, Hernando."

"Go, Delta-1."

"Have all SWAT team members respond to the scene. We're en route with the van."

"Delta-1, do you have an ETA?"

"Leaving the SO now."

"Four-04 to Four-05, I need to know who has the perimeter and who has the back covered, all that stuff. I need it A-sap!"

"Six-37, I'm in the trailer park behind the Shell Station."

"Six-90, I'm at the east northeast, in the park behind the Shell Station."

"Alpha-10 and Four-19 are in front of the Shell Station."

"Four-04 to Sergeant Campbell."

"Campbell, go ahead."

"We're assuming he's inside the station. You've got to try to make communication inside the station first."

"The negotiators are now coming to Ten-97. We'll have contact established in just a moment."

"Four-04, Hernando, give me the latest up-to-date description of the suspect."

"Four-04, the latest we have is a white male, 5 feet 10 and 175, shoulder-length hair, light-colored eyes. Last seen wearing a white shirt and blue shorts. Be advised subject is armed with a revolver and has a handcuff on the right wrist."

Having looked at Carr up close and straight on, Deputy Stockton called in. "Tango-8, Hernando."

"Tango-8."

"The person I saw in the store had on a black T-shirt with print on the front. He was balding on top with long hair."

"Ten-4."

"Tango-1, Hernando."

"Tango-1."

"Hernando, I need forensics to respond to the first overpass south on the interstate for processing of a scene."

"The first overpass south on 75?"

"Correct. The first overpass south of Highway 50. We should have a unit standing by."

Gary Kimble, the HCSO supervising Crime Scene Tech, piled into his Sheriff's Jeep and headed for the crime scene at I-75 and 50. His associates, forensics technicians Judi Banks and Rick Swain, took the shortest route to the interstate location where the truck driver took a bullet in the arm.

Working in forensics for only a year, Banks had seen gunshot wounds before, but this one gave her a chill knowing it came at the hands of someone who had killed three police officers. After all, her husband, Detective Tom Banks, was on duty that day, and like many law enforcement officers, they had a young child expecting Mommy and Daddy to arrive home safely that night.

Paramedics rushed Espinosa to a hospital in Spring Hill, where he underwent surgery to repair extensive damage to his upper arm.

Lieutenant Rivenbark moved his command post to the median of SR 50, 30 yards west of the station, which provided a clear view of the front entrance. At that location, he noticed a deputy had moved into position behind a gas pump and ordered him to move back and find cover behind a vehicle.

Major Nugent called Rivenbark. "Four-03, Four-04."

"Go ahead."

"Have our negotiators tried to make contact yet?"

"They're just arriving at the hotel. They're at the Days Inn."

"Tell them to expedite it if they can."

"Four-04, Sergeant Campbell."

"Go ahead."

"How soon can you make communication with this guy? We need communication A-sap."

"I'm less than a minute away."

"Six-47, Hernando."

"Go ahead."

"Have Sergeant Blade go to SWAT frequency. See if we can get him to come up on Tactical."

HCSO Sniper Scott Card had just come off duty when he arrived at his home north of Brooksville. The 28-year-old SWAT officer planned a snack and a nap prior to finalizing arrangements for his annual deer-hunting vacation in Alabama, but a text-message page from the Comm Center abruptly altered his plans. It was identical to the message Deputy Kelly received. *Go to Interstate 75 and State Road 50.*

Card changed into a Woodland Camouflage uniform, jumped in his official vehicle and streaked toward the interstate. On the SWAT frequency, he called to team leader Jim Blade. "Delta-5, Delta-1."

"What's your location, Delta-5?"

"I'm on Mondon Hill."

"SWAT van will be just east of the overpass on the median."

"Delta-4, Hernando."

"Go ahead."

"Get supply to have everything ready. I'll need 37 milimeter. I'll be there in a couple minutes to grab 'em from him."

"Ten-4."

"One-10, Hernando."

"One-10."

"See if you can get hold of One-11 by radio. Have her call me."

"Hernando, One-11."

Deanna Dammer, the Public Information Officer for the HCSO, responded to the call. "One-11."

"Call One-10 on his car phone," said the caller. "ASAP."

Dammer responded with a Ten-4.

Depending on her appointment schedule, Deanna Dammer often wore slacks to her job. Not on Tuesday, May 19. With the weather report identical to the previous day, extremely hot and humid, the petite, dark-haired mother of two grown children came to the office looking like a fashion model in pink pumps, flowered print skirt, and a short-sleeved, olive-green shirt.

Like everyone at HCSO, Dammer had great respect for Sheriff Mylander. After attending broadcasting school near her hometown of Northfield, Minnesota, she moved to Brooksville in 1988 and started her own radio show on WWJB. When Mylander ran for reelection, Dammer invited him to an on-air interview.

"I remember feeling that he was an extra-special person," she said. "Way above anyone I had interviewed during that election."

In 1994, Sheriff Mylander hired Dammer as a trainee under PIO Sergeant Frank Bierwiler, and when Bierwiler retired, Deanna took over the position.

"I was in my office when they told me to go to I-75," Dammer said. "Lieutenant Paez handled the media from the Sheriff's office, and I headed straight for the interstate to locate Sheriff Mylander and Major Nugent."

The drive to I-75 on State Road 50 turned out to be an adventure in itself. When Dammer neared the freeway, a deputy in a marked car helped her weave through the growing maze of backed-up traffic, media and curious on-lookers.

The next update came on the SWAT channel. "Four-87, I just left the Tampa Bomb Squad. They got a hold of me on the phone. They have the equipment loaded up and ready to move in case you need breaching charges."

"I'll pass it along to One."

"I have them on a hard line right now," said Four-87.

"Tell them to stand by. I appreciate it."

The radio ID *One* belonged to Sheriff Tom Mylander.

The Sheriff was attending a meeting when beeped by the Comm Center. He rushed to the interstate in an unmarked car, where he and

Major Nugent set up the command post and communicated with field supervisors through liaison personnel. Typically, Mylander exhibited complete confidence in his officers and eschewed micro management of personnel, but the scene at SR 50 presented unique problems.

"Having numerous agencies and high-ranking individuals present added to the difficulties," Mylander said. "I had to be sensitive to the emotional state of the officers from Tampa and FHP. They wanted to be involved, and I understood that."

Regardless, the buck stopped at One.

Lieutenant Rivenbark contacted Campbell. "Four-05, Six-10."

"Six-10."

"Have you made contact with the suspect?"

"We're trying to get in there now. We're dialing the number we received from the Comm Center."

Dispatch called Sergeant Campbell with an update. "Hernando, Six-10."

"Six-10."

"The suspect is landline with his mother in Tampa at this time. Tampa has a SWAT negotiator en route to her residence."

With full SWAT gear and a sniper rifle, Deputy Card found the SWAT van and checked with Sergeant Blade.

"Set up and hide," Blade instructed his sniper.

"By hide," Card explained, "he meant for me to find a final firing location. I took a quick survey in front of the station and selected a visual from the median where I was protected by a highway patrol unit. Once in position, I adjusted the Laser Range Finder on my scope, showing the target was exactly 49 yards from my location."

Sniper Jim Walker selected a hide position near the Indian River fruit bins.

Major Nugent authorized his snipers to shoot the suspect if they had a clear shot.

"Given the violence already performed, "Nugent articulated, "we had a clear indication of what his intentions were. We decided it was best to end the situation as soon as possible."

With permission to shoot, the highly trained snipers only needed to see Carr's head and the drama would end with one squeeze of the trigger. And although Carr could not see his chief adversaries, he knew they were outside the building somewhere—waiting patiently for the opportunity to fulfill their assignment whenever necessary.

The walls continued to move closer, leaving Carr nothing more than a twelve-by-eight crawl space and a frightened young woman to hide behind.

11

1913 East Paris Street
Tampa
May 19, 1998; 1520 hours

While returning to Elmore and Floribraska, Detective Bert Batista received a page requesting a hostage negotiator at 1913 East Paris Street. "I contacted the supervisor and advised that I was en route. Upon arrival at Paris Street, I ascertained that Detective Wolff had been speaking with the suspect for approximately thirty minutes, and that 'Boo' stated he would not hurt his hostage if he was allowed to speak with his wife, Bernice Bennett."

Batista got on the phone with Carr and confirmed the information.

"Okay, I'll try to bring your wife up there," Batista assured him, "but only if you'll let the hostage go unharmed."

Carr agreed.

Batista verified the telephone number of the call initiated by Carr, then told him to remain calm and not do anything until he heard back from him.

Batista released the phone line so Hernando could take over. "I advised Chief Kenneth Taylor and Captain Siling of the situation at that point. Since the detectives were interviewing Bowen at Franklin Street, they advised me to pick her up at the station and transport her to Hernando County via the DEA helicopter."

When Detective Batista arrived back at the station, he updated Sergeant Reynolds, leader of the Hostage Negotiation Team. "Than I attempted to connect with suspect Carr," he said, "but the line was busy and I couldn't get through."

The shift commander notified Hernando Command that the DEA helicopter would deliver the suspect's wife and the detectives to the scene as quickly as possible. When informed that the DEA chopper was currently under repair, Ten-7, they switched to the department's Hughes 500.

"Bowen agreed to fly to Hernando County," Massucci said. "She insisted I go with her."

"Detectives Holland, Stanton and Massucci responded along with Carr's wife and myself to the parking lot at the Tampa Dog Track at I-75 and Bird Street," Batista explained. "We were met by Corporal McKinnon, Sergeant Zaleski and Flight Officer Jeffery Fife from Air Service. I was advised that only four people could be transported in the helicopter, therefore it was decided that Corporal McKinnon and I would escort Bowen to Hernando County."

Detective Massucci would return to Franklin Street.

*

Deputy Marisabel Kelly set up negotiation operations in rooms 101 and 102 at the Days Inn motel, 200 yards east of the Shell Station, with Sergeant Doug Campbell serving as liaison between Kelly and the command post. When Kelly moved into room 102, she placed a chair in the middle of the room away from the window and pulled a telephone, headset and writing equipment from the gear box. With assistance from her crew and the telephone company, she attempted to contact the Shell Station.

However, with the news media broadcasting the location and showing live video at the scene, the telephone inside the station took hits, which prevented negotiators from connecting with Carr.

"We're trying to make contact with him again," Campbell told dispatch, "but the phone keeps ringing. They must have call waiting. Go ahead and make contact with the phone company. Have all the bells and whistles taken off the phone immediately."

"Ten-4."

"Eleven, Six-10. What number you showing? I havc a telephone employee with me."

"What number is he giving you?"

"He has 796-7938."

"I'm not getting an answer at that number."

"Six-10, Hernando, advise the phone company we need a direct line into the station."

"Ten-4."

Calls from the media came in fast. Lieutenant Paez could only provide broadcast information until Deanna Dammer got set up at the scene. Over half an hour after the hostage situation began, Betty Paez called to say everything was okay. With a sigh of relief, the lieutenant then took another call on a landline.

"Lieutenant Paez here."

"Joe, Deanna Dammer is positioned at the Mobil Station west of I-75 on 50 when people want to meet with her."

"Okay, thanks."

"Four-05, Hernando."

"Go ahead Four-05."

"We need to notify Hernando units on the perimeter of the station that they are soon to be relieved on the front by Hernando SO SWAT, and in the rear by Pasco SO SWAT. Do not leave your post until you are relieved."

Hernando dispatch relayed the order to all Hernando units.

"Hold your positions until you are relieved," repeated Rivenbark.

"Air-1, Four-05, I believe we have four troopers on the back side of the station."

"That's a Ten-4."

Sergeant Campbell called to Rivenbark. "Six-10 to Four-05."

"Oh-5."

"I'm now at room one-zero-one. I have the captain from FHP Ten-12. He wants to know where is the command post?"

"The command post will be on 50 by the interstate, right under the red light."

"He'll respond at that location."

"Six-10, Hernando."

"Six-10, go ahead."

"We're still receiving a busy signal at that number. Can the phone company clear the line so we can get through?"

"Stand by."

"See if you can keep the operator on the phone until we can get communications established."

At that point, Major Nugent issued the order to release the Tampa Bomb Squad. "Have them start heading this way."

Another update came through the utility channel. "Be advised, DEA is flying the suspect's wife to the scene."

"Advise DEA to land in the field east of the Days Inn. Take the subject to room one-zero-one."

"Four-21, Hernando."

"Four-21, go ahead."

"I wasn't able to raise Air-1. Advise him Air-2 is ready to go. Does he want us to come out there and stage?"

Sergeant Nowlin answered on the utility channel. "I've got about 15 minutes of fuel. Have you been briefed on this?"

"Ten-4, I've been keeping up to date. Four-22 wants to know if the helicopter has been hit."

"I've got one hole through the front of it, but it looks like it went out the glass okay. I want you to come up and take position over 75 and 50. I've been holding at 500 feet, looking at the perimeter and the back. Basically a seeing-eye for the ground troops."

"Four-22 wants to come out and check on the helicopter before you return."

"I'm in the air at this time. I'll put down on the west side of the Holiday Inn if you want to talk to me, but we have about six other aircraft here so be careful when you get in the area."

"We have helicopters at the airport also. They're from all the television stations."

"I'm going back to Patrol-2. Call me when you get in the area."

Tampa PD informed Captain Bob Henning that a helicopter was Ten-51 to Hernando with Bernice Bowen. He radioed Sergeant

Campbell at the Days Inn. "ETA for DEA helicopter with the bad guy's wife is 15 minutes."

"Ten-4."

"Do you want the wife brought to your location?"

"That's Ten-4. We're in the process of getting connected."

"Four-05, we have a helicopter coming in."

"That's Air-Med arriving, oh-5."

"Advise Air-Med will be landing behind McDonald's."

"Go a little farther east," Rivenbark advised. "Bring it down at the Sunrise Plaza."

"Ten-4."

"Six-10, Four-04."

"Oh-4."

"All the operator can do is confirm he is talking on the telephone. She cannot tell us what the conversation is and she cannot disconnect the line so we can dial in. Do you want to go to the throw phone?"

"Can the phone company advise where he is calling to?"

"Ten-54. The operator says it sounds like he's talking to another male, but she can't even confirm that."

"Six-10, are you talking to an operator or supervisor?"

"We're speaking with the supervisor."

"Per Four-04, standby on the bag phone for now. If we need it we'll have SWAT deploy it."

"Hernando, Four-05."

"Go ahead."

"One-11 is at the Mobile Station. Send the media there."

Deputy Mike Coburn called dispatch with a Ten-86, *starting tour of duty*, reporting that he and Deputy Phil Johnson were Ten-51 to the interstate in Air-2.

"Six-10 to Four-05. We got a call from the Orange County Sheriff if we want armored vehicle to respond."

"Hold off for now, Six-10."

"Tango-1 to Hernando. Notify fire department to set up at the scene. Respond to command center under the interstate."

"Please advise SWAT that the original truck has not been cleared. We have SWAT members between the truck and the station."

"Ten-4."

"Six-10, Tampa PD advising that DEA helicopter is 10 minutes ETA with the wife. Will landing zone on the east side of the motel be satisfactory?"

"Come again?"

"DEA helicopter landing in 10 minutes, east side of the motel."

"Air-1, Hernando. Air-2 has now taken position at the scene. I'm returning to the hanger for fuel."

The director of aircraft maintenance advised Sergeant Nowlin to first land the LOH-6 in the Holiday Inn parking lot northwest of the Shell Station.

"I need to check it out before you go," Bill Borcherding told Nowlin through the headset.

"I appreciate it."

When Borcherding approached the helicopter, Nowlin pointed to the splintered floorboard adjacent to his right foot. "That's where I took the hit."

"Well, it looks clean," Borcherding told him after inspecting the damage.

"Okay." Nowlin stuck a finger through the hole above him. "It exited right here."

"Damn! How did it miss your head?"

"I ducked."

Borcherding hitched a ride back to the hangar and Nowlin went to refuel. Only later did the maintenance chief find evidence that the second bullet had nicked the tip of the rotor blade.

Deputy Johnson guided the NOTAR into position while Deputy Coburn rolled video footage of the activity surrounding the station.

Lieutenant Mike Richie flew in from Citrus County. After making contact with Sergeant Nowlin, he staged in the parking lot of the Holiday Inn and waited for a call to service.

*

Detective Randy Scott Bell
Tampa Police Department
Killed in the line of duty: May 19, 1998

Detective Julie Massucci
At the Wall of Honor
Tampa Police Museum
411 Franklin Street

Detective Ricky "Chilly" Childers
Tampa Police Department
Killed in the line of duty: May 19, 1998

Detective Henry Duran
The Ricky Childers Interrogation Room
Tampa Police Department

Trooper James Bradford Crooks
Florida Highway Patrol
Killed in the line of duty: May 19, 1998

TROOPER
JAMES "BRAD" CROOKS
HIGHWAY
The portion of State Road 54 running through
Wesley Chapel, Florida has been named
after Trooper Crooks, who valiantly gave his
life protecting the citizens of this state.
Trooper Crooks was the third law enforcement
officer to give his life on May 19, 1998
following a tragic chain of events that left a
little boy, Joey Bennett and two Tampa police
detectives, Randy Bell and Ricky Childers dead.
This memorial was erected to honor not only
those lost, but those who serve the citizens of
Florida in public service everyday of every year!
The citizens of Wesley Chapel thank you!

DRIVE
SAFELY
IN MEMORY
TROOPER
JAMES B CROOKS

Memorial and Safety Marker
In Memory of Trooper James Crooks

Deputy Lonnie C. Coburn
Hernando County Sheriff's Office
Killed in the line of duty: February 21, 1978

In Memory of Deputy Lonnie C. Coburn

Dwight Hopkins
"I couldn't just let him get away."

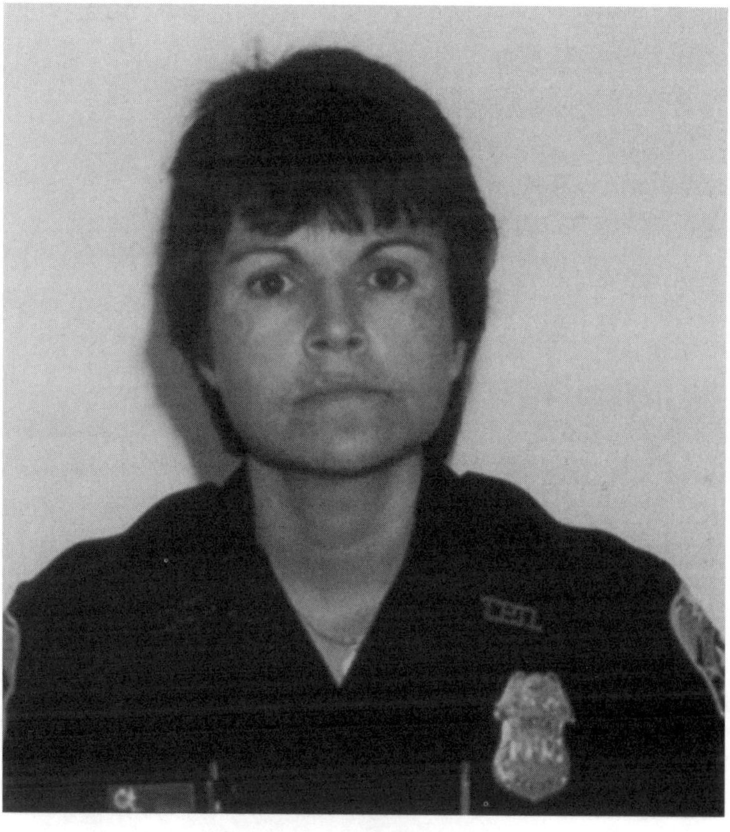

Officer Lois M. Marrero
Tampa Police Department
Killed in the line of duty: July 6, 2001

Sergeant Tom Nowlin
Hernando County Sheriff's Office
"The Lord was my co-pilot."

Officer Mary Ann Collura
Fair Lawn Police Department
Killed in the line of duty: April 17, 2003

Shell Station
Interstate 75 & State Road 50

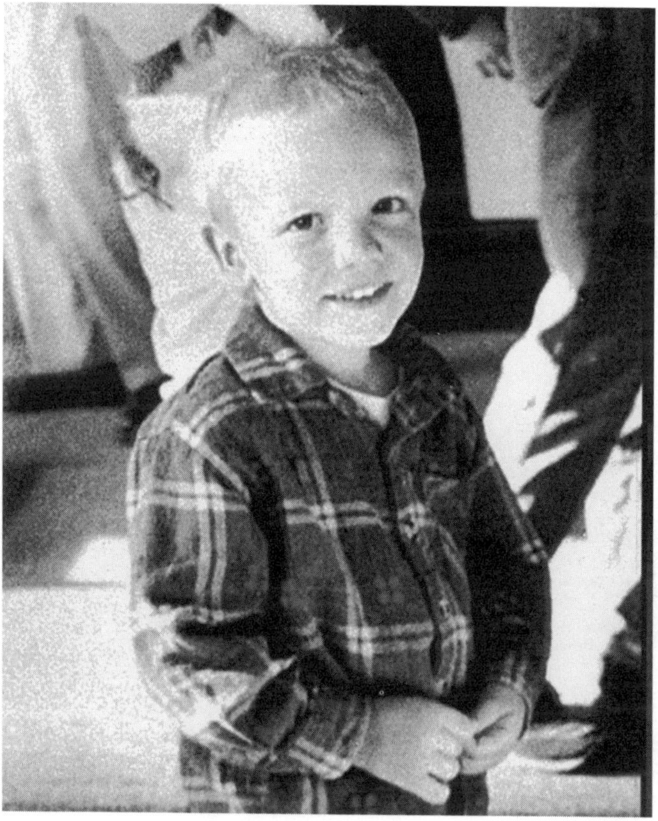

Joey Bennett
Four years old
"Daddy, I dreamed I could swim."

1997 Ford Ranger
Deliver Truck
Carjacked at gunpoint

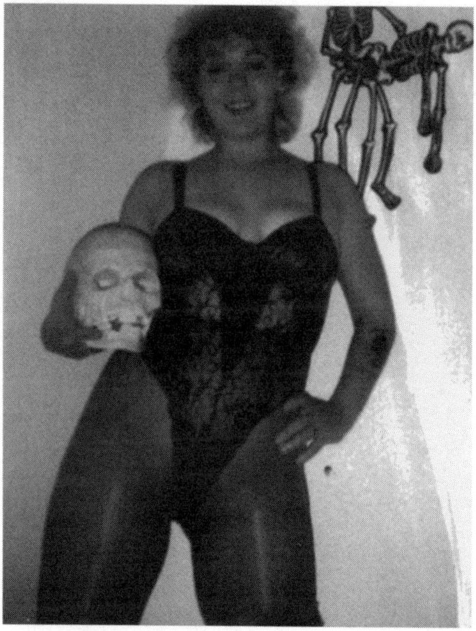

Bernice Bowen
Working at the Starlite Lounge

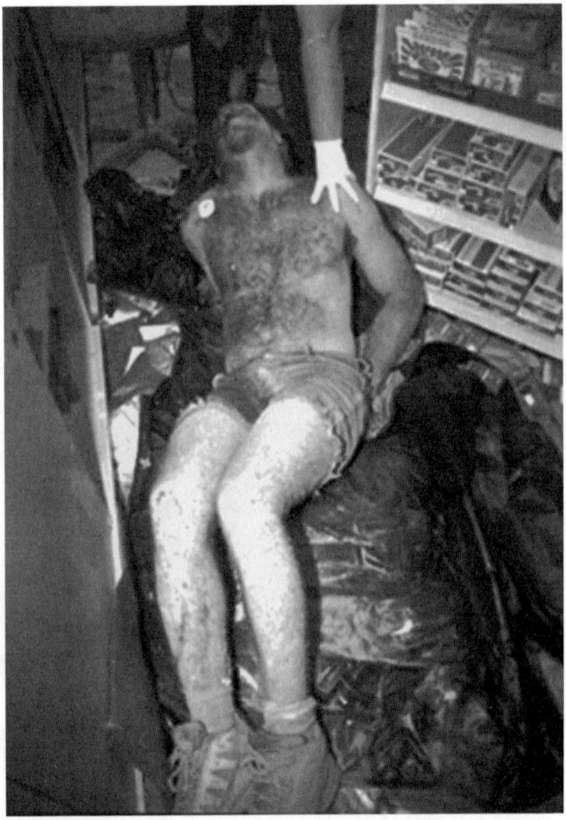

Hank Earl Carr
May 19, 1998

Hernando County negotiators made repeated attempts to contact the suspect at the phone number given to them by Detective Batista, but the instant Carr hung up the phone, a caller from a radio station in Tampa completed the connection first.

"We were covering the incident," said Susan Treccase, head of the 970 WFLA news department. "I made the decision to contact the Shell Station."

Treccase instructed her staff to locate the station and make the call, which Carr answered. "He asked us to call back in ten minutes, so we set up our recording system and called him back."

As Carr mentioned to Kramer, he wanted to make phone calls to friends and former girlfriends. His next call went to the mother of his children in Ohio.

"Hank wanted to talk to my daughter," Evelyn Sacks said. "But I refused to let him talk to her because I was afraid, and I didn't want her talking to him and getting upset."

The call from Carr brought back painful memories of constant beatings, the woman lamented in an interview. "He called to tell me he loved me, that this was goodbye."

The moment Carr hung up, WFLA snagged the open line.

"To verify we had the suspect," Treccase said, "we asked to talk to anyone else in there and he put the hostage on the phone. She wasn't crying, but her voice was trembling."

After verifying they had the right suspect, on-air newsman Don Richards took control of the interview. To the chagrin and frustration of the negotiation team, WFLA then broadcast the conversation live. It was heard all the way to Hernando County, where the officers and media on scene listened incredulously on their car radios.

Richards first asked Carr what occurred that day. His rambling detail of events began with the family plans; he talked rapidly, giving the newsman little time to interject questions.

CARR: Well, it started out this morning. We got up. I was gonna take the kids swimming. I was gonna buy me a new wallet cause mine's tore up, and the wife had some runnin to do. We were gonna get a VCR fixed. We were in the bathroom talkin and I heard a noise. I came out. My son had somehow knocked a rifle that I was holdin for a friend overnight. It was only there overnight. I took the gun from him. I said, "No, you're not supposed to be playin with these," and I turned around to put it up, and I guess the butt hit the side of the wall and it went off. It discharged a round right through my son's face. I didn't know what to do. I was scared and I panicked. I flipped out. I knew he was still alive so I tried to get him medical attention. We threw him in the car and we took him up. I seen a cop on the side of the road. I stopped him, and he was acting like, he was just moving too slow for the emergency situation. I told him, "Look, I can't wait. My son's been shot, I gotta go." He hollered at me, "Go to the fire department down the street." I pulled into the fire department down the street. All this was an accident.

While talking to Richards, Carr glared at his hostage, a reminder to do exactly as he had said.

CARR: When I pulled him out of the car and gave him to the paramedics, I felt his pulse again. It was gone. I knew at that time my son was dead. We left our little girl with the neighbors because my wife Bernice didn't want Kayla in the car with Joey, with him bleeding, because it would have freaked her out. So I took off in the car again. I wasn't under arrest. I left and went back to get my daughter and to get the rifle for the cops, to show them. Well, while I was there, the cops showed up and one of the cops grabbed his gun and said, "Don't move!" So I didn't move. They were sitting there talking to me. I said, "Am I under arrest?" They said no. I wanted to go be with my wife and see if my daughter was all right, so I took off to be with my wife. I hurt my leg. The cops surrounded me, they threw me in the back of the car, they took me downtown, they asked me a bunch of questions, they called me a liar. I tried to tell them it was an accident. They took me back to the scene, which was bad enough. My son's blood was all over the floor and the walls. And I tried to explain to them exactly what happened. They started calling me a liar, and this and that, and I was going to prison, and blah, blah, blah…

During the one-sided conversation, Kramer began to understand what had transpired earlier in the day, which intensified her anxiety and fear for her own life. Carr took a breath and continued his story to Richards.

CARR: They put me back in the cop car and I asked them, you know, "Am I going to prison?" They said, "Yes." I got one of the handcuffs off. I reached up front and got the pistol away from the officer that was driving. The other one jumped in the back seat trying to get it away. I shot them both. I got in the truck that was parked behind me and made the guy get out. I opened up the back of the cop car and grabbed my rifle that they had took. Then I took off up north. I was heading north when the cops started chasing me. They were shooting at me, every underpass I went under they would shoot at the truck. They were shooting at me. They blowed my tires out. Ninety miles an hour, I almost wrecked twice. I finally got the car on the road. They were shooting at me. They shot me through the truck. I was hit in the ass. It's a big hole. I think it's a 45. I'm bleeding bad. They've surrounded this place now. I fell off into this gas station, running for my fucking life, and here I am. And that's the story. What happened to my son was an accident. It was a terrible accident, and I don't even think I deserve to live. It's unlikely that I'll come out of this alive. I can't see giving myself up to fry in the electric chair. I know I'll fry for the cops.

RICHARDS: Who's in the Shell Station with you?

CARR: The lady that works here. No harm will come to her. She's been very nice, very cooperative. If anything, I'll shoot myself. But my wife is supposed to be on the way. They're gonna let me talk to her. Hopefully she can talk me into making the right decision here. Basically, I want to tell her that I'm sorry, and that it was an accident. She was in there. She knows that it was an accident. And I'm waiting on them.

RICHARDS: Joseph, could you let that lady out?

CARR: Not at this time. Not until I hear from my wife. Which may be time to call now. I don't know what's going on.

From room 101 at the Days Inn, Sergeant Campbell contacted Hernando. "Six-10, Hernando."

"Six-10."

"Tell 'em to discontinue communication with him so we can get back on the phone."

"Tell who to discontinue communications?"

"The subject is giving a live interview on the air," Campbell said, his frustration apparent. "All we're getting is a busy signal. We need to worry about the hostages not an interview. Tell them to get off the phone."

"He's now talking to 970 AM," an officer working with the phone company informed Sergeant Campbell. "It's WFLA radio. We'll have to disconnect it at the telephone office."

"Ten-4."

Sergeant Nowlin called dispatch. "Air-1, Hernando."

"Go, Air-1."

"Be advised, we have refueled. We will be staged by the Holiday Inn with the Citrus County helicopter."

"Ten-4."

"Hernando, Four-05."

"Oh-5."

"We received teletypes from Citrus County. They're making their services available for hostage negotiator release if needed. And they also employ the services of a victim advocate if needed."

"Have them standby. We'll advise later."

"Four-86, Four-05, on utility."

"Go ahead."

"I have several of the news media here. Lieutenant Guzman with the FHP is advising them to come up here."

"We have a PIO at the Mobile Station to take care of them. Have them respond to the Mobile Station."

"Ten-4."

Inside the station, Carr answered questions from the newscaster.

RICHARDS: Joseph, what is preventing you from putting down that weapon and just walking out?

CARR: I don't have the weapon. The weapon is laying right here beside me. I haven't had the weapon in my hand for over 15 or 20 minutes now. I'm not in no way threatening this lady. She's visibly upset, but she knows she's going to live. She will live.

RICHARDS: Why don't you just open that door and walk out very slowly?

CARR: Well, there's sniper shooters, and they're all laying under their cars. The police have me surrounded. There's cops everywhere. I'm not going out there. They done shot at me all day. They've been shooting at me for the last 30 miles.

RICHARDS: But if you are not a threat to them, then you should be able to get out okay. Isn't that sort of logical?

CARR: I'm already shot. Logically, I don't want to fry in the electric chair. I don't want to go to prison. I don't want to have to eat the food. I don't want to have to live with people. I just, I don't want to go to prison. I don't want to go.

RICHARDS: The best advice I can give you would be to let that lady, who has nothing to do with any of this, out of that store. And, you know, and to follow her yourself.

CARR: Do me a favor. My real name isn't Joseph Bennett.

RICHARDS: What is it?

CARR: Hank Earl Carr.

RICHARDS: Hank Carr?

CARR: Yep.

RICHARDS: How do you spell that?

CARR: C-A-R-R. H-A-N-K.

RICHARDS: Can we call your wife, Hank?

CARR: I'm trying to get them to get hold of her so I can talk to her now. That's why I'm fixin to get off the phone in case she calls. In case they're bringing her in to try to talk me out of this. She's the only one that can. I know you're trying and I appreciate that.

RICHARDS: That lady has nothing to do with any of this, and, you know, she's treated you well.

CARR: She's only served her purpose. She's just keeping me alive long enough to where I can see my wife. I just wanted to tell my story. My son was an accident. We don't keep loaded guns around the kids. That gun was supposed to be empty. I don't understand what happened.

RICHARDS: A lot of people will be asking a lot of questions for a long time about this particular day in the history of Tampa Bay. Hank, let the lady out and then follow her with your hands up. What's your wife's name, Hank?

CARR: Bernice Bowen.

RICHARDS: Bernice?

CARR: Yeah.

RICHARDS: Let that lady out and then follow her with your hands up and the situation can probably come to a—

CARR: Right after I talk to Bernice. I'll probably give her the guns and let her go out and then I'll just lay on the floor here and they can come and get me. But for right now, I want to talk to my wife before I do anything.

RICHARDS: This situation could end peacefully, Hank. Okay?

CARR: Y'all got the story?

RICHARDS: I think we do.

CARR: Thanks, buddy.

RICHARDS: Okay.

CARR: Bye.

While returning to the station from Bird Street, Detectives Stout and Massucci listened to the radio interview in rapt astonishment.

"I couldn't believe what I was hearing," Massucci said. "That was the first time I heard the name Hank Carr."

*

As events unfolded, more questions required answering. Corporal James Herren and Detective Bobby Holland interviewed Bowen.

HERREN: Who shot your child today?

BOWEN: I guess my boyfriend did.

HERREN: Were you in the room when your boyfriend shot the child?

BOWEN: No, I was not in the room.

HERREN: Where were you?

BOWEN: I had walked up the steps from taking my VCR to my car.

HERREN: Where did you see your boyfriend?

BOWEN: I didn't see my boyfriend at that time.

HERREN: Was he in the house?

BOWEN: He was in the house, but I didn't see where at in the house.

HERREN: Where was your child in the house?

BOWEN: My child? Which one?

HERREN: The one that was shot.

BOWEN: The one was shot was laying in front of my couch.

HERREN: Okay. Who was in the house when you walked outside to put the VCR in the car?

BOWEN: Two was in the house. One was my daughter Kayla, I believe. And my son and boyfriend.

HERREN: And your boyfriend's name is what?

BOWEN: Uh, he says his name is Joseph Bennett.

HERREN: And does he go by that name?

BOWEN: He goes by several different names.

HERREN: And those names are?

BOWEN: Uh, let's see, uh, Joseph Bennett. He goes by Hank Carr. Let's see, Earl Reid. Ah, Boo…

HERREN: How old is he?

BOWEN: He's between the age of thirty and thirty-two, I believe.

HERREN: How tall is he?

BOWEN: I believe he's about five foot six.

HERREN: Does he have a mustache or sideburns?

BOWEN: He has a mustache and a goatee.

HERREN: Earrings in his ear?

BOWEN: No.

HERREN: Does he have tattoos?

BOWEN: Yes, he has three tattoos. One on his left leg of a skull.

HERREN: A skull?

BOWEN: A skull with blue flames, like a smoke scene is what it is. And then he has a spider on his right arm. He has a little cross on his left arm, on the, uh, upper part of the arm. On both upper parts of the arm.

HERREN: Okay. How did you come to meet him?

BOWEN: I came to meet him on, uh, Valentine's Day. Through some friends.

HERREN: Valentine's Day of this year?

BOWEN: No, it was last year.

HERREN: And you met him where?

BOWEN: I met him, I believe, at a bar.

HERREN: Here in Tampa?

BOWEN: In Marietta, Ohio.

HERREN: Were you living there at that time?

BOWEN: I was living there.

HERREN: And he was living there at that time?

BOWEN: No, I wasn't living there at the time. I was visiting. I'm sorry.

HERREN: How about him, was he living there at that time?

BOWEN: I don't, uh, no, I don't think so.

HERREN: Did y'all decide to come to Tampa together?

BOWEN: No, I came down here by myself. I moved down here by myself.

HERREN: And when did he come down?

BOWEN: He came down before I did. His father was going to have a heart attack or something. Or he had a heart attack and he came down here. And then later on I moved down.

HERREN: Did he call and ask you to come live down here?

BOWEN: Uh, yeah, I think so.

HERREN: How long have y'all been dating in Tampa?

BOWEN: In Tampa, I would say, I don't know.

HERREN: How long have you lived in Tampa?

BOWEN: Probably about a year and a half, two years.

HERREN: Has he ever been arrested before?

BOWEN: No.

HERREN: ...Something happened last night at your house about midnight, is that correct?

BOWEN: Yes. A friend had brought over a gun last night and dropped it off at the house and said he'd be back today, Monday, to pick it up.

HERREN: Who's the friend?

BOWEN: His name is Lawrence.

HERREN: Lawrence have a last name?

BOWEN: Uh, yeah, he does, but I'm not sure what it is. I don't know. I have no clue.

HERREN: How did you meet Lawrence?

BOWEN: Through some friends.

HERREN: Is he a friend of yours or your boyfriend?

BOWEN: A friend of my boyfriend.

HERREN: Has he ever asked you to hold a gun for him?

BOWEN: No, not me. He's asked my boyfriend to hold a gun, but not me.

HERREN: What kind of gun?

BOWEN: I think it was an SKS.

HERREN: How long did he stay?

BOWEN: He stayed maybe fifteen, twenty minutes.

HERREN: What did he leave behind?

BOWEN: He left behind the gun. The rifle.

HERREN: What did your boyfriend do with this rifle?

BOWEN: I'm not really sure. I believe it stayed in my bedroom on the top shelf. Um, I really didn't see where the gun was put or anything.

HERREN: Was it loaded or unloaded.

BOWEN: I believe it was unloaded.

HERREN: How do you know it was unloaded?

BOWEN: Cause I thought that I saw my boyfriend check the chamber. And he said it was unloaded, I think.

HERREN: Earlier you told me you didn't see your boyfriend check it.

BOWEN: I seen my boyfriend check the chamber and he said it was unloaded. He told me it was unloaded.

HERREN: So, apparently, somebody today had to load that gun. Are your kids capable of loading that gun?

BOWEN: No.

HERREN: Did you load the gun?

BOWEN: No.

HERREN: Was anybody in your house today that could have loaded the gun? A baby sitter? An in-law? A mother in law?

BOWEN: Nope.

HERREN: So the only people in the house today was your son, your daughter, your boyfriend and you. And you didn't load it?

BOWEN: I wasn't in the house when it occurred. Like I said, I took my VCR downstairs to my car.

HERREN: Let's go back to the loading of the gun. You actually saw your boyfriend check to see if the gun was loaded or unloaded. Did you ask him, was it loaded or unloaded?

BOWEN: I didn't ask him anything. He usually, whenever he messes with a gun, he makes sure it's unloaded.

HERREN: What kind of guns do you have stored in your house?

BOWEN: I believe I have a SKS, a shotgun, and I believe a Glock maybe.

HERREN: What kind of Glock?

BOWEN: It's a 40 caliber.

HERREN: And where is the Glock kept?

BOWEN: On the top shelf in the bedroom.

HERREN: What is your daughter's name?

BOWEN: Kaitland Nicole Bennett. Kayla.

HERREN: In talking to her today, she says Joseph carries the Glock in the waistband of his pants. Is that correct?

BOWEN: Yes, sir.

HERREN: Have you seen him carry it in the waistband of his pants?

BOWEN: I have seen him carry it in the past.

HERREN: Does he carry it all the time in his pants.

BOWEN: Most of the time, yes.

HERREN: Did you tell the police officers today that he may have a gun in his pants?

BOWEN: Nobody asked me that question.

HERREN: Did you ever think to tell them that he may have a gun and he's possibly dangerous?

BOWEN: I never thought about it. I had too much going on with my son, and I worried about my daughter.

HERREN: How do you know he shot your son?

BOWEN: The police officers told me.

HERREN: When you ran out of the house, was he nearby?

BOWEN: I don't know where he was.

HERREN: Did you ever think about going inside the house and asking him what happened?

BOWEN: He came down the steps with my son.

HERREN: Did he tell you what happened?

BOWEN: I asked what happened and he said Joey was shot and that was it.

HERREN: Did you ask him if he shot your child?

BOWEN: No, I didn't ask him.

HERREN: Why not? I mean—

BOWEN: Because I didn't think he did it.

HERREN: Why not?

BOWEN: Cause he's not that type of person just to be shooting kids, you know.

HERREN: Did it ever occur to you to tell the officers he may have a gun in his waistband?

BOWEN: I know whenever he left the house with me with my son, he did not have a gun on him.

HOLLAND: How do you know that?

BOWEN: Because he had his shirt off. I didn't see it in his pants.

HERREN: What was he wearing today?

BOWEN: When he put his shirt on, I think blue jeans. Blue jean shorts.

HERREN: Did he ever go back in the house after he brought the child down the stairs?

BOWEN: No, sir.

HERREN: He stayed downstairs with you the whole time?

BOWEN: Yes, sir.

HERREN: When he came downstairs, he didn't have a shirt on?

BOWEN: No, wait. Wait. Okay, I came down the steps. He came down behind me and he told me that Joey was shot. Okay, he ran back up the steps. I told him, I said get Joey and come on. I said we got to get an ambulance. I ran back down the steps. I hollered out the door for my friends, they were all standing around. . . .By that time, he had Joey in his hands and he had his shirt on. He had Joey in his hands and put him in the back of the car. And I told Alisha to watch my little girl.

HERREN: And Joey was in the living room, right?

BOWEN: Yes.

HERREN: You went upstairs. Did you go in the living room to pick him up? Cause I see no blood on you.

BOWEN: No, I have a little blood.

HERREN: Who did you ask help from?

BOWEN: Uh, the neighbors. Uh, Linda was standing out there, Alisha was.

HERREN: Linda and Alisha have a last name?

BOWEN: Linda's last name is Yonce. Alisha's last name is, ah, Mace, I believe.

HERREN: Did you take the child to the hospital or something? Did Fire Rescue respond?

BOWEN: What I did is, we put the child in the car. We took him down the street and we saw an officer at the O and B Deli. So we pulled over there and asked the officer to call an ambulance.

HERREN: Where was the child bleeding from?

BOWEN: The head, I believe.

HERREN: Did you ask your boyfriend what happened?

BOWEN: No.

HERREN: You never asked him?

BOWEN: I already knew what happened. He told me my son was shot. All I wanted to know if my son was going to live. I wanted to get him somewhere to where he could get medical attention.

HERREN: But you never asked him?

BOWEN: No, I didn't.

Among the aliases Bowen mentioned in the interview, Hank Carr finally appeared. And since Carr had in fact previously been arrested in Hillsborough County, he knew it was only a matter of time before the officers would learn his real name, and once they had that, they'd find his booking photograph, fingerprints, prior criminal history and the outstanding warrants.

A career criminal like Hank Carr knew the officers would lock him in jail, a place he loathed and vowed never to return.

12

Hernando/Hillsborough Counties
Interstate
May 19, 1998; 1530 hours

The Tampa Police officers at Floribraska and Interstate 275 soon learned that the killer made it all the way to Hernando County and had taken a female hostage.

"Nothing more could be done on Elmore," Detective Duran said. "Since Gene Black and I are both negotiators, Lieutenant McNamara grabbed us and said, 'Let's go!'"

Duran—a congenial SWAT officer who worked Sundays during the football season providing personal security for the head coach of the Tampa Bay Buccaneers—retrieved a vest and helmet from the trunk, leaving his car for Paul Southwick.

At speeds over 100 miles an hour, Lieutenant McNamara drove a marked unit up the interstate.

"He had tears in his eyes," Duran said of the lieutenant. "When I realized how fast we were going, I told him we better slow it down or we'd have more deaths."

Referring to the Shell Station scene, the detective added, "I had never seen so many officers. There were police cars everywhere, from every agency."

Detective Todd Lunge said, "I took a position with other Tampa officers west of the Shell Station. We heard the assailant was talking with a radio personality over the air, so I used my cell phone to call the radio station, requesting that a copy of the taped conversation be created for TPD."

The detective advised station manger Alan Ryan that a uniform officer would come by and pick up the tape. He then telephoned TPD dispatch via cell phone, instructing them to send a uniform officer to the station to collect the tape.

"I heard the live broadcast," Officer Raymond Sheridan said, his disapproval apparent. "I came Ten-8 from a call on South Drexel and immediately responded to the radio station at 4002 West Gandy. With Corporal Robert Wagner as backup, we contacted management and obtained a copy of the tape. We then marked it, dated it, removed the security tabs, and remanded it to the custody of Sergeant Long on the 8th floor at 411 Franklin Street."

"Officer Seal and I heard the pursuit," Richard Zytczak said. "We ran to our vehicles and drove north on 75. When we arrived at State Road 50, we met with Corporal Jerry Clark, who asked us to take a position on the east side of the Shell Station. Officers Timothy Grams and Michael Hollifield arrived along with us."

Lieutenant Guidara, Sergeant Robert Weinhold, Detective Grady Snyder, Investigator Chuck Hudson, as well as Officers Hernandez, Paz and Balkcom promptly hooked up with the Tampa contingent. Units from the Florida Highway Patrol swarmed in, led by Major Morris Leggett and Captain Gary Odom. Members of the Florida Department of Law Enforcement also joined the effort. An estimated 200 officers rushed to the scene prepared for whatever action was necessary to end the reign of terror.

Lieutenant Guidara said, "I assumed command of Tampa officers at the scene until Captain Small arrived. Deputy Chief John Bushell was the first command staff member to arrive, later followed by Chiefs Sawyer, Holder and Taylor respectively."

Although Carr had already terminated the interview with Don Richards, he immediately made another call, continually tying up the phone line.

"Six-10, Hernando, you guys having any luck getting hold of that TV station?"

"We're trying to get through."

"It's a radio station and he's talking about it on 970 AM right now."

"Have the ground units see if there's a mobile unit referencing that radio station."

"Hernando, we've been advised they have now hung up with him. We do not want him calling out."

"Okay, we're trying to block outgoing calls."

"Get ready to go."

"Wait," Sergeant Campbell said, further angered by the impasse. "The phone is still busy."

Before they got through, Carr made another call.

*

Albeit a horrendously traumatic day for all law enforcement officers, the most difficult assignment fell on the shoulders of Detective Kevin Durkin: documentation of the crime scene on Elmore Street. The assignment required Durkin—a robbery detective who was also being urged to join the homicide squad—to scrutinize and report everything inside the vehicle, including the blood-splattered bodies of his two friends.

Durkin examined and noted the precise positions of the bodies, as well as the location of each bullet wound and the amount of blood loss. He itemized personal effects and articles of clothing that had recently been dry cleaned and wrapped in plastic. He located the spent shell casings from a 9mm gun. He logged every detail, then stood by solemnly as CSI technician Richard Garvin took pictures of the slain officers.

From the position Detective Bell died, he apparently put up a fight, but was no match for a 9mm slug at close range. His upper torso laid draped over the seatback, half his body hanging in the rear seat, with a small pool of blood directly below his head. The first bullet hit his neck and slowed him, but the second found his forehead above the right eye.

An anguished Kevin Durkin observed many curious bystanders gawking at the lifeless bodies of his friends. "That's when I decided the vehicle would be placed on a flatbed wrecker just as it was. We would leave both officers inside the vehicle and take them to the Hillsborough County Medical Examiner's Office."

Durkin choked back tears as he closed the doors and watched a tow truck driver load up the vehicle and drive away. Under the escort of several officers in patrol units, the Taurus arrived at the Medical Examiner's Office at approximately 1600 hours. After further scrutiny and additional photos, Officers John Aleman and Rocky Ratliff assisted Detectives Stanton and Durkin in removing the bodies and placing them on gurneys.

Then Durkin completed documentation of the interior portion of the vehicle. Personal items documented included a traveler coffee mug and a sales tag for a DeMarini softball bat; Childers and Bell both loved the game and often played on the same team.

Identification Technicians Mitchell and McIlwaine processed the interior and exterior of the vehicle for latent fingerprints.

"I placed security seals on all the doors," Durkin reported. "Then Officer Pemberton escorted the vehicle to the impound lot."

The day offered additional suspense and terror for Joe Durkin, Kevin's brother, a civilian supervisor in the reports department.

"Corporal Mike Morrow and I watched the noon news from a restaurant in Ybor City," Durkin said. "When we returned to Franklin Street, a female officer told us two detectives had been killed. My first thought, of course, was *Kevin*."

Joe Durkin had experienced several close encounters with death back when he was an officer with the Tampa PD. While on patrol in 1994, a drunken driver slammed into the driver's side of Corporal Durkin's cruiser at 50 MPH. It ended his career as a law enforcement officer and nearly ended his life. It took rescue crews with the *Jaws of Life* over an hour to remove his twisted body from the mangled patrol car. Joe Durkin had little memory of that day, but his brother Kevin certainly remembered.

Stella Castillo, a Police Department employee who witnessed the accident, ran to Durkin's aid. She also remembered the day well.

"I saw the crash," Castillo said. "The van pinned his patrol car against a telephone pole."

Castillo dutifully remained at the scene, offering support and comfort until paramedics arrived.

On a hot summer day three years earlier, Durkin responded to one other call involving alcohol that could have easily taken a life, either his own or that of the suspect. "I took a stabbing call on 22nd and Idlewild. As I approached the house, the EMT advised me of a large man inside with a butcher knife."

Durkin went inside with gun drawn, only to find himself staring into the menacing eyes of a six-foot-four, 305-pound black male with a bloody towel covering his outstretched hands.

"Freeze!" Durkin demanded.

"You ain't gonna shoot me," the huge man snarled, lumbering slowly closer.

"I didn't know if he still had the knife," Durkin reported. "I couldn't see his hands."

"You ain't gonna shoot me! You ain't takin me to jail!"

"Stop right there!"

The suspect refused to stop, eventually crossing that invisible and protective line defined in the *21-step* rule. As per policy, Durkin had authority to fire his service weapon and terminate the threat.

"I had my finger on the trigger, ready to squeeze, when I again yelled for him to stop. Fortunately, he finally stopped."

When backup officers took control of the suspect, Durkin ran to a bedroom looking for the victim. He found a black female lying prone with knife wounds to her back and shoulder. He gently turned the blood-covered victim to her side and checked for vital signs.

"Hi, Joe." The woman forced a smile at the man who saved her life. "Good to see you."

"The victim was Stella Castillo," Durkin discovered. "One of our most dedicated employees."

Stella had worked over twenty years in the records department, at times reporting directly to Vickie Childers.

"Joe was there for me," Castillo said respectfully of Durkin. "And I was there for him."

*

Sitting in the center of room 102 at the Days Inn, Deputy Mari Kelly transformed from a COPPS officer to her critical role as team leader of hostage negotiations. With an innocent life perilously on the line, she mentally focused on the awesome responsible ahead, an assignment where success is relatively unnoticed by anyone outside the circle, but failure leaves scars that last forever.

Deputy Rick Ruiz placed a "Situation Board" in the room so the team could take notes and mark progress. With members of the FBI and the Tampa Police Department huddled around an external speaker in room 101, Kelly prepared for action.

"Hold on a minute," Sergeant Campbell grumbled. "Somebody else just called him. . . Someone told him to kill himself."

"It's gonna take us a little bit longer," the telephone employee said to Campbell. "We'll have to manually connect the line when you tell us to go."

"Okay, just tell us when you're ready. We're standing by to dial."

"People are calling in and tying up the line. We're trying to dump them so we can reestablish."

"Ten-4. We're in the process of changing the number. Let us know when we can dial."

"Six-10, he's now on the phone with somebody from Spring Hill who's telling him about God."

"Cut the line and tell us when."

The negotiator's persistence paid off. "Go ahead and go. They dropped the line. Go ahead and go."

"Six-10, we got it. We are in contact. Don't do anything more."

"Ten-4."

"Four-97, Hernando."

"Go ahead."

"Have Deputy Nelson standby with the phone man at the box in case we get disconnected."

"We'll keep him on it as long as we can."

"Do not disconnect this call. We have a landline."

"Six-10 to Four-05. We are now talking to the suspect ourselves."

A few minutes past 1600 hours, Deputy Kelly took over.

After identifying herself and verifying she was talking to Joe Bennett, she went directly to questions regarding the detectives. Her primary objective was the safe release of Stephanie Kramer, but she also needed information, subconsciously knowing that everything she said would one day be scrutinized by her superiors, peers, the media, the public, jurors and lawyers.

Although talking rapidly as usual, Carr remained as calm as if he were interviewing for a job.

KELLY: Yeah, and then what happened?

CARR: Then I shot the guy next to the door.

KELLY: And how did you get a gun to shoot the two officers?

CARR: I took theirs.

KELLY: Oh, you were sitting in the back seat?

CARR: Yeah.

KELLY: And then what'd you do, drive their car?

CARR: No.

KELLY: How did you get here?

CARR: I carjacked a guy that was behind us. I got out the car, pointed a gun at him and told him to get out of his car. He got out of his car, no problem. I jumped in it. Went and filled it up with some gas and was headin out of state. I was goin to visit with my little girl before I died 'cause I was planning on killing myself. I just wanted to see my baby girl one more time before I died.

KELLY: Oh, we don't want you to do that.

CARR: Well, I need to get my wife on the phone or somehow get her to talk to me.

KELLY: Okay, they're doing that for you. They're bringing her up here. You know that there's a little bit of distance between Tampa and here.

CARR: Yeah, I drove for some time at 90 miles an hour.

KELLY: Wow.

CARR: With the tires blowed out and everytime I went under a bridge cops shot me, and every time I went by an exit or underpass they shot me. The trucks all shot up. They shot my tires out. They shot me. I'm shot. I've got bullets in me now.

KELLY: I thought you were only shot once in the butt?

CARR: I guess I was shot in the butt but I may have been shot in the back. I don't know. There's a huge hole in my butt and it's probably just the one shot. But there's something mashin on my spine. I can feel it. I think it's the bullet.

KELLY: Wow. So, tell me this, how could you get their guns if you were cuffed? Were you cuffed?

CARR: Yeah.

KELLY: In the front?

CARR: Yeah.

KELLY: Oh. It must have been quite a struggle, huh?

CARR: No. I pulled one of my hands free from the handcuff, reached up, grabbed the gun. They jumped back and was trying to get the gun and I just shot 'em both in the face.

KELLY: Were they wearing shoulder holsters?

CARR: One was. The other one I don't know. I think I pulled his gun out of his side holster after he was dead. Then I pulled the gun they confiscated from me out of the back of the trunk, throwed it in the truck, loaded everything up and was ridin. And then the big shootout happened all the way down the interstate. All the way fuckin down it.

KELLY: Okay.

CARR: Finally my car wouldn't go no more. The tires were fucked. I had an exit there, they were shooting at me bad. At that point I'm runnin for my life. I ran in here. I'm held up in here until I can talk to my wife, in which case I'll either turn myself in and let 'em fry me or I'll blow my brains out right here.

KELLY: Well, I'm hoping that we can work some things out. I know it's not the best scenario that you have.

CARR: There's no way out of this. I'm surrounded. They've got more bullets. I've only got a few left. I'm not gonna hurt the person I'm with. She's very sweet. She's helping me out a lot. Being very polite. Very nice to her.

KELLY: Um, how about the clerk?

CARR: That's the clerk I'm talking about.

KELLY: Okay, she's being nice to you?

CARR: Yeah, her name is Stephanie and no harm will come to her.

KELLY: You're not gonna hurt her?

CARR: No sir. No ma'am. No way.

KELLY: Okay, that's great.

CARR: I'm not an evil tyrant guy, you know.

KELLY: You don't sound like it. You just sound like you got in a really bad situation.

CARR: Right. People act weird under stress, I guess.

KELLY: Yes, they do.

CARR: Cops talkin and shootin at you is about as stressful as you can get.

KELLY: Yeah, that's for sure. Um, can I call you Joe? Do you go by Joe?

CARR: It don't matter, yeah.

KELLY: I want to make sure I call you by the right name.

CARR: It don't matter.

KELLY: Um, did you run into anybody else on the road when you were traveling?

CARR: Yeah, some people tried to run me off the road. I guess citizens.

KELLY: No, I mean like any more law enforcement?

CARR: Yeah.

KELLY: Did you run into a Highway Patrolman?

CARR: Yeah, I think so.

KELLY: You think so?

CARR: I'm not sure what they were.

KELLY: Oh.

CARR: They were cops.

KELLY: Okay, um, the clerk, her name is Stephanie or Deb?

CARR: Stephanie.

KELLY: Oh, okay, that's what I thought. . . Okay, how are your injuries?

CARR: Pretty bad.

KELLY: Are you bleeding a lot?

CARR: Yeah, I got a leg I can't even walk on.

KELLY: Oh, wow.

CARR: I'm bleeding a lot. I got a huge hole in me. I think it was a forty-five. It had to a been a forty-five. A nine don't make that big a hole.

KELLY: Were you running when you got shot in your butt?

CARR: No, they shot me right through the truck.

KELLY: Wow.

CARR: I mean, I ducked down and smashed the gas but they hit me with I don't know how many rounds. It was at least seven or eight cops out there just blastin away at the truck as I went by. And that happened at every fuckin interstate I went under. They were all out there settin up roadblocks and shootin at me. I'm surprised I even made it this far. With any luck they woulda put one in my head but I guess their sharpshooter missed.

KELLY: Hey, Joe, so where did you go? The two detectives went to your house to talk to you?

CARR: Uh, those detectives took me to the house, asked me to recreate the scene what happened, which was stressful enough. I told 'em what happened, they called me a liar and confiscated my wife's rifle. They confiscated a bunch of shotguns, or a shotgun next door.

KELLY: Oh. And after you went to the house, you guys got in the car and were supposed to go to the jail, huh?

CARR: Yeah, they were taking me downtown to book me.

KELLY: What road were you going on?

CARR: I don't even know. They took an exit.

KELLY: Oh, an exit? You were on the interstate?

CARR: Yeah. They were drivin up the interstate and they took an exit. I guess a downtown exit or somethin. That's why I said fuck it, I want my freedom and I was just runnin for my freedom. Then the fight over the gun happened and I was just fightin for my life. So I got out of there and I've been fightin for my life ever since.

KELLY: Yeah. So, you were fighting with the detective that was in the passenger seat first?

CARR: No, the first one, I grabbed the one drivin's gun, and I reached up and I grabbed his gun. He tried to stop me and I snatched it loose, then the other one dove in the back trying to stop me and I just started pullin the trigger. I shot 'em both in the face.

KELLY: Oh. Ummmm, so you must have shot one person then the other?

CARR: I don't remember. I think so. I shot one twice. I had to shoot one twice 'cause I shot him and he was still tryin to get the gun, so I shot him again. Blood poured out everywhere. I just jumped out. I couldn't even get out of the car door. I had to reach around and open up those doors. I got out, went in the trunk and grabbed the rifle and took off. I wish I had somebody else driving.

KELLY: So, what was going through your mind at this point? It must have been pretty tough?

CARR: I just was hopin I could slip through and get up north and see my baby and then I was gonna go off into the woods and just shoot myself. I feel so bad about killin that little boy. I loved that little boy. I taught him everything.

KELLY: How old was he?

CARR: He was four. He's so beautiful. Blonde hair, brown eyes. Cutest little bugger. Tough. Strong. Brave.

KELLY: Were you watching him that night?

CARR: No.

KELLY: Was it at nighttime?

CARR: These are our kids. They live with us.

KELLY: Oh, they live with you.

CARR: A family unit. We've been out of trouble for so long. I got in a fight with a next door neighbor and they called HRS on me, just to, what do you call it, a call where they don't need to be there but the people call and they try to get me in trouble. I told them if they had a problem with me, they should just jump on me and beat me with a stick or something. Don't have my kids snatched away from their mother. Everybody apologized. They said that HRS was wrong, but anyway HRS was up our ass for about a month. And they finally found out that the kids aren't being abused. The kids are fine. They got food. They know we love them.

KELLY: Oh, you've got more than one kid?

CARR: Yeah, there's two there. Kayla and Joseph. Well, Joseph is no longer with us.

KELLY: Oh. The two guns that you have in there, are they the ones you got from the police?

CARR: Yeah.

KELLY: So, they're nine millimeters?

CARR: Yep. One's a Glock 17 and one's a Glock 26.

KELLY: I guess you know things about guns, huh?

CARR: A lot.

KELLY: I don't know much about 'em.

CARR: I bought most of my guns from law enforcement.

KELLY: Well, uh, if you don't mind we'll continue to stay on the phone until your wife gets here.

CARR: No, I'm gonna hang up. My ear's gettin kinda tired.

KELLY: Put it on the other side. If you want, I can give you a break for a little bit.

CARR: Yeah, give me a break and let me hang up and call me back here in a little bit, all right?

KELLY: Uh, well—

Carr promptly hung up the phone, leaving the deputy with no chance to object.

13

Hernando County
Shell Station
May 19, 1998; 1630 hours

Over twenty minutes passed before the negotiators got Carr back on the phone. During that time, he told Kramer how much he hated cops, admitted intentionally killing the two detectives, but insisted that shooting Joey was an accident. His captive played along, expressing sympathy for the death of his son. Carr showed her pictures of Joey and Kayla, and once Kramer perceived he loved his children, she told him she was pregnant and looking forward to being a mother. For the time being, the ploy may have saved her life.

"Four-05, Hernando."

"Go ahead, oh-5."

"I need you to check back and advise of any unit who is Ten-25 with the parents of our possible hostage."

"The parents are now at the command post."

"Ten-4."

"Six-10, the helicopter carrying the wife is Ten-97."

"Bring her to the Days Inn, room one-zero-one. We'll step out and get her."

Corporal John Bennett, a sniper with the Tampa Police Department, selected a hide location near Deputy Card and took aim on the window in front of the cashier's compartment. "I didn't have enough time to change into my black fatigues," Bennett said. "I showed up in a long-sleeved, black polyester uniform. The heat was unbearable."

At 1630, Carr answered the phone.

KELLY: …We were talking when you said you wanted a break.

CARR: Uh-huh.

KELLY: And then I couldn't get back through.

CARR: Yeah, right, people's been callin up here from the news and all kinds of things.

KELLY: Oh, man, you don't want to talk to them right now.

CARR: I just wanted everybody to know it was an accident.

KELLY: Yeah, I can understand that.

CARR: I never shot my son on purpose. I didn't even know the gun was loaded. It was unloaded the night before. I don't know where the bullet came from.

KELLY: (sympathetically) Yeah.

CARR: It was an accident. I feel like shit and I don't even think I should live.

KELLY: No. I want you to live. I mean we got things that you can work through and you do have your wife and your daughter. What's her name?

CARR: Kayla.

KELLY: Kayla?

CARR: They're beautiful. Have you seen her?

KELLY: I haven't seen her yet, but I'll be seeing her soon.

CARR: Joey is beautiful too.

KELLY: Oh.

CARR: He was a cute little bugger.

KELLY: Yeah, I bet he was.

CARR: I'm so sorry. . . So ashamed.

KELLY: I know you are, but it was an accident.

CARR: That's what I tried tellin them, and they were callin me a liar and all kinds of shit. And they tried to act like me and her got in some kind of fight or something and the cop goes did she, did she shield herself with the child and you shot him anyway or somethin. And I was like no way, man, it was an accident. I mean I immediately grabbed him up and ran for the medical assistance. It was just too late. He was shot point blank in the face and I felt so bad. God!

KELLY: It's a lot of things that you have to work through. But—

CARR: I guess you got my wife on the way?

KELLY: Yeah, they do.

CARR: Well, call me whenever they're here. I want to talk to her. I gotta get off the line now.

KELLY: Well, why don't you let me talk to Stephanie while you do what you do?

CARR: Here she is.

KELLY: Okay.

STEPHANIE KRAMER: Hello.

KELLY: Stephanie?

KRAMER: Yes.

KELLY: How are things?

KRAMER: Okay.

KELLY: How's he treating you?

KRAMER: Very good. He's a very nice man.

KELLY: You just be real nice to him, okay?

KRAMER: Of course.

KELLY: I'm sure you're really a nervous wreck, but just try to be strong, okay?

KRAMER: Okay.

KELLY: Um, is he bleeding a lot?

KRAMER: Yeah, he's bleeding. All we have are Kleenex to put on it.

KELLY: All right. Is he shot in his back like he said?

KRAMER: He just found the bullet.

KELLY: All right. Is he shot in his back like he said?

KRAMER: He said it's in his butt.

KELLY: Oh, it went through his butt and then into his back?

KRAMER: Yes.

KELLY: Okay, I'm gonna ask you a question. Just say yes or no, okay?. . . Are the guns on him?

KRAMER: No.

KELLY: Are they on the counter?

KRAMER: Yes.

KELLY: Do they have bullets in them? That you know of?

KRAMER: One.

KELLY: One. Okay. Do you think he's at a stage where he might pass out from the injuries?

KRAMER: He already gave me one gun.

KELLY: He gave you one gun?

KRAMER: Yes. I've got it in my hand.

KELLY: Is it unloaded?

KRAMER: Yes, it is. So he told me. I'm looking at it. I don't see anything in it.

KELLY: Okay, but that doesn't mean there isn't anything in it.

KRAMER: He's very nice. He knows I don't like guns so I don't think he'd give me a loaded gun.

KELLY: Well, be careful. That doesn't mean that particular gun is unloaded.

KRAMER: Okay. He just took everything out of it and it's not loaded at all.

KELLY: Is the chamber open then?

KRAMER: Chamber is open. I can see in it.

KELLY: Okay, I'm gonna ask him if he'll let you go. You think he'll let you go?

KRAMER: He wants to talk to his wife. Before he lets me go. That's what he wants.

KELLY: Okay, and the gun that, uh, that has the bullet in it, is it on the counter?

KRAMER: Yes.

KELLY: Is he near it now?

KRAMER: Yes.

KELLY: Okay. . . Does he look like his injuries will. . . Will he be passing out any time soon?

KRAMER: He is weak. And he's in pain. I know it hurts him. I can see it.

KELLY: Okay. You be real sympathetic with him and we're gonna get you out of there, okay?

KRAMER: Okay… He said please keep the cops back away from here.

KELLY: They're not gonna move in. They're gonna stay right where he sees them.

KRAMER: Okay.

KELLY: I can't ask them to move back any farther, but if he works with us, we can work with him. Is there any question you want to ask me since he's resting? What's he doing? Sitting?

KRAMER: Yeah, he's sitting. He's resting I would say. (she speaks to Carr) Are you resting?

KELLY: Did he mention anything about the trooper? The highway patrolman, anything?

KRAMER: No.

KELLY: Is the front door locked?

KRAMER: No.

KELLY: Are you guys in the cubicle where the cash register is?

KRAMER: Yes.

KELLY: Is it locked?

KRAMER: The one door is. The window is open.

KELLY: You didn't tell him it's bulletproof did you?

KRAMER: No.

KELLY: Okay. He's just letting you talk, so you can ask me whatever you want. I don't want him to hang up. Maybe he'll pass out from losing a lot of blood. Is he losing a lot of blood?

KRAMER: You feel faint or anything? (she asked Carr) No, he doesn't feel faint. I've been making sure he has something to drink.

KELLY: Okay. You're feeling okay as far as feeling strong about this whole thing, that you can do it right?

KRAMER: I looked at him and I've looked in his eyes and he has told me he is not gonna hurt me, and I believe him.

KELLY: Okay, you believe him.

KRAMER: I believe him.

KELLY: All right, well, we would like to keep you on the phone, so we'll just chat. . . My name is Mari and I work for the Sheriff's Office. Your family is here. Anything you want to tell them?

KRAMER: Just that I love them and I'm doing fine. That he's not gonna hurt me. Tell my mom that he promised he would not hurt me.

KELLY: Okay. How old are you, Stephanie?

KRAMER: I'm gonna be 28 in June.

KELLY: You have any kids?

KRAMER: I can see it in his eyes when I'm talking to him. I trust him. He's not gonna hurt me.

KELLY: I'm glad about that. I wish he would turn himself in so we can get him some help and then he can be around for his daughter and his wife, who obviously cares for him.

KRAMER: You've talked to her?

KELLY: She's on her way here. Our ultimate goal is to get you out safely. And then him.

KRAMER: I hope things stay safe. I believe it was an accident what happened to his son. I honestly believe it was an accident. He's pretty tore up, and I can understand why. . . He's wanting to use the phone now.

KELLY: Who does he want to call?

KRAMER: (to Carr) They want to know who you want to call.

CARR: Hello?

KELLY: Hi.

CARR: I'm probably gonna try to call my mom again.

KELLY: Uh, you want to call your mom? I believe your mom is traveling this way. I don't think she's home because she was worried about you.

CARR: All right then. Let me get off of here an y'all call me when she's here.

KELLY: Well, I don't want to break the line because I definitely don't want the press calling you. We don't want any bad publicity for you, you know?

CARR: It's already bad enough. I mean, it can't get no worse. Killing a cop ain't a good thing.

KELLY: No, there's always hope sometime.

CARR: Shootin a cop ain't a good thing.

KELLY: Well, I want to work for you so, if you—

CARR: Well, right now I just wanna make a couple phone calls. I might not get to talk to these people again. These people I want to call are old friends and stuff and tell 'em that everything is all right and that I'll probably be goin to jail or prison or whatever, and that it was an accident today.

KELLY: Joe, we're trying to keep this line clear so when your wife gets here we can get her on the line.

CARR: All right, then let me hang up. Everything is fine here. I'm gonna sit and wait on my wife. I'm gonna make a few phone calls and that's it.

KELLY: Okay, well listen to me. Your wife, they were flying her up here, so they're telling me to hold on, okay?

CARR: All right.

KELLY: She may be close. Let me check and see how far away she is and then—

CARR: Well, I'm gonna hang up. Go ahead and call me back in a little bit.

KELLY: Joe, wait. Joe, there's a chopper in the parking lot—Joe? Joe? Are you there? ... He hung up on me.

Whether or not the chopper landed, Kelly didn't know for sure. Her comment in that regard was intended to keep him on the line, but the attempt failed. He immediately tried to call out, but the telephone company employee now controlled the line, ensuring that no more calls originated from that number.

*

Sergeant Jim Diamond III, the Regional Bomb Squad Commander, conducted a training session at the SWAT facility on Highland Street in Tampa. While members of the squad discussed detonation tactics, Diamond went inside the shop and found a message on his pager: *No further information available on the two detectives killed.*

Diamond's jaw dropped. With over 20 years on the force, he knew every detective in the county. His formative years involved law enforcement, with his father retiring as a Deputy Chief in the Police Department, and now his son, Jim Diamond IV worked the Southwest Gangs Unit for the Los Angeles PD. When it came to crime-fighting families, the name Diamond topped the list.

"Randy and Ricky have been shot," radio dispatch informed the burly sergeant when he called for specifics. "We're now in pursuit of the shooter."

"Ricky and Randy played on our 40-plus softball team," Diamond said. "They were my friends. Very close friends. I was determined to do whatever I could to help get that guy."

As regional commander, Diamond made the decisions where and when to deploy, and when he learned the killer was holed up in a gas station, he loaded equipment onto the Bomb Disposal Truck and hitched up the 3 ½ ton Bomb Containment Vessel.

"I dispatched immediately to the scene," said Deputy Garrett Haskins, a Hernando County Bomb Squad and SWAT member who was in Tampa training that day. "While driving north, I maintained radio contact with Sergeant Diamond."

Shortly after the field commander in Hernando County advised his coordinator to release the Tampa Bomb Squad, Sergeant Diamond and four TPD SWAT officers rolled the equipment onto Interstate 275, only blocks from where the heinous murders were committed a few hours earlier.

With the situation at a dangerous stalemate in Hernando County, the Pinellas County Sheriff's Office also responded to support their brethren across the bay. Lieutenant Dan Simovich, commander of the Special Operations Division, picked up the telephone and contacted Sergeant Robert Holloway, his SWAT team leader.

"Hey, Bob, is the Peacekeeper ready to roll?"

"Sure is. Are we going to Hernando County?"

"Yep. You want to drive it or take it on the flatbed?"

"We'll drive."

"Ten-4."

From the Sheriff's Office in Largo, Holloway and SWAT team member Raymond DeCunto loaded their SWAT gear and piled into Peacekeeper One, a converted military surplus armored personnel carrier. By way of Ulmerton Road and Howard Frankland, they rolled north: destination Hernando County.

*

Detective Batista and Corporal Lawrence McKinnon hustled Bowen to the Days Inn, where Deputy Cinda Moore took control of Bowen and escorted her to room 103 for briefing. Detectives Duran and Black went to room 102 with Deputy Kelly.

"Perhaps by divine intervention," Henry Duran commented, "but I placed my micro cassette recorder near the speaker and recorded the negotiations. Only later did we learn that their equipment had failed and mine was the only recording we got."

Duran sat near Deputy Kelly with a pen and notepad.

Batista and Black stood by to assist when needed.

"I did not want to get on the phone," Batista confessed. "It was nearly impossible for me to suppress my hostilities toward that—"

Once the telephone company completed the necessary operation, the phone rang inside the Shell Station about fifty times before Carr finally answered.

CARR: Yeah?

KELLY: Hi, this is Deputy Kelly. Was that enough rest?

CARR: What did y'all do, turn off the phone?

KELLY: I didn't.

CARR: Somebody here turned off the phone where I can't make any outgoing calls.

KELLY: I didn't ask anybody to do that. I was able to dial in.

CARR: Where's my wife at?

KELLY: She is definitely on her way. They're gonna get her ASAP because we're trying to work things out for you. We know that's who you want to speak to.

CARR: Thank you.

KELLY: Um, Joe, when your wife gets here, since we've done this for you, Stephanie's family is really concerned for her. Can you let her out at that point? Can you do that for me?

CARR: Let me talk to my wife. At this point I just want to talk to my wife.

KELLY: I understand that, but you know how you were talking about family and what everybody means to you. Well, her family is really upset.

CARR: Nothing's gonna happen to Stephanie as long as the cops stay away. I want to talk to my wife before I turn myself in.

KELLY: Yeah, I know. We're gonna do that for you. Can we get Stephanie out first?

CARR: Stephanie is not gonna come to any harm by my hand.

KELLY: I understand that.

CARR: But at the same time I was just fightin for my life with all those cops. They're out there with sniper rifles, all aimed and trained on me. Waitin on me to make a move. I'm not gonna do anything but sit back where it's safe until I can talk to my wife.

KELLY: Okay.

CARR: Cause I've already been shot. I know they will shoot me. Okay?

KELLY: We can do that for you.

CARR: I'm in the middle of writin a letter to my daughter right now, tellin her how sorry I am about her brother.

KELLY: Okay. All right.

CARR: I'll be back as soon as she gets here. . . Listen, I have some money here that's mine. I haven't robbed nobody or done nothin bad. I have some money here that's my own money. It's like 180 bucks.

KELLY: Okay.

CARR: I want to make sure my wife gets that if anything happens to me because she doesn't have no money.

KELLY: All right. Well, we don't want anything to happen to you either. And we'll let you talk to your wife. My concern also is for Stephanie. You know that, right?

CARR: Right. Stephanie is in no trouble whatsoever.

KELLY: Okay, she's being really nice. And she's treating you really well.

CARR: I don't even think I pointed a gun at her have I? I'm not gonna. I don't even have one in my hand. I gave her the other one. I'm being cooperative as I can. I'd just like to see my wife. Please don't jerk me around.

KELLY: I'm not. Do you feel that I am?

CARR: I don't know. I tried to call out. I was gonna call a buddy of mine and tell him to forget the money I owed him. And to tell a few friends of mine that it was an accident.

KELLY: Well…

CARR: I feel so ashamed and I'm so sorry for it.

KELLY: Well, you were on the news pretty much. I'm sure lots of people heard it. You told quite a few people on the air that you did not mean to hurt your child. And you really sound sincere. Stephanie said you're sincere about it, and I know you feel bad about it.

CARR: Oh, terrible.

KELLY: Yeah, that's why you're having a difficult time with this. And maybe in—

CARR: I mean they could have locked me up for anything, man, and I woulda just went no problem and done my time, but I didn't shoot my son on purpose.

KELLY: Yeah, I don't think you did either.

CARR: It was an accident.

KELLY: Yeah.

CARR: The rest of the day just went wrong.

KELLY: It sure did. But there's always a chance to turn it around, don't you think? There's always hope. You'll go to court on it, and you know that's what they have good lawyers for.

CARR: I can't afford a lawyer. They'll give me a public defender that'll railroad me and I'll either take the chair or life in prison. You don't shoot cops in Florida and not fry.

KELLY: Well, I can't really answer that… I won't lie to you. If I have to tell you the truth no matter how bad it is, I'll tell you the truth. I feel that you have been sincere with me, and Stephanie says you are sincere. But, Joe, I would really love to give Stephanie back to her family. Her family is very upset. And you have to admit, this is probably traumatic for her. Even though it—

CARR: She has no reason to fear me.

KELLY: Well, it's an unusual situation, don't you think? She's got to have some kind of fear. So as soon as your wife gets here, I will definitely make that arrangement for you, but you have to give me your reassurance that you'll let Stephanie out after that.

CARR: Yes. I will.

KELLY: Great. How are you feeling?

CARR: I'm hurt. More inside than outside. Hell.

KELLY: You're probably not even thinking about that bullet wound are you?

CARR: The bullet is lodged in my back and it hurts, but inside my heart. I saw my son's head blowed off, for Christ's sake.

KELLY: Yeah.

CARR: (crying) I didn't mean to.

KELLY: You could probably get some therapy and talk this out, Joe. Not that you will ever forget it, but you can work things out and forgive yourself for that, you know.

CARR: What's Bernice saying? She said it's an accident, right?

KELLY: I haven't had a chance to talk to her. When she gets here, I can ask.

CARR: It's an accident. She has to know.

KELLY: When did it happen?

CARR: This morning.

KELLY: Oh, okay.

CARR: We were getting ready to take him swimming and buy him some toys. And I picked up the gun, I went to turn it around and put it back on the shelf and I hit the wall with it and it went off. I blowed my little son away. (sobbing loudly)

KELLY: Oh, I didn't realize that happened this morning.

CARR: I've been cryin all day. The detectives, they were really being pricks.

KELLY: They were?

CARR: They told me if I didn't admit to having a gun, I couldn't seek medical treatment. My knee was hurtin bad… They called me a liar and all kinds of shit, and I took 'em and showed exactly what happened and they still didn't believe me and were talkin about chargin me with all kinds of shit. Put me in prison and being real nasty, so I tried to make a break for it. We got into a gun fight, a gun came loose. It was either they were gonna shoot me so I shot first.

KELLY: Oh, you felt the cops were gonna shoot you?

CARR: Yeah, and then I fuckin ran. Hauled ass and ran. And they been shootin at me ever since.

KELLY: You ran? I thought you shot them in the car?

CARR: Yeah, I did those two. That's where the fight happened, in the car.

KELLY: Oh, you took the driver's gun first?

CARR: Right.

KELLY: That's the guy that had the shoulder holster, right?

CARR: Right.

KELLY: So, with his gun, you shot the passenger cop?

CARR: Yeah.

KELLY: Oh, wow…

Negotiators determined that Bowen now understood the situation, and like it or not, they had no choice but let her talk to Carr. They knew he was a desperate animal at the end of his leash; an armed and dangerous killer, ready to strike with minimum provocation. And at his disposal, an innocent woman who served only one function.

"We had to be careful what we said," Kelly acknowledged, the understatement obvious. "It was very tense."

*

Deputies escorted Bowen from room 103 to 102. They prompted her one last time on what to say and what not to say. To help elicit the desired information, Detective Duran sat next to Bowen so he could pass notes and coach her along.

As minutes ticked away, tension mounted.

BOWEN: Hey, sweetheart, what are you doin'?

CARR: Oh, Tater, I'm so sorry.

BOWEN: It's okay, baby. I know it was an accident, sweetheart.

CARR: Baby, I didn't mean to take your boy from you. (sobbing pathetically) Baby, I didn't mean to take your boy from you.

BOWEN: It's all right.

CARR: I'm so sorry.

BOWEN: Let Stephanie go, okay?

CARR: I am.

BOWEN: Let her go now.

CARR: I'm gonna let her go in a little bit. Not right now. They're not gonna rush me right now. Give me a minute to talk to you.

BOWEN: Okay, I love you.

CARR: Do you hate me?

BOWEN: No. I love you. I know it was an accident, okay?

CARR: But baby I didn't mean to. My God, how can you ever forgive me?

BOWEN: Baby, I forgive you. I know it wasn't your fault, okay? I know it was an accident, sweetheart. I love you.

CARR: I love you, baby. And I'm gonna give you some money. I got a note in an envelope. I wrote a letter for Kayla telling her I'm sorry and I wrote one for you and I'm gonna send it out. It's only 180 bucks. That's all I had.

BOWEN: Okay, but let Stephanie go. Okay?

DURAN: (to Bowen) Have Stephanie bring the note out.

BOWEN: Have Stephanie bring the note out to me, Okay?

CARR: She will.

BOWEN: Can I see you in person?

CARR: I don't know if they'll let you.

BOWEN: They should let me. Let her out, okay?

CARR: But you won't be able to see me. They'll rush me and they'll shoot me.

BOWEN: No, baby, they're not gonna shoot you. They don't want to hurt you. They have no intentions of hurting you at all.

CARR: But I already shot three cops. And Lord knows how many other people. They already shot me.

The admission officers wanted finally came: three cops, not two. Bowen continued doing as told, assuring him, keeping him calm. She told Carr he was loved, wanted and safe. She said exactly what Carr wanted to hear. He repeated that it was an accident, even describing to her what happened between himself and the officers.

CARR: Baby, I'm shot. I'm bleedin bad.

BOWEN: You're all right. Calm down.

CARR: Listen, there's no way we could ever be together again, okay?

BOWEN: I'm listening.

CARR: I love you with all my heart.

BOWEN: I love you.

CARR: And I wanted to have another baby with you so bad. I loved Joey and it hurt me when that happened. It shocked me so bad I couldn't believe it. It was like a nightmare.

BOWEN: Listen, let Stephanie go and we'll talk about it, okay?

CARR: I love you baby and I'm not gonna make it through this.

BOWEN: Yes you are. You're strong.

CARR: Baby, I can not live the rest of my life knowing that I've killed your precious boy.

BOWEN: Baby, it was an accident.

CARR: The cops weren't. I got in a fight with them. The gun came loose.

BOWEN: Just a minute…

DEPUTY KELLY: Joe, it's Kelly again. Listen, you're upsetting your wife a little bit. She wants you to let Stephanie out and then you can talk with her. She wants to be near you and you can't do it from in there. Okay, Joe?

CARR: Could you let her talk to me some more?

KELLY: I'm gonna give her a couple of minutes, and then I'm gonna come back and talk to you. We want Stephanie out now, okay?

CARR: Let me talk to her.

KELLY: Okay.

BOWEN: Hey, baby.

CARR: Hey.

BOWEN: Let Stephanie go, okay?

CARR: They're gonna put me in prison forever.

BOWEN: No they're not. No they're not.

CARR: Baby I shot two cops in the face and shot one with the SKS in the face and I shot a bunch of other fuckin cops and people. There was a big shootout. Every time I went under an interstate they were shootin at me, they were shootin at me. They hit me. I'm shot. They shot my wheels out from under me. Now they're out there with snipers right now aimed at me.

BOWEN: Baby, calm down, listen. Let the girl go.

CARR: Listen, I'm gonna let this girl go.

BOWEN: Please do.

CARR: I'm gonna let her go for you. I've been nice to her. She's a nice lady. I didn't mean to flip her out, but I was fightin for my life. I want to tell you something, okay? I'm gonna take my own life.

BOWEN: No you're not.

CARR: I cannot live knowing that you're gonna be in this pain the rest of your life. I'll never see you again anyway.

BOWEN: You will. I may only get to see you through a glass window but I'll get to see you and you'll get to see my face.

CARR: Did you tell them it was an accident?

BOWEN: I told them the gun accidentally went off baby, okay? Please, I love you.

CARR: I love you baby, and I'm gonna send out this 180 dollars. I wish I had more to give.

BOWEN: Let her go, okay?

CARR: There's some gold in the house. I don't know what all. I think they took all the guns outta the house in the other apartment.

BOWEN: That's fine. Let her go, okay?

CARR: Is anybody listening on this line?

BOWEN: No. Nobody is listening.

What he did next shocked even the most experienced detectives. As one neighbor had reported, Carr and Bowen often spoke in some obscure language or code that sounded like gibberish. Carr suddenly spat out the esoteric words as fast and fluently as he spoke English.

Without translation, his recorded words phonetically sounded like the following:

CARR: *goodagar dadagiv na guvada guy unaga gura gokada dicka gina gotima gitima gova dagata gavada ga.*

BOWEN: (a sigh) Baby, listen. I love you. Please just don't—

CARR: I'm smokin cigarettes.

BOWEN: (a small laugh) Are you?

CARR: Yeah, I done smoked half a pack. I figure they ain't gonna kill me. The cigarettes ain't gonna kill me.

BOWEN: Listen, please let her go so we can talk, okay? After you let her go, I want to be able to talk to you.

CARR: Baby, as soon as I let her go, they're gonna rush me.

BOWEN: No, they're not. They're not.

CARR: I saved two bullets for myself. I can't let them put me in prison. Baby, I don't want to live with niggers again.

BOWEN: Baby, listen, I love you. Don't do this.

CARR: The time we had together was the sweetest time I've ever had. Even though we fought a lot sometimes. I was takin the kids swimming. We was getting the VCR fixed. They was all through the house, they took your SKS but I got it back. I pulled it outta the cop's trunk… but you won't get it back no more cause it's been involved in a homicide of a police officer.

14

Deputy Kelly took the phone from Bernice. While she cautiously pleaded for Carr to release the hostage, he insisted on talking longer to his wife. As the situation dragged on, media helicopters flocked to the scene, congesting the sky and creating a hazard for police and emergency helicopters. Reporters on the ground rushed to the Mobile Station to find Deanna Dammer.

"In situations like this," a Channel 10 reporter asked, "what goes on at this point?"

Viewers throughout the country watched the PIO calmly field questions on national TV.

"Our negotiators first try to develop a rapport with the suspect. The bottom line, we just try to talk them out. The goal is to make sure no one else gets hurt."

Forensics Supervisor Gary Kimble meandered back and forth near the interstate, snapping photos from every angle and taking shade wherever he found it. "Most of my work comes later. After SWAT clears their gear, Bomb Squad clears the building, Fire Department clears the area and Sheriff Mylander gives the okay." The former science teacher added a touch of humor. "That's when everyone else is back home watching us on the television."

The TPD Bomb Squad arrived in the Bomb Disposal truck and met up with Deputy Haskins, who cleared a path near the command post. The SWAT crew from the Pinellas County Armored Unit also rolled in with Peacekeeper One, available for support and protection if requested by the Sheriff.

Sergeant Diamond reported to Sheriff Mylander in the command post. "Can you make a tactical entry?" Mylander asked.

"Yes, sir, but I want two entry points."

"Okay, it's your call. Advise me when ready. We're going in as soon as he releases the hostage."

Once Haskins had gone over the layout of the Shell Station and Food Mart, Diamond concluded egress would occur on the north wall away from the large refrigeration units, and another on the west wall where Carr remained hidden inside the office behind the bulletproof Lexan glass.

As negotiations continued, Sergeant Diamond marked an *X* on each wall where he wanted the charges. To penetrate the north wall, he selected an explosive called RDX—a material packed in 5-inch strips similar to PVC pipe and weighing approximately one pound each. On the west wall, he utilized a charge labeled PETN.

"We'll rig the west wall," Corporal Stan Diokas told Diamond.

"We'll get the north wall," said Detective Paul Rockhill.

Corporal Diokas and Officer Steve Metzler taped the ordnance and detonation cords to the west wall directly behind the cashier's cage, approximately where they determined Carr was hiding.

"It may not kill him," said Diokas, a long-time friend of Detective Randy Bell. "But he won't walk away from it."

To limit damage yet create an opening large enough for SWAT entry, the RDX charges on the north wall would have to go inside the concrete blocks. In order to accomplish deployment, the team of Haskins, Rockhill and Robert Nicholson needed to bust through the concrete block and lower charges inside the wall at the appropriate location. The question, however, was how to punch a small hole in the concrete wall without the suspect hearing it and alerting him to the intended entry point. Sergeant Diamond had the answer: "We called for a helicopter to hover directly above the target."

With the deafening noise and wind concussion vibrating the small station, no one inside heard the sledge hammer smash the concrete. With that mission accomplished, the helicopter ascended to 1,500 feet. Diamond and his team had everything in place except for the detonation device.

"We connect that later," Diamond explained. "After successful removal of the hostage."

*

Carr grew increasingly frustrated as the standoff stalled.

Deputy Kelly had been on the telephone for hours and needed a breather, so Detective Batista offered to have a go at it, hoping he might have better luck at that point. Kelly continued another minute or so before Batista took over.

KELLY: ...This is what we're gonna do. We want you to come out. Then, of course, you're gonna answer all the commands they give you. Then we'll let you talk with Bernice. The SWAT guys are gonna come when she steps out. They're gonna take her out of the area cause that's what they're trained to do. Then we want to work on getting you to come out, okay?

CARR: Let me talk to Bernice one more time.

KELLY: No. You said one more time two times ago.

CARR: Yeah, but I didn't get to talk to her. I've been talkin to cops more than I have her. At least let her talk to me and hear my last words.

KELLY: Joe, you promised me. We've been on the telephone for a long time.

CARR: The only way this thing is gonna go down smooth is if I get to talk to her. Until I'm satisfied I'm done talkin with her, then I'm gonna let the girl go. I'll either come out or I'll shoot myself. It ain't askin much. The phone's right there, hand it to her. I promise I'm lettin Stephanie go. She'll live to see 28 and she's pregnant so she's gonna live to have a child.

KELLY: You gave me your word, Joe. You spoke to her twice.

CARR: Look, I gave her the gun like y'all asked. I'm wantin to talk to my wife. As soon as I'm done talkin to her, we'll do it. But I wasn't done talkin with her. Y'all keep pullin her off the phone. Please, this is aggravatin me.

KELLY: Okay, hold on. Bert wants to speak to you now.

DETECTIVE BATISTA: Boo?

CARR: Yeah.

BATISTA: We kept our word. I flew her up here in a helicopter.

CARR: I know, but I only talked to her for a little bit and y'all—

BATISTA: Let Stephanie go and you can talk to her as long as you want. I promise you.

CARR: That's not true and you know it. The only time I'm gonna get to talk to her for a while is right now.

BATISTA: We're not gonna rush you. You have a gun. We don't want to hit anybody. We don't want anybody else hurt.

CARR: I don't want to hurt nobody.

BATISTA: Let Stephanie go. We're not gonna rush you. I gave you my promise. Stephanie is scared. She's been there for a long time. She has a family. Let her go.

CARR: Please let me talk to my wife and Stephanie's coming right out the door.

BATISTA: You said you'd let her go.

CARR: I didn't get to finish talkin to her.

BATISTA: You can talk to her as long as you want as soon as you let her go.

CARR: I'm not gonna argue with y'all. Put my wife back on the phone. Y'all are aggravatin me.

BATISTA: Okay, let me talk to Stephanie first.

CARR: (handed the phone to Kramer) Tell him to let me talk to my wife.

KRAMER: Please let him talk to his wife.

BATISTA: Okay. She just went to use the bathroom. Believe it or not, she had to go to the bathroom.

KRAMER: (to Carr) She had to go to the bathroom. They said she went and she's coming back… We can wait until she comes back.

BATISTA: His wife says she doesn't want to talk to him until he let's you go. That's what she's saying. I'm not making this up.

KRAMER: Well, she needs to tell him.

BATISTA: Okay, as soon as she gets out of the bathroom, I'll tell her. Does he still have the gun in his hand?

KRAMER: No. It's sitting next to him. He's been very nice. He's been very polite.

BATISTA: Okay. We don't want anybody else hurt. We're gonna let him talk to his wife as long as he wants, as long as he lets you go. Just calm him down. We don't want to excite him.

KRAMER: Okay. He doesn't want to talk to you guys. He wants to talk to her.

BOWEN: Baby? Hello?

CARR: Baby, yeah, let me talk to you for a little bit, baby.

BOWEN: What's up? What do you want to talk about? Want to talk about the blue skies and the birds and trees and birds and the bees? Talk about me and you? Listen, I want you to stay alive and I want everybody else to stay alive too, baby.

CARR: They're gonna fry me in the electric chair anyway.

BOWEN: No they're not.

CARR: Baby, I've got a record. I've shot three fuckin cops point blank. I've shot a little boy that I love to death. That's bad enough.

BOWEN: It was an accident. They know it's an accident.

CARR: Did you hear what the detectives were sayin to me? They were tellin me I was gonna fry and I was a liar and that you held the kid up and I shot the kid.

BOWEN: Baby, you're dealing with us now. You're dealing with these people here. That's totally different from them, okay?

CARR: Yeah, they're dead. I ain't dealin with them no more. They're dead.

BOWEN: You don't have to deal with that no more. Just deal with Hernando County, okay? They know it was an accident. I know it was an accident.

CARR: Yeah, but the rest of it wasn't. That's what they're gonna fry me for.

BOWEN: Baby, you're not gonna fry.

CARR: Baby, I'm shot. They already shot me. I'm shot in the butt and it's lodged in my back somewhere. I'm hurtin like a bitch. I'm losin blood.

BOWEN: You're all right. You're tough.

CARR: I know I'm tough, but I cannot live my life in prison and you know that.

BOWEN: Baby, I'll be there to see you everyday, okay? I love you. Don't do this to me. Don't be stupid.

CARR: I'm sorry but my last thoughts are gonna be of you and the babies. (crying) I'm sorry.

BOWEN: Baby, don't do this to me. Boo, don't do this to me.

CARR: I got no choice. You think I'm gonna go out there and let 'em shoot me?

BOWEN: They're not gonna shoot you. They do not want to shoot you, okay?

CARR: Listen, I'm not goin to jail.

BOWEN: Baby, listen. Do me a favor and let Stephanie go so I can come over there and talk to you. Please.

CARR: I'll let her go, and as soon as she's out the door I'm gonna blow my fuckin brains out. This is the last time we're gonna talk. I saved a coupla bullets just for myself.

BOWEN: Baby, don't do this to me.

CARR: I only wanted to see my Little one more time. I called Evelyn and she said I would never be able to see Little again and that she's off with some other guy, and Little, she won't even let me talk to Little.

BOWEN: That's a bunch of bull.

CARR: No, I called her. Evelyn said.

BOWEN: Baby, don't be stupid. I love you, okay? Kayla still loves you. Baby, you just gonna leave me here? Is that what you're gonna do? Is this your easy way out?

CARR: You don't understand. I'm leavin you there cause I'll be in prison the rest of my life. They ain't gonna let me see you. At least Joey didn't feel no pain when he died.

BOWEN: No. Joey's all right. All right.

CARR: Joey's in heaven. (crying) I'm so sorry for that, baby. I never meant to. God! I wanted to go swimming and buy the little arm things. I was gonna fix the VCR and we were gonna have a good day together. It was your day off and I didn't mean to fuck it up.

BOWEN: Everything is fine. Don't worry about it.

CARR: I'm gonna go now. I'm gonna let this girl outta here and I'm gonna do what I gotta do... She's been real cooperative. I'm sure she's scared out of her wits but she ain't showed it. She's brave. I wish it was you in here talkin to me.

BOWEN: I can be but you've got to let her go first.

CARR: They won't let you in here.

BOWEN: Yes they will.

CARR: No, because they're scared I'll hold you hostage.

BOWEN: No they won't.
CARR: What did you tell the cops?
BOWEN: I didn't tell them anything.
CARR: The cat's out of the bag that I'm not Joseph Lee Bennett.
BOWEN: Yeah, we know.
CARR: Are you in any trouble for that?
BOWEN: No. Hang on a second and I'll let her talk to you, okay. Hang on.

Many officers eavesdropping on the conversation cringed at the thought of Bowen *not* being in trouble. In their minds, three of their brothers were now dead because she continually lied and withheld information that would have kept them alive. Had they known about his criminal record, they believed the slain detectives would have treated Carr as a criminal rather than a grieving father.

Deputy Kelly returned to the phone.

KELLY: Okay, Joe, you ready? This is Deputy Kelly.
CARR: Yeah, give me a minute.
KELLY: Okay, okay.
CARR: Listen, this is what's gonna happen. I'm gonna send her out. She can take the empty gun if she wants. I've still got a gun in here and I plan on shootin myself. I'm gonna send her out and I'm gonna do it where she ain't gotta see it, okay?
KELLY: Can we talk after you send her out?
CARR: No. I'm gonna shoot myself. I don't deserve to live after what I done to that baby. The cops, I'm sorry I know you're a cop, but those detectives were being pricks. I just wanted to get away. It was a wrestlin match ensued. I ended up with the gun. The other cop was goin for his gun. I had to shoot or they were goin to shoot me. It just went all outta hand. I didn't mean for this to happen. And on the freeway I don't even know who I was. I was so fuckin flipped out on adrenaline and people shootin at me and cops chasin me, I think I shot some people. I'm a bad person and I don't deserve to live.
KELLY: Oh, I haven't heard about any of that.
CARR: Please let me have just a little bit longer, okay. It's my last request.

KELLY: Joe, I've bent over backwards for you. You've gotta let Stephanie out. As soon as they tell me on the radio that Stephanie's out the door, I will hand the phone to Bernice. She's right here next to me. Okay, Joe?

CARR: Tell her to pray for me, okay?

KELLY: Okay, just don't hang up on me.

CARR: I'm gonna set the phone down. I need a few minutes to think. I'm gonna sit here and bleed a little bit and then as soon as I get the balls enough to pull the trigger on myself, I'm gonna let her go and then I won't have no choice. They'll come to get me.

KELLY: What are you gonna do? You're gonna let Stephanie out, right?

CARR: I'm gonna let her out and then I'm gonna kill myself.

KELLY: Okay, where is Stephanie? She by the door now?

CARR: No, she's sittin right here in front of me.

KELLY: Okay, but let me talk to her while you take a minute to compose yourself.

KRAMER: Hello?

KELLY: Stephanie, as soon as the door is unlocked, you run out, okay?

KRAMER: Okay.

KELLY: Run straight ahead.

KRAMER: Okay.

KELLY: There'll be some SWAT guys to meet you. Don't be frightened, just run as fast as you can to the closest car you see.

KRAMER: Okay.

KELLY: All right, don't hang up on me. Tell him that you're ready to go now.

CARR: (he took the phone from Kramer) I'm going to hang up now. I'm gonna do a few things. I'm really gonna let her go. I'm really gonna shoot myself.

KELLY: Don't make that decision yet, Joe. Joe?

CARR: (spoken to Kramer) Can you turn your back for a second? I gotta pee. I don't wanna die and pee on myself. Just turn your head away, okay?

KRAMER: You want me to hold the phone?

CARR: No, just turn your head away.

KELLY: Joe? (hears Carr moaning) Joe? Hey, Joe? Joe, you okay? Is Stephanie coming out? Joe? Joe?

CARR: ...Hello?

KELLY: Joe, I was getting worried about you there. I heard you moaning.

CARR: Yeah.

KELLY: Is Stephanie coming out?

CARR: Yeah, I'm gonna let her go. No sense in her dying.

KELLY: Okay, well Bernice wants to speak to you, Joe. Come on out now.

CARR: Let her speak to me.

KELLY: We had an agreement, Joe. Let her walk out the door.

CARR: All right, give me a few minutes to compose my thoughts and she'll be right out.

KELLY: I thought you did that?

CARR: You can sit and listen, but I'm gonna put the phone down cause I don't want to talk to you no more unless Bernice is gettin on the phone then.

KELLY: Well, okay. All right, then I'll talk to Stephanie while you compose yourself.

CARR: Don't worry about that.

KELLY: Come on now. Come on, Joe. Joe? Joe?

Kelly pleaded for him to get back on the phone, but apparently, the man with a near-genius IQ was preparing for the tragic day to end, and he alone would determine the ending.

When Carr placed the phone on the floor, officers heard him talking to the hostage. With an occasional moan from pain worsening in his knee and buttocks, Carr handed Kramer his car keys, handcuff key, some money, the letters he wrote, photos, his gold chains, and the shirt off is back; all of it for Kramer to give to Bowen.

Negotiators could only listen.

CARR: ...Pretty much done fucked up.

CARR: ...I don't deserve to live after killing my son. It was an accident, but for me to even have that gun in the house was wrong.

CARR: …My knee is swollen bad, ain't it?

CARR: …I wish I had more to leave her with. I wish I had more to give her. Guess I'm a cold-hearted killer now, huh? There's the car keys.

CARR: (moaning loudly) Aaaahhh!

CARR: (gives Kramer the handcuff key) Been carryin one for five years. Just in case. It all started when I was a little kid.

CARR: …If you keep a gun in your house, please keep it away from your children.

CARR: …They're all out there waitin for me.

CARR: …I bought her an engagement ring. I was just thinkin last night when I got that SKS. I keep one for protection. We live in a bad neighborhood and we always have. We can't afford to live in a good neighborhood. Seems like every time I get somewhere in life, cops show up and fuck with us and I'd have to move again.

CARR: …I always thought I'd be able to go somewhere and die. I always wanted to die in North Carolina where my dad died. Always knew I'd kill myself. I didn't want to die of old age or get crippled, you know. Even if I live, I'm gonna be crippled for the rest of my life. I've got a big bullet hole in me.

CARR: …I guess the news had me recorded on air so everybody in the world knows I didn't mean to shoot my son. It was an accident. Cops whoever else got shot. It's just crazy shit.

CARR: …Everyday I would pray, God bless my babies. God bless Little. My children, little Joey, he loves to pray at the table. The food he'd say "We gotta pray, we gotta pray."

CARR: …They're gonna put her away. God, how could I do that? I didn't mean to. I feel so bad.

CARR: …They took me back to the scene. I could see my son's blood, everywhere pieces of him. And they callin me a liar, fuckin with me.

KELLY: Joe? Joe? Joe let me know what's happening. Joe, talk to me. Joe, can you hear me? Joe?

Carr picked up the phone.

CARR: Hey.

KELLY: Thanks for coming back on the phone. Kind of hard when you're not able to talk to anybody on the other end.

CARR: I'm sending some things out for Bernice. So make sure she has her money so she can pay her bills. She's got an insurance payment comin up she's gonna need to pay and life goes on.

KELLY: Okay. All right. We'll do that for you.

CARR: All right. This is gonna be where I die. So y'all don't have to worry about no confrontation with me or no crap like that.

KELLY: You're not gonna let Stephanie see anything like that, are you?

CARR: No, I'm gonna let her run out of here in just a minute. I'm gettin weak anyway. I can't be much longer. I'll be passed out from loss of blood.

KELLY: Are you gonna let me talk to her? I just need to tell her family that I actually got to talk to her, okay? Just let me say a couple of words to her.

CARR: Okay.

KRAMER: Hello?

KELLY: Stephanie, don't continue the conversation. Tell him you want to go to your family, okay?

KRAMER: Okay.

KELLY: Now gear yourself that this is the way you want to go, otherwise we're gonna continue this way. You're family wants you outside, so that's what you need to tell him you want, and that you're ready to go.

KRAMER: Okay.

KELLY: All right. I know you're feeling sorry for him, but your family is concerned, so you need to say that you're ready to go.

KRAMER: Okay

KELLY: All right, just give the phone back to him. Wait like a minute, then tell him that you're ready to go. Then just start walking towards the door.

KRAMER: Okay. (gives the phone to Carr)

KELLY: ...You okay, Joe?

CARR: Yeah.

KELLY: All right, I'll tell her family that she's fine.

CARR: She's comin out. Just give me a few more minutes.

KELLY: All right, but don't hang up the phone cause I want to make sure you're okay and can at least hear what's going through your mind. Okay?

CARR: All right, I'm just gonna sit it down. Just give me a few minutes.

With the standoff going into the fourth hour, Carr again placed the phone on the floor and spoke only with Kramer.

CARR: ...There really ain't nothin left to do. Let you go and kill myself. Good day to die. Sunny day.

CARR: ...Take life for granted anymore. My dad died of cancer. Her dad died of smokin. Both our dads died of smoking.

CARR: ...Don't worry, I'm not gonna let nothing happen. Tell everybody I'm the nicest bad guy you ever met. You probably never met anybody.

CARR: ...I'm hackin up blood. That's a good sign.

CARR: ...I wish I had a picture of Bernice. If I could just see her pretty face one more time before I die.

CARR: ...Tell her my last thoughts were of her. How sorry I am.

CARR: ...They'll put me in prison and I'll never get out. They'll fry me in the electric chair. I'd rather die by my own hands, you know what I mean?

CARR: ...Dear Lord, forgive me for my sins.

KELLY: Joe? Joe? Hey, Joe? Joe?

CARR: Hey.

KELLY: Hey, Joe.

CARR: Where's Bernice?

KELLY: She went out to have a cigarette.

CARR: Is she outside where I can see her?

KELLY: No, not directly outside.

CARR: Do me a favor. Don't let her see 'em draggin me out dead. She's already witnessed her son get his head blowed off, okay?

KELLY: Okay.

CARR: Y'all got a lot of cops out there?

KELLY: I don't know. I'm not out there.

CARR: Yeah, there's plenty. Had all fifty chasin me.

KELLY: All right, let's send her out.
CARR: Give me a second left. I'm gonna let you go.

He dropped the phone again. He asked Stephanie for water, then began repeating everything he already told her and the negotiators, including his trip to South Dakota and the Harley Davidson Bernice bought him. He praised Kramer for her strength, saying she only broke down when she cried for him.

CARR: ...My babies are gonna grow up thinkin their dad was some loser that killed himself.
CARR: ...I'd go out in a blaze of fuckin bullets if I thought they'd kill me. I'm scared they'll only wound me and I'll be locked up wounded. The only way I can feel I can make this right is to kill myself. Maybe somehow that'll make Joey's life better.
KELLY: Joe? Joe, pick up the phone.
CARR: Hello.
KELLY: I'm so glad you picked up the phone. We're ready. Send Stephanie out.
CARR: I will.
KELLY: Send her out now.
CARR: Yeah, she's on her way out.
KELLY: She's out?
CARR: All right. This is hard for me.
KELLY: I know it is. I know that.
CARR: I can't even bring myself to kill myself much less her. So don't worry about her, okay? (to Kramer) I just can't. I wouldn't be able to take it, her comin, me wonderin if she's all right, not being able to help her. Not being able to get her. Sorry I caused you bad nerves and stuff. I'm sorry. But I'm gonna let you go. I want all my personal affects and all my property, anything taken from me released to Bernice. Tell her I only wanted to live to help her. Me livin right now ain't gonna do her no good. It's only gonna cause her pain comin to see me...

As Carr rambled on, negotiators attempted to calm him by putting Bowen back on the phone.

BOWEN: Hey, Boo? Boo?

CARR: Is this my wife?

BOWEN: Yes.

CARR: Hey.

BOWEN: Listen, let Stephanie go.

CARR: I ain't gonna hurt her, baby.

BOWEN: Let her go.

CARR: You got my word.

BOWEN: Okay, Stephanie's pregnant.

CARR: Yeah.

BOWEN: She's got a baby carriage. Okay, now the stress is gonna cause her to lose that baby so you need to let her go now.

CARR: They're gonna fry me in the electric chair.

BOWEN: They are not.

CARR: Baby, I don't want to argue with you. I know they are. Somebody shoots a cop in Florida they fry 'em .

BOWEN: No, they are not. Now let Stephanie go.

CARR: She's gonna live. She's gonna walk right outside. She's got some things, a coupla letters I want you to give momma, a letter to Kayla, a letter to you. Pictures of me and some money. I'm givin you my wallet. It's got blood on it.

BOWEN: Boo, I love you and I don't want you to do this. Don't let me live the rest—

CARR: Baby, you've already lost me. When fuckin Joey got shot, you lost me.

BOWEN: Let her go right now, okay? Don't do anything stupid.

CARR: I'm gonna let her go. But when I do I'm gonna kill myself so I want to talk to you.

BOWEN: Baby, the sun is going weak. It's getting weak. Let Stephanie go, please. Don't do this. I love you and I want to hold onto you. Please let me hold you one last time.

CARR: I woulda got away but my knee went out.

BOWEN: Baby, listen to me. Don't be stupid. Let Stephanie go and let it be me and you. Do not kill yourself after you let her go, okay? Let her go so me and you can talk.

CARR: As soon as they act like they're comin in, I'm gonna put the gun to my head and blow my brains out. I'm so sorry. I've been shot, my leg is broke, but the worst pain is in my heart because I've done you wrong.

BOWEN: Nobody's gonna do anything. They have done everything I've asked them to do for me.

CARR: They're not chargin you with anything?

BOWEN: They're not charging me with anything. I didn't do anything wrong, okay? It was an accident.

CARR: Okay, I'm gonna let her go and kill myself as soon as she leaves.

BOWEN: Baby, don't do anything stupid. Let Stephanie go.

CARR: (sobbing) I want you to know baby that I love you. Please let me go to heaven knowin that you love me too.

BOWEN: No. No. You're not gonna do any of that stupid shit. Now straighten up!

CARR: Baby, I knew this day was comin. I'm gonna kill myself. They're not putting another pair of handcuffs on me.

BOWEN: Baby, let Stephanie go. Don't be stupid. Please, for me.

CARR: The CD of Nazareth. It's got Sunshine on it. I want you to hear that song and think of me, Sunshine.

BOWEN: Boo, listen to me. Don't be stupid. Let Stephanie go and let it be me and you. Baby do not kill yourself after you let her go. Let her go so you and me can talk.

CARR: I'm gonna shoot myself. As soon as they fuckin launch the gas and shit, I'm killin myself.

BOWEN: Baby, they're not gonna do nothing stupid. Let her go now. Please, I'm still on the phone with you and while I'm on the phone let me talk to you.

CARR: Are they gonna let you talk to me when she leaves?

BOWEN: Yes, they are, I swear to you, okay? We're still gonna be able to talk. I don't want you to do nothing stupid, okay?

CARR: I'm gonna kill myself.

BOWEN: Please, no, don't! Let Stephanie go.

CARR: I'm gonna.

BOWEN: Tell her to walk out the door now. Please let her walk out the door now.

CARR: Pray for me, baby.

BOWEN: I love you, baby. Please don't.

CARR: The gun's to my head right now.
BOWEN: Don't you dare! Baby, don't you dare!
CARR: I don't have a choice.
BOWEN: Baby, don't do this!

At approximately 7:20 p.m., while Bowen hysterically begged her desperate boyfriend to release the hostage, Stephanie Kramer dashed to freedom. Although reluctant to turn her back on a cold-blooded killer, she fled for the front door, appearing first in the scopes of Scott Card, Jim Walker and John Bennett. The trio of highly skilled marksmen anticipated Carr might pop into view next, but he didn't.

Following directions from the negotiators, Kramer ran toward the first squad car she saw, where members of the SWAT team rushed into action. Sergeant Rick Kramer intercepted her near the closest vehicle. With officers in full body gear running on each side, they hustled the terrified woman to safety at the west end of the station, past the Indian River Fruit stand and down a grassy ravine.

A collective sigh of relief followed.

High-fives and hand slapping spread through the congested area of I-75 and S.R. 50. Word reached the Days Inn instantly, where tears of joy flowed from Kramer's family members and her boyfriend Chris Hill. Media swarmed to the Mobile Station, where Deanna Dammer shared the long-awaited news.

"The hostage has now been released," she said, as a slight smile surfaced. "The hostage is safe."

Officers queried Kramer regarding any other hostages, weapons, and exactly where Carr was located when she left the station. That, along with other pertinent information, went directly to Mylander, Nugent and SWAT leader Jim Blade.

"We were taking no chances of him walking out and firing shots in a suicidal last gasp," Major Nugent said. "We would not allow him to get the upper hand again."

PART IV

15

State Road 50
Shell Station
May 19, 1998; 1924 hours

As the standoff between cops and the cop killer neared conclusion, negotiators and Bowen attempted to coax Carr out peacefully while the Bomb Squad and SWAT teams prepared for forced entry. The field coordinator warned media helicopters to move at least 1,500 feet away from the station, indicating officers planned to use something far more powerful than a concussion grenade.

The bomb teams set the detonators and cleared the area. Sergeant Diamond and his team took cover on the northwest corner where he maintained visual on the SWAT teams. "I cautioned the SWAT teams to stay below the rise until after they heard the noise. We don't have a countdown because if you anticipate the explosion and look up too soon, the back frag can take your head off."

SWAT leader Minnax assembled his Tampa squad northwest of the station. Sergeant Blade, leader of the Hernando Squad, hid his troops in a ditch west of the station and behind the east wall. With cameras capturing aerial footage a quarter mile away, news anchors reported what they saw.

Channel 8 newscaster Bob Hite described the scene. "As you can see on the right side of the building, there is now what appears to be a SWAT team. The building is being completely surrounded by law enforcement."

Channel 13 news anchors John Wilson and Kelly Ring offered the following account. "If she was the only hostage, he's in there alone right now," Wilson speculated. "If we are correct about that, we can assume that now they will take some sort of action, and we are near what appears to be near the end of a very tragic day for the Tampa Police Department and the Florida Highway Patrol. Based on my experience, the first thing that would happen would be a concussion grenade to distract the suspect, then there would be tear gas fired and officers would rush in and hopefully overpower him before any shots are fired."

"That's a good indication why they put their gas masks on," Ring agreed. "That could be happening."

One on-scene reporter mentioned that SWAT officers converged at the back door. However, no door existed on the north wall. Not a problem. At the appropriate time, Jim Diamond would create one.

"Hernando SWAT is in position," Sergeant Blade reported.

"Tampa SWAT in position," echoed Sergeant Minnax.

For the detonation device, Diamond connected detonation cord to an electronic blasting cap with a hand generator. As negotiations went on inside, he stood by for a signal from Sheriff Mylander.

BOWEN: Baby, the girl's pregnant! Don't do this to her!

CARR: Baby, she's—

BOWEN: Don't do this to her!

CARR: She's gone.

BOWEN: Don't do this to her, Boo!

CARR: Listen, she's gone. She's free.

BOWEN: Okay. Okay, baby, don't do this to me. I love you, please don't do this.

CARR: Listen.

BOWEN: Okay, baby, don't do this to me. I love you, please don't do this.

CARR: Baby, the gun is to my head.

BOWEN: Baby, please don't.

CARR: Listen.

BOWEN: Don't.

CARR: I'm so sorry for killin your son.

BOWEN: Where is Stephanie?

CARR: She's outside. The cops got her.

BOWEN: Okay baby, I love you.

CARR: I'm in here by myself.

BOWEN: Baby talk to me. Listen to me.

CARR: Get your stuff from her.

BOWEN: No, listen it's just me and you now. Nobody else is in the room with me. It's just me and you. Don't do anything stupid. I need you. I need you to help me get through this.

CARR: Listen to me. Are you listening? Listen to me. Today is my last day.

BOWEN: Baby, don't. Please don't.

CARR: They'll never let us be together. I'll sit in jail for years and years.

BOWEN: So what? I'll still be able to see your face and hear your voice and that's what matters to me. And if that doesn't matter to you, then you really don't love me.

CARR: Don't say that. You know I love you. If you think I can live after what I did today—

BOWEN: Baby, it was an accident. I love you. Please don't do anything stupid.

CARR: Do me a favor. Quit beggin me not to cause I'm gonna.

BOWEN: Don't do this to me.

CARR: Quit sayin that. Quit sayin that, baby.

BOWEN: I'm not gonna quit until you put the gun down.

CARR: Okay, I'm puttin the gun down.

BOWEN: Put the gun down.

CARR: It's down. Okay, now quit talkin about the gun.

BOWEN: I'm not gonna until you kick it out of your reach and I know you're safe. I'm gonna stay here and throw my little temper tantrum, okay? Tater made her tantrum. This is Tater and she is showin her ass.

CARR: If you'll just shut up—

BOWEN: Huh-uh. And I'm not gonna shut up until you fuckin straighten up.

CARR: Okay, I'm straightening up, but you gotta listen to me. I love you baby and I'm sorry for what I did.

BOWEN: Okay, they even agreed to give me conjugal visits. See, we can be able to see each other.

CARR: Listen, all that's bullshit. Tell them to quit talkin to you.

BOWEN: Listen to me. I love you.

CARR: Please let me get these last few words out.

BOWEN: No I'm not cause you're not gonna do anything stupid. I'm gonna sit here and keep throwin a fit until you fly right.

CARR: You keep throwin a fit and I'm just gonna hang up the phone and shoot myself.

BOWEN: No you're not!

CARR: Please.

BOWEN: Baby, I love you. Please don't do this to me. Please, I beg of you. I'm on my hands and knees right now praying to God that you don't.

CARR: Baby, I can't.

BOWEN: If I can't hold you, I can at least hear your voice and you can help me get through this.

CARR: Baby listen, I wrote a letter to my mom tellin her to help you out in any way she can, you understand?

BOWEN: I don't care, Boo. Don't do this to me.

CARR: There's a suitcase at momma's. I want you to have everything in it, okay.

BOWEN: Boo, don't do this.

CARR: One day I want you to tell my daughter how much I love her.

BOWEN: Boo, don't do this.

CARR: Quit beggin me to quit. You're makin me—

BOWEN: It doesn't make a difference, Boo. Your daughter is gonna see that her daddy was a punk pussy boy who blowed his fuckin head off. Okay, that's what she's gonna see. And she's gonna say my daddy was weak. Okay. So don't be stupid and don't let her see that.

The crazed and desperate man who held two hundred officers at bay for over four hours steadfastly refused to surrender peacefully. With the hostage now safely tucked away, Sheriff Mylander made the decision to end it: "Hernando-1, we're going in!"

Protected by a small contingent of SWAT troops in battle dress and bullet shields, Grenadier Brandon Ross charged toward the Shell

Station carrying a launcher loaded with a canister of chemical irritant. The weapon roared once, penetrating the first window with a 6-inch shell packed with the chemical agent CS. The canister exploded into the back wall and landed on the floor, and as Ross reloaded, a cloud of gas filled the Food Mart.

CARR: Please, baby, I don't think... They just busted something in here!

BOWEN: Boo, I love you, don't do anything stupid!

CARR: They just busted off a gas bomb or something!

BOWEN: Boo, they did not! Don't do anything stupid!

CARR: I'm dyin here! I gotta go! I love you! I love you with all my heart, baby!

BOWEN: Boo, don't! No! No!...

Ross fired a second canister, reloaded and fired several more. Through the phone and speakers, negotiators in the Days Inn heard the first and second canisters crash through the windows, followed by the faint sound of one gunshot.

When the grenadier and SWAT contingent returned to the safety zones, Sergeant Diamond activated the breach charges and the station exploded. Through a cloud of gas and construction dust, a doorway appeared on the north wall and a gaping hole on the west wall; debris from the walls and roof few everywhere.

Dumpsters at the northwest corner nearly toppled and sections of the Indian River Fruit bins crumbled. A quarter mile away, airborne helicopters rocked and swayed from the concussion.

"It sent a shock wave over our heads that you could feel," Deputy Tom Brooks related with mild surprise. "It really felt like something substantial, not just air."

The Tampa SWAT teams streamed in from the north. Hernando SWAT raced to the west wall, but with the hole too small for entry, they scampered to the front of the station and entered through the front door, where Deputy Mike Beckwith covered them from outside the first window.

The phone line at the Days Inn fell silent.

"I don't hear anything," Deputy Kelly whispered.

"He blew his head off!" Bowen wailed mournfully. "He blew his head off! I know it!"

When the phone went dead, Detective Duran marched directly over to the sobbing Bowen. "I demonstrated tremendous restraint," he said bitterly but honestly. "All I did was yank the headset off her and walk away."

"I could barely see through the irritant," said Deputy Stockton, the first officer to approach the cashier's cage, where he found the door locked. "Once Deputy Fortunato penetrated the cage with a sledge hammer, I reached inside and unlocked the door. The suspect was covered with debris."

Through the headset, Stockton informed Sergeant Blade he had located the suspect. The deputy then pulled out a set of handcuffs and secured Carr's lifeless hands behind his back.

"You don't need handcuffs," Blade growled. "This piece of shit is Signal-7."

"I'm sure he is," the deputy responded. "I'm taking no chances with a possum."

Stockton came up with blood on his hands.

"You better go out and decontaminate," Sergeant Blade advised. "We're finished in here."

Stockton complied. He went outside, located the EMS truck and flushed his hands with fresh water.

Sergeant Jim Diamond poked his head through the oval-shaped hole on the west wall and peered inside. He spotted Carr on the floor, almost within reach, lying shirtless and cuffed behind his back. At the risk of contaminating the crime scene, Diamond spat on the body and succinctly expressed his thoughts.

"Checkmate, sucker."

"The suspect and Deputy Kelly seemed to get along very well," Major Nugent said, commending his lead negotiator. "She was able to keep him talking." Regarding Carr's actions, Nugent said, "Trying to rationalize what an irrational person does isn't worth the time. Three cops and a little boy are dead. You can't rationalize that."

*

The end came just as it started—violently. Along with it, a new phase began: the grief, recovery, questions, opinions, trials and conclusions; in general, the process of dealing with the sobering reality of events that changed an untold number of lives.

Sergeant Kramer assisted in securing the area and setting up the crime scene tape. "That's when I learned that Rick Childers was one of the slain detectives. He and I worked together on the investigation of a woman in Hernando County. They found her with her arms tied and shot in the head."

Once again, the media scrambled around Deanna Dammer to hear the official update. With sunglasses perched on top of her head, she simplified the ending. "We continued to negotiate with him, but that didn't work, so the officers set off a bomb at the end of the building. We entered and found him dead."

Exhausted from the long afternoon, the burdensome heat and the emotionally draining event, Dammer arrived home to an answering machine overloaded with callers who watched the horrific events unfold. The calls came from all over, including several from friends in Minnesota she hadn't seen in ten years.

Reporters zoomed in for an interview with Paula Hill, mother of Stephanie Kramer's boyfriend. "I feel badly for the officers and their families… But now I'm just glad that Steph's okay and we still have her with us."

Friend Brian Hill choked back his emotions and expressed his thoughts of Kramer. "Stephanie is a very open-hearted, down-to-earth person who is always willing to help anybody she can. We're just glad it's over and she's okay."

SWAT teams cleared their gear and loaded the vans. Once the Bomb Squad finished inside the station, the Fire Department checked the entire area and Sheriff Mylander authorized the Crime Scene Technicians to take over.

"To prevent contamination of evidence," Gary Kimble said, "we cleared the outside area first, including documentation of the truck, weapons, shell casing, damage, that sort of thing."

When the CSI team finished examining the white Ford Ranger, a flatbed wrecker transported it back to Tampa. With the fumigant still hanging heavy inside the station, Kimble and Judi Banks obtained air packs from Fire Department personnel, and with nose and mouth covered, latex gloves on their hands, they went inside to document and photograph everything from the floor up.

"The blast homogenized the immediate area," Kimble explained. "The deceased was covered with drywall, concrete, glass, dust, and even money."

Much later that evening, the Medical Examiner removed the body and transported it back to Tampa for an autopsy and later release to Gail Cox, Carr's mother. With little consolation from Carr's death, officers filled out required reports and returned to their respective homes and agencies.

Detective Holland wrote the following: "CS Technician Kimble pointed to the location where the weapon was recovered and Agent Davenport took photographs. A Glock model 20 was recovered from beneath the decedent's body. The magazine was inside the weapon with the slide in the closed position. The decedent appeared to have a wound on the right side of his head, approximately two inches above the right ear… All photographs and video tapes of the crime scene were turned over to the Tampa Police Department."

"If I had my 20 years in," Detective Jerry Clark said, somberly recalling the life-altering event, "I would have resigned the next day. The entire ordeal was surreal, like we were in a movie."

Hank Earl Carr's rampage left an endless list of victims, yet the numbers could have been far greater. Most of his bullets missed the intended targets. Chris Espinosa took a bullet, Deputy Jim Campbell a fragment, and Kevin Luke felt the sting of shattered glass, but Carr's intent was to kill them. Henderson and Kramer looked into the barrel of a loaded gun; many officers and civilians took random fire.

"If Mike Coburn had flown the LOH-6 today," Sergeant Nowlin surmised, "the bullet probably would have hit him. He's a lot bigger than I am."

Tom Nowlin received a phone call from a grateful Ridge Manor resident. "I just want to thank you," Dave Hill told the sergeant. "My wife was on the interstate today. If you hadn't risked your life as a decoy, she may have been killed."

Detectives Batista, Romanyak and Thomas Stefan drove Bowen back to Tampa and turned her over to Captain Price.

"Detective Black and I returned to 411 Franklin Street around 2100 hours," Detective Duran stated. "I told Captain Price that we wanted to interview Bowen one more time. He told us to go on home, but we insisted."

Duran anticipated a difficult challenge convicting Bernice Bowen for obstructing justice and accessory to the murders of his friends. He had a gut feeling that once she recovered and understood the reality of her situation, and that her son and boyfriend were indeed dead, she might not be so vulnerable, and in fact would feel she had nothing to gain by being truthful.

Price acquiesced and gave Duran the green light; the questioning began with Duran trying to determine why she continually refused to reveal Carr's name.

DURAN: You and I know each other from activities earlier today when we were in Hernando County, is that correct?

BOWEN: Yes, sir.

DURAN: What Detective Black and I want to clarify, if you will, the entire chain of events that occurred today. I'd like to start out by setting the stage as far as your relationship with the gentleman that became known to us today in Hernando County, who you were talking to on the phone. Could you please tell me what that gentleman's name is?

BOWEN: Uh, I guess his name is Hank Carr.

DURAN: I'm sorry, could you repeat that?

BOWEN: I guess his name is Hank Carr.

DURAN: I understand that you have two young children, a boy and a girl. Is Hank Carr the biological father of either of these two children?

BOWEN: No.

DURAN: Hank Carr, how long have you known him?

BOWEN: I don't know. Maybe a year or two years. Two and half years.

DURAN: And when you were introduced to him, how were you introduced?

BOWEN: I was introduced to him as Boo.

DURAN: As Boo?

BOWEN: Yeah, his name was Boo.

DURAN: And when you didn't refer to him as Boo, what did you call him?

BOWEN: Baby or Tater.

DURAN: Okay, when did you learn his real name. I mean, some people carry a driver's license and have identification.

BOWEN: I never got to see his drivers license, so I really never knew his real name for the longest time that I knew him. I don't know. I guess I just… I'm not really sure. I don't really know.

DURAN: Try to remember. I mean, did he work somewhere? Did he have a paycheck?

BOWEN: He worked as a lumberer at truck companies. He never got paid by a check. He always got paid cash.

DURAN: How about mail that came to the residence?

BOWEN: He never got no mail that came to the residence that I know of.

DURAN: Did y'all live together?

BOWEN: For a little while, yes.

DURAN: How soon after you met?

BOWEN: I mean, after HRS came out, he moved out. He just came by occasionally to visit.

DURAN: This is in Ohio?

BOWEN: No, this is here in Tampa.

DURAN: Okay, let's go back. I'm trying to get a little sequence of events here.

BOWEN: Okay.

DURAN: When you met him and started dating him—

BOWEN: I didn't live with him until I moved here.

DURAN: When did you move here?

BLACK: Was it shortly after you met him?

BOWEN: I'm not real sure. I just know it was February. I'm not sure what year it is.

After a series of questions, Duran established that she met Carr on Valentine's Day in 1996 or earlier. Sometime later, she moved to Tampa with him, where they initially lived with Carr's mother.

DURAN: Did you know him as Hank Carr prior to coming to Tampa, or was it when you got to Tampa?

BOWEN: After I got to Tampa, I knew him as Hank.

DURAN: How did you do that? Did he get arrested or probation?

BOWEN: It was his mom or something. I'm not really sure how I came to find his name.

DURAN: Okay, you know that his name is Hank Earl Carr 'cause you've already lived with his mother, even though you call him Boo or Tater. You know that Hank Carr is his name, correct?

BOWEN: I just want to go home.

DURAN: I realize that, Bernice, but we still need to clarify a few things.

BOWEN: Am I in trouble?

DURAN: You're not in trouble. I'm just trying to clarify some things about his identity. I know that you knew he was Hank Earl Carr, and I'm just trying to ascertain if it was prior to you leaving Ohio or when you moved in with his mother.

BOWEN: I think it was when I moved in with his mother. I think.

Now obvious that Bowen had lied all along about not knowing Carr's real name, Duran directed her to the subject of guns.

DURAN: What identification was he using to purchase the guns?

BOWEN: He wasn't. He would go to the gun show and buy them, um, from people there. Just from individuals.

DURAN: How many guns are you aware that he purchased?

BOWEN: He had the Glock and the shotgun. And then there's an SKS Paratrooper that's in my name. And it's in the pawn shop under my name.

BLACK: Why was it put under your name and not his?

BOWEN: I don't know. I always wanted it in my name.

BLACK: Why?

BOWEN: The one, because I'm licensed to tote.

BLACK: But a weapon this powerful?

BOWEN: No, I would never carry that gun nowhere.

BLACK: Why was it in your name instead of his?

BOWEN: Because I pawned it in my name.

BLACK: Why didn't he pawn it?

BOWEN: I don't know, sir. I have no clue.

BLACK: He never told you that he couldn't pawn it because he might be wanted?

BOWEN: Huh-uh.

DURAN: When did you take the Paratrooper to the pawn shop?

BOWEN: Um, I just got it out, I believe, at the beginning of this month.

DURAN: Is this the gun we're talking about today?

BOWEN: No, no, no. That's a totally different gun. The gun that shot my son is a totally different gun. The gun that shot my son came from Lawrence just last night. He dropped it off last night. It wasn't exactly like mine.

DURAN: Yours was a Paratrooper. It had a folding stock?

BOWEN: Yeah, mine had the folding stock on it, and it had the, um, the bayonet.

DURAN: Bayonet? A knife at the end?

BOWEN: No, it's not a knife. This wasn't a knife. This is like a real long object and it's not a knife.

DURAN: Why would you use a different name if you knew his real name? What were you trying to save him from?

BOWEN: I wasn't trying to save him from anything, sir.

DURAN: Sure you were. Anybody who has had a tragedy in their life is not even gonna think twice about coming up with a fictitious name, right? I mean, you would have to think about it. You'd have to intentionally do it. So answer me honestly. Why would you identify him as Joseph Bennett?

BOWEN: He asked me to at the fire station.

DURAN: At the fire station?

BOWEN: We were standing on the side of the station and he told me to tell everybody his name was Joseph Bennett.

DURAN: Was your child still in the station at that point?

BOWEN: Yes. They were working on my son.

DURAN: Did you ask him why?

BOWEN: I didn't think about it. My baby is, you know, my baby was all I could see was my son and his teeth. Blood was everywhere.

DURAN: Okay. So the first time you told detectives his name was Joseph Bennett was here at the Tampa Police Department?

BOWEN: Yes.

DURAN: Did you also tell them he was the biological father?

BOWEN: I don't remember.

DURAN: If Joey and Kayla are Bennetts, it would make sense.

BOWEN: I don't remember if I did. All I know is that today was very upsetting for me.

DURAN: I understand that, Bernice. I guess the bottom line here is that when you were at the fire station, the gentleman who you know as Hank Earl Carr told you to tell the police that his name was Joseph Bennett.

BOWEN: And the next thing I knew, he, he kept telling the police officer if you'll just go with me, I'll show you where it's at.

DURAN: Where it's at?

BOWEN: Yeah, where the house was. And then the next thing I know, I'm sittin on the side of the station there and the next thing I know the police officers are chasing after him, and I guess he took off in the car. In my car.

DURAN: But you heard him tell the police his name was Joseph Bennett?

BOWEN: Uhhh, I'm not sure. I don't recall.

DURAN: Okay, but you come down here and tell the detectives his name is Joseph Bennett?

BOWEN: Uh-huh.

DURAN: Knowing he was actually Hank Earl Carr, correct? And did you know he was wanted?

BOWEN: No, I didn't.

DURAN: Let me tell you, when somebody with an extensive criminal history like he has, he's gonna tell you. You must have talked about it at one time or another. You can set there and tell us that you never knew he was in prison?

BOWEN: I think he was in jail before in Ohio.

DURAN: For what?

BOWEN: I don't know. He just told me he's been in jail before and that's it.

DURAN: So, if I understand you correct, you didn't know he was a convicted felon?

BOWEN: No, sir, I didn't.

DURAN: You didn't smell a rat, so to speak, when he tells you to identify himself as Joseph Bennett?

BOWEN: Earlier today when he did that, I kinda thought something was up and then, uh, everything just went crazy today.

DURAN: Did you ask him why?

BOWEN: No, like I said, he had hopped in my car and left.

DURAN: And how about the handcuff key? How long did he have that?

BOWEN: Um, I don't know. Maybe four or five months.

DURAN: What was his reason for having the handcuff key?

BOWEN: I don't know. He just always carried it around with him and I don't know why.

DURAN: Carried it where?

BOWEN: Anywhere he went.

DURAN: On his person?

BOWEN: Yes.

DURAN: Concealed?

BOWEN: I guess.

DURAN: Where did he conceal it?

BOWEN: I guess he would always carry it in his pocket.

DURAN: Front pocket? Back pocket?

BOWEN: Back pocket, I believe.

DURAN: What was his obsession with this key?

BOWEN: I don't know.

DURAN: Whose name is on the lease at Crenshaw?

BOWEN: Uh, I believe there is no lease. It's a month.

DURAN: Is there a lease?

BOWEN: There is no lease, but the rent receipts are in my name.

DURAN: Okay. So you pay cash to someone?

BOWEN: Yes.

DURAN: He receives no mail at that address?

BOWEN: Never. The only thing I pay is gas and that's in his mom's name.

DURAN: In his mom's name?

BOWEN: Yeah, she put it in her name because I have an old gas bill. I didn't have the money to have it all turned on. All the other utilities were included in the rent.

DURAN: Then, today was the first time that he ever used the name Joseph Bennett?

BOWEN: That I know of.

DURAN: And you knew his real name was Hank Earl Carr.

BOWEN: Yeah, I knew that that was his name.

DURAN: You knew Joseph Bennett was not his name, correct?

BOWEN: Yes.

DURAN: Did you know he had that handcuff key on him?

BOWEN: No sir, I didn't. I didn't think of anything like that cause the only thing I could see was my son's face. Okay, his teeth were hanging out…

The detectives obtained the information they needed, but it came too late to save three members of the law enforcement family. Three wonderful sons were already lost—two fathers; two husbands and a fiancée; a grandfather and grandsons. Three dearly loved friends.

Chief Bennie Holder summarized his thoughts during an evening news conference. "It's going to be very difficult…Unfortunately, we're in a business where whenever we suffer a loss, we can't close up shop and grieve."

At approximately 2245 hours, Detectives Batista and Romanyak transported Bowen back home to her empty apartment at 709 ½ East Crenshaw Street. A day never to be forgotten had mercifully neared an end.

When Sheriff Mylander arrived home at 2300 hours, his wife of 32 years seemed to put everything in perspective.

"Hi, honey," she said when he walked in. "Long day, huh?"

Long day indeed.

*

Results of a TPD Gun Trace revealed more disturbing information. Many of the weapons found belonged to Bowen. She had pawned them under aliases such as Bernice Brown, Bernice Bowdon, Denise Bennett, Venus Taylor, Shayla Livingston.

Weapons included:

Remington 1100, semi-automatic 12-gauge shotgun
Norinco SKS assault rifle
Beretta A303 semi-automatic shotgun
Taurus .38 Special
9mm Ruger P89
Ruger P90
Sundance .25
Russian SKS
Astra A74
9mm Kel-Tec P11.

Detectives obtained a warrant for Bernice Bowen, and on May 28, 1998, officers conducted a traffic stop on a Ford Escort with Ohio tags. Bowen was a passenger in the vehicle. She had visited Kayla at the Child Advocacy Center and was on her way to a funeral home to see Joey before his body was flown to Ohio for the funeral.

Detectives Noblitt and Stanton took Bowen to TPD Headquarters for an interview, subsequently informing her that she was under arrest for two counts of aggravated child abuse.

"Bowen then stated she wanted to talk to an attorney," Stanton said. "The interview concluded and a uniformed officer transported her to the Hillsborough County Jail."

16

With consideration for the overwhelming number of mutual friends and co-workers, the families of Detectives Bell and Childers decided on a single memorial service at the Tampa Convention Center for the slain officers. Reverend Daniel Dempsey presented the invocation. Lieutenant George McNamara delivered the eulogy to Randy Bell; Detective James Noblitt to Ricky Childers.

The choir groups united to sing several beloved hymns, including a tear-invoking rendition of *Amazing Grace*.

The funeral procession filled the streets for miles, with police motorcycles and thousands of uniformed officers accompanying their fallen friends to the Garden of Memories Cemetery. The poignant ceremony included the traditional 21-gun salute, helicopters flying in formation overhead, and presentation of the American flag to widows Donna Bell and Vickie Childers.

An emotional outpouring of cards, letters, poems and telephone calls flowed into the eighth floor at 411 Franklin Street, where flower bouquets blanketed the marble monument at the street entrance. The Gold Shield Foundation, a non-profit organization created by George Steinbrenner, issued $5,000 to each family for immediate financial assistance. At the Governor's request, flags on all state property were flown at half-mast. Grieving Americans around the country paid their final respects to the fallen heroes.

"This incident has touched every citizen in the area," Mayor Dick Greco lamented openly. "The people needed a forum to say goodbye and to thank public safety officials for protecting us every day."

"I even received a phone call from a convicted murderer who Chilly and I arrested," Detective Massucci said, remembering her friend lovingly. "He called to offer condolence."

Although the detective pool in the homicide division remained understaffed, volunteer replacements for Detectives Randy Bell and Ricky Childers responded immediately.

"I transferred before the day ended," Henry Duran announced. "It seemed like the right thing to do after what happened to my friends."

Kevin Durkin respectfully did the same.

At John Boy Auditorium in Clewiston, Florida, a town with less than 25,000 citizens, more than 3,000 mourners came from all over the state to honor the trooper and offer support to Michael and Vivian Crooks in their darkest moment.

"The public auditorium was the only building large enough to hold everyone," Lieutenant Guzman pointed out, observing those in attendance. "Just look at the faces of these people. This community will never be the same."

In many ways, the *world* will never be the same.

CHILDERS

Detective Ricky J "Chilly" Childers, 46, of Valrico passed away Tuesday. Funeral services will be held Saturday, 11:00 A.M. at the Tampa Convention Center with Rev. Dan R. Dempsey, Rev. Ken Whitten and Rev. Jerry Sweet officiating. The family will receive friends at the funeral home chapel Friday evening from 6:00-9:00 P.M. Interment will be in Myrtle Hill Memorial Park. Det. Childers was a 19-year veteran of the Tampa Police Department, working 12 years in Homicide. He was a member of the Police Benevolent Association and Tampa Classics Softball. He managed his own softball team, the Terminators III. He is survived by his wife, Vickie Childers of Valrico; two sons, Glenn Corky Harris of Plant City and Ricky Jo Childers II of Plant City; one sister, Fay Childers of Plant City; one brother, Randy Childers of Plant City; and his parents, Roy and Jane Turner of Plant City. Flowers will be accepted and/or donations may be made to the Tampa Police Department Memorial Fund, 411 N. Franklin St., Tampa, FL 33602.

BELL

Detective Randy Scott Bell, 44, of Odessa, passed away Tuesday. Funeral services will be held 11:00 A.M. Saturday at the Tampa Convention Center with Rev. Dan R. Dempsey, Rev. Ken Whitten and Rev. Jerry Sweet officiating. Interment will be in Myrtle Hill Memorial Park. The family will receive friends at the funeral home Friday evening from 6:00-9:00 P.M. A native of Des Moines, IA, Det. Bell had lived in Odessa since 1996 coming from Tampa. Randy was a member of the Police Benevolent Association and a 20-year veteran of the Tampa Police Department, with 10 years in Homicide. Survivors include his wife, Donna Bell of Odessa, FL; son, Chris Hill of Odessa, FL; four daughters, Demetra Jones of Fort Myers, FL, Ashley and Kacey Bell of Odessa, FL, Amanda Hill of Odessa, FL; grandson, R.J. Jones of Fort Myers, FL; brother, Jeff Bell of Norcross, FL; sister, Jennifer Neal of Tampa, FL; mother, Barbara Setzor of Tampa, FL; father Dave Bell of Des Moines, IA; paternal grandfather, Jim Bell of Des Moines, IA. Flowers will be accepted and donations may be made to the Tampa Police Department Memorial Fund, 411 N. Franklin St., Tampa, FL 33602.

Bell and Childers Memorial Service
Tampa Convention Center
May 23, 1998

CROOKS

James Bradford Jean Crooks, 23, of Tampa, passed away May 19, 1998. Services will be held in the John Boy Auditorium, Clewiston, May 22, 1998 at 3:00 P.M. with the Revs. Harold Taylor and Ron Thomas officiating. He is survived by parents, Jean Michael Crooks and Jewell Vivian Hazel Crooks, Clewiston; paternal grandmother, Virginia Crooks, Clewiston; maternal grandmother, Lois Hazel, Okeechobee; great-grandmother, Alma LaConti, Okeechobee; brother and sister-in-law, Jonathan and Michelle Crooks, Chicago; nephew, Logan Crooks, Chicago; niece, Savannah Crooks, Chicago. Flowers will be accepted and/or donations may be made to the James Crooks Memorial Fund, First Bank of Clewiston, 300 E. Sugarland Hwy., Clewiston 33440.

A reporter for the Tampa Tribune spoke with the widows of Ricky Childers and Randy Bell. She captured the affecting essence of their painful recovery progress. On October 9, 1998, the following article appeared in the Tribune.

POLICE WIDOWS STILL GRIEVE FOR HUSBANDS
By Patty Ryan

TAMPA – Relatives of slain police officers will take part in a memorial run Saturday. Two widows describe their own paths.

She goes to a spa, hoping for anonymity and a facial.

A therapist recognizes her name. "Are you *the* Donna Bell?"

The answer brings heartfelt silence.

For the next hour, compassion drives a stranger's fingers. Tears stream down Donna Bell's face into a stranger's hands. Randy Bell's widow would rather cry in private, but hers is a public grief.

Likewise for Vickie Childers.

Their husbands, Tampa police detectives, were torn from them in May by gunman Hank Earl Carr, who also killed a child and Florida Highway Patrol Trooper James B. Crooks, before ending his own life.

"People say you have your memories to console you," says Childers, widow of Detective Ricky Childers. "In the beginning, they don't console. They only hurt you more."

No one demands that the two women be strong. No one expects them to give more. Yet, they will be there Saturday at Curtis Hixon Park in downtown Tampa, along with more than 1,000 others, for a foot race to honor police.

Family of slain officers—recent and past—will wear ribbons. Some, like Donna Bell and Vickie Childers, will walk in the fourth annual Tampa Police Memorial Run, despite their emotional wounds.

"It's a great tribute," Donna Bell says.

Last year, Vickie and her husband nearly attended the third annual run. It meant something different to her then. Then, she thought Ricky Childers was invincible, that somehow, because he arrived late to crime scenes, he would be insulated from the worst of danger.

She worked in TPD records. They had known each other for years. A friendship turned romantic Valentine's Day 1989. She had lost a boyfriend and Childers stepped up with a red rose. Married, they lunched together on Fridays, suffering jokes because they ate spaghetti so often.

Now she can't bear to enter police headquarters. She can't look at photographs.

"I'm hoping it gets better because it's still extremely painful," Vickie Childers says.

She returned to a new city job, away from the sculpture that honors fallen officers. People find it hard to know what to say.

"How are you?" they ask, thickly.

In the beginning, Donna Bell, the eternally cheery nurse, would always answer, "Fine."

It was hard to mean it.

"The counselor said that I need to let go," she says.

"I do, but sometimes it's in my closet or at home or in my car."

She always knew life could be hard. She oversees emergency and intensive care at Town & Country Hospital. She used to make Randy kiss her goodbye every morning, just in case something bad should happen. Her stomach would knot up at night when he got dragged out of bed to a crime scene. He called to say he was okay, but the knot always returned.

That's the only relief now. No more knot.

"When people see us, *they* have the knot," she says. "They have that uncomfortable feeling."

She and Randy had known each other eight years. They met on Friday the 13th and were married on Friday the 13th, each bringing children to the marriage, with a dog for good luck.

Now the dog mourns his master's absence, and Fridays bring another lonely weekend for Donna and her daughter.

Her son has gone away to college.

She sees less of Randy's children. She misses cooking for six. She misses the NASCAR weekends and Sundays holding hands in church.

He was an usher at Wesley Memorial Methodist.

She's reading a book called "I Love a Cop."

It helps her understand some things.

She wears Randy's wedding band on a chain around her neck, next to a police badge and a charm of tiny handcuffs.

Vickie Childers keeps a journal. In it, she writes letters to Ricky. He was the extrovert; she, the introvert. So now, she closes herself off, stays at home.

She wonders what kind of person she will become. Once a week, she visits the cemetery with fresh flowers. One day, she had to dodge bees. She told Ricky about it in the journal.

She finds herself walking around, talking to him.

"Ricky, I've got to get out and pull these weeds," she'll say.

When Donna Bell speaks of Randy, she does so in the present tense.

"He's not here physically, but his spirit is in the community," she explains. "Everybody still feels it. Everybody still feels the pain.

"When you say Randy Bell or Ricky Childers, the name hasn't faded yet. And I'm sure it will, maybe in time, but I hope it doesn't."

She wants to teach children that police are human beings who buy Beanie Babies, coach youth football and raise kids. They cry, get mad, and, by necessity, put up walls.

She remembers the wall of police at the funeral.

"All I could see was the pain in every one of their eyes. They stand so stern, so straight, but I could see it," Donna Bell says.

She goes home half expecting to see her husband's car. She never got to say goodbye.

If God would change the rules, she would make that request. Let people say goodbye.

"Sometimes at night, especially when it's late, I'll be laying there and I'll be reading," she says. "He used to work off-duty. It's like I'm waiting for him to come through the door—and he doesn't come.

"So, no," she says. "I say I'm okay, but I'm not okay. I'm never going to be okay again."

BELL and CHILDERS INTERROGATION ROOMS

Before Hank Carr took the lives of Detectives Bell and Childers, the Franklin Street police facility had no designated interrogation rooms. To conduct interviews, therefore, detectives had questioned suspects inside a large conference room adjacent to the homicide supervisor's office. With deference to the exceptional interrogation skills of Bell and Childers, a consequent renovation on the eighth floor converted a section of space into three interrogation rooms.

Bronze plates with inscriptions commemorated two rooms by naming them after Bell and Childers, with the third room fitted for observation. Vickie Childers and Donna Bell attended the emotional dedication, and Linda Greco, wife of the mayor, formally recognized and honored the widows for their endless strength and support.

*

Kayla Bennett spent many months in state foster care before the court granted custody to her maternal relatives back in Ohio, with Joseph Bennett allowed limited supervised visitation. Although emotionally scarred, the child found a home and happiness back with the people she loved most.

Law enforcement agencies and individual officers throughout the country acknowledged the efforts of Deputy Marisabel Kelly. Better than anyone, they understood and respected her accomplishment.

In all likelihood, Kelly's persistence and patience determined the life or death of Stephanie Kramer. The fact that Carr repeatedly said his hostage would not be harmed meant nothing: with the reality of his situation and immanent death, the outcome teetered precariously on every word Kelly said. With the slightest provocation, Carr may have chosen to make one final statement of defiance and rage, and Kramer was the only person available to facilitate his desire.

"A killer with nothing more to lose is willing to take another life before pulling the trigger on himself," Detective Duran said, when he summed up the pressures on hostage negotiators.

"She put the subject at ease," Detective Batista added. "He felt very comfortable talking to her. The importance of that can never be over emphasized."

Others extolled her calmness under pressure.

In a modest response, Deputy Kelly said, "After receiving many requests to speak about the incident, I developed a training program. Everyone usually wants to hear all the juicy details, but I try to limit each presentation to about two hours."

In addition to a departmental "attaboy" from Sheriff Mylander, Kelly received an invitation to attend a two-week FBI Negotiator Course in Quantico, Virginia, which she happily accepted.

Six months after accepting the PIO position at the Hillsborough County Sheriff's Office, Sergeant Rod Reder incorporated the lessons of May 19 into training sessions on domestic/family violence and law enforcement practices.

Disregarding the fact that Detectives Childers and Bell did not breach department policy, many critics faulted and second-guessed them for cuffing Carr in the front—even though "Joseph Bennett," the boy's "father," had earlier freed himself when cuffed *behind* the back. The officers themselves determined the method of restraint, for they alone knew best how to deal with each individual suspect based on information available. As elsewhere, hindsight rules do not apply. For future safety, however, and to avoid controversy and criticism, the Tampa Police Department issued an official order that no future suspect would be handcuffed with hands in front of the body.

Not unexpectedly, the telephone call and interview by 970 WFLA radio created a furor among law enforcement agencies and various public watchdogs.

"We train professionals to handle those situations," one officer said sourly. "I don't think they teach that in broadcasting school. What would they say if he killed that girl during the interview?"

Many in the news media questioned themselves in that regard.

"Police are obviously listening to this and paying attention to this," a male news anchor stated, referring to the coverage he and his co-anchor presented during the standoff.

"Yes," his partner responded. "And *he* may be listening to this and paying attention. We don't know, there may be a television inside the station."

"Uh, right. Yeah."

Sheriff Mylander and the Florida Sheriff's Association petitioned the Florida legislature to enact laws that would prevent the media from encroachment at a crime scene. The reasons were many: WFLA had interfered with the negotiations, allowing an untrained reporter to obstruct professionals, thereby increasing peril to the hostage; news helicopters swarmed the airspace, endangering officers and civilians in aircraft around them; suspects viewing the television coverage had firsthand information of everything happening on the outside, not unlike having an accomplice infiltrating the perimeter. Aerial footage left TV viewers—and possible suspects—with little question where the Bomb Squad would penetrate the building for SWAT entry.

"In that regard," Deputy Stockton theorized, "if Carr had found his way into a walk-in beverage cooler, effects from the chemical irritant would be minimized. He may have then fired in the general direction of the entry team, possibly leaving another officer dead and a family mourning."

The Florida House agreed and passed the legislation.

The Senate blocked it.

"The news media has plenty of clout with elected politicians," Mylander said, clearly disappointed. "The best we could get was a 'handshake' agreement."

"Sheriff Mylander downplayed his accomplishments," Deanna Dammer said respectfully. "Because of his efforts, the FAA restricted media air space during ongoing crime scenes."

In an informational police video titled *Crossing the Line: When the media becomes the story*, Deanna Dammer revisited the events of May 19. The video opened with the voice of Hernando County dispatcher Peggy Brooks broadcasting the initial BOLO regarding the shooting of two Tampa police officers, then following it with a police siren and the voice of Deputy Bierwiler calling dispatch. "Alpha-10, Hernando, I'm Ten-51 via 476 the Lake Lindsey area…"

Then came the dramatic call from the FHP to Mary Booth. "We got a trooper shot."

"You got a trooper shot?"

"Hernando, all units responding to the interstate, be Ten-18."

"Four-05, Ten-9 that?"

And finally, the emotional call from Peggy Brooks to Lieutenant Rivenbark: "Four-05, we're receiving calls that the trooper is now Signal-7."

The video displayed chronological footage of the news coverage, including photos and names of the three slain officers and the four-year-old boy. Dammer provided the voice over. "On any given day, law enforcement officers expect the unexpected. But on the morning of May 19, 1998, no one could have predicted how many lives would be changed by the actions of one man. The television coverage was immediate, extensive and dramatic during the four-and-a-half hour standoff.

"Early in the hostage situation," Dammer continued, as the video showed reporter Mike Deeson holding a Channel 10 microphone next to a speaker in his automobile, "one radio newscaster crossed the line between observing and reporting the news to being a participant. He was, in effect, interviewing the suspect before the law enforcement officials could start their negotiations."

Excerpts from the interview by WFLA personality Don Richards followed, which incorporated the piece where Carr admitted his name was not Joseph Lee Bennett.

Dammer mentioned that reporters had a need to continue coverage even thought they relied on hearsay and conjecture to describe events leading up to the hostage situation. She provided examples, including footage from the Channel 13 helicopter circling the Shell Station while the news anchor offered his opinion on how the SWAT entry would take place.

The video ended poignantly with the co-anchor who said, "And *he* may be listening to this and paying attention. We don't know, but there may be a television inside the station…"

"In any situation," Dammer said, after making the point visually, "where an innocent person is being used as a barricade between an armed criminal and law enforcement is just a heartbeat away from tragedy. Not all standoffs end peacefully, but they should always be left to those who are trained to take that risk without interference."

In closing the informational video, Ms. Dammer referenced a commentary from the Tampa Tribune written by Kevin Walker and Jennifer Barrs. The title: *Ethics watchdogs wonder about propriety of a Tampa radio station's talk with Hank Earl Carr.*

"Ethical issues related to the live coverage of Hank Carr's radio interview have become a source of concern for law enforcement," said Dammer, "and members of the media have been asked to carefully evaluate the role they played. As one reader advocate wrote in response to the coverage of the Hank Earl Carr incident…"

Dammer then quoted an advocate, Mike Clark, from the Florida Times-Union newspaper.

"News organizations should stick to reporting and let the police handle hostage negotiations."

On a sunny day in Marietta, Ohio, Joseph Lee Bennett and three friends carried a flower-laden casket containing Joey Bennett to his final resting place.

Joseph Anthony Bennett
Rest in peace

17

Hillsborough County Courthouse
Tampa, Florida
May 1999

In two separate trials, the State Attorney prosecuted Bowen on two counts of aggravated child neglect and accessory after the fact in the deaths of three law enforcement officers. The case attracted considerable public and media attention, with the community overwhelmingly agreeing that Bowen was morally responsible for the deaths.

In her opening statement, Prosecutor Shirley Williams told jurors they would be hearing from approximately forty witnesses. She then summarized the events of May 19 based on witness testimony. With nearly every sentence, Williams underscored lies and deception on the part of Bernice Bowen.

In defense of Bowen, attorney John Kromholz emphasized the timing of relevant events, then presented evidence that Bowen did, in her mind, cooperate with detectives.

The first witness, neighbor Alisha Webb, identified the defendant as Bernice Bowen. Webb stated under oath that she was outside the apartment when she heard the gunshot.

"Did you see Bernice Bowen outside?" Williams asked.

"No I didn't."

"Did you see her on the staircase?"

"No."

"When is the first time you saw her after you heard the noise?"

"When she came running down the stairs."

"Did you see any blood on her?"

"Um, I seen little spots on her arm."

Webb testified that Kayla came down the steps next, stating that the child also had spots of blood on her neck and forehead.

"When did Boo come down?"

"After Bernice came down, then she went back upstairs. Then he came down."

"When he came down, what did he do?"

"He went to her car and just sat there for about a second, freaked out like he didn't know what to do. Then he ran back up the stairs and got the baby and brought him down to the car."

Officer John Simmons testified Carr presented ID with the name Joseph Bennett, confirming it as exhibit number 10. Officer Pederson stated that Carr and Bowen were extremely evasive, refusing to tell him where they lived. Corporal O'Connor testified that Bowen said Carr was her husband, Joseph Bennett. Detective Clark took the stand and talked about the weapons he found on Crenshaw Street.

The prosecutor called Howard Bassano.

"What did you know him as?" Williams asked.

"Well…a crazy man."

"I mean, what name did you know him as?"

"Boo."

"Did you ever ask his real name?"

"Yes, and he told me it was none of my business."

Bassano testified that Bowen came to his house complaining that Boo was always beating up on her, but she wouldn't leave him. When asked about an incident he witnessed involving Joey, Bassano said, "He had done something and Boo called him up to the table and Joey was really scared. He put him on his belly on the table and pulled his shorts down and hit him several times. Hard."

"Were you ever with Bernice Bowen when she discussed what would happen if the police ever came?"

"That one way or the other, he would get away. He would kill or do what ever he had to do to get out of it."

"Were you aware that he had been to jail?"

"No, but he mentioned that he'd never go back to prison, so I took it that he'd been in prison before."

"Were you aware that Boo had a handcuff key?"

"He kept it on a necklace or in that little pocket in his jeans."

"After all these killings happened, did Bernice Bowen ever talk to you?"

"Yes."

"What did she say?"

"She came up to the house after this happened and pulled out a bag of marijuana, set it on the table and wanted to roll one, and I said 'Don't do that, I have my daughter right here.' And she—"

The defense interrupted, requesting permission to approach the bench. Judge Daniel L. Perry said, "Come on up."

Williams informed the judge that her line of questioning involved comments Bowen made on a taped interview she would introduce during the course of the trial. After a five-minute recess, Judge Perry denied the defense attorney his motion for a mistrial.

"Mister Bassano," Williams began, "when Miss Bowen came to your house after Joey had been shot, did she make any remarks to you about Joey?"

"She said that, well, my son is dead, they have my daughter, that she felt that now she's a free woman and she's glad that the cops were shot and dead."

"Did she talk to you about missing Joey?"

"No."

"Who did she miss?"

"Boo."

"Did she say that?"

"Yes."

During cross-examination, Bassano admitted a previous felony conviction. Then the court called Detective Massucci to the stand.

At one point during questioning, Williams asked if Bowen ever mentioned her own mother. "Yes she did. She said her mother was going to be real mad at her for what happened to Joey."

"Did there come a time when she told you that Joseph Bennett was not her husband?"

"During interviews at the fire station, Detective Stanton came in and she told him that he was her ex-husband, and that he was not the father of her children. I remember specifically asking her if he was not the father of your child, then how can they have the same last name, or the same name as Joseph Bennett. She got all hysterical and upset and I never got that question answered."

Massucci testified that she witnessed Detective Stanton obtain a Consent to Search the apartment on Crenshaw, which Bowen signed as Bernice Bennett.

Williams asked Massucci about the blood on Bowen's dress. "I noticed the blood splattered on her jumpsuit, so I asked where she got it because I remembered that she said she never hugged her son. She said, 'I don't know, I hugged somebody. It was my husband.' I said, 'Are you sure you didn't hug your son?' and she said no."

The prosecution presented a tape recorder and played the entire interview between Bowen and Detectives Massucci and Noblitt. The tapes and witnesses made it clear that Bowen had lied.

Williams called in Terrance LaVoy, a senior crime lab analyst with the Florida Department of Law Enforcement; a ballistics expert. When presented with the assault rifle that killed Joey Bennett, he was asked if that particular weapon could be accidentally discharged with the safety device engaged. After a lengthy discourse, LaVoy testified that throughout rigorous testing, the gun never fired accidentally, but concurred with the defense "anything is possible."

Detective Jerry Keith explained to the court how he obtained the name and address of Gail Cox, Carr's mother.

"Did she ever mention the name Carr?"

"Yes, that was one of the names."

"Did she give you a first name?"

"No. The names she gave were James and Joseph."

They played the second taped interview, in which Herren proved Bowen had many opportunities to reveal Carr's identity.

Officer Marilyn Lee answered questions regarding Kayla. She said the child told her she was in the room at the time of the shooting. "When I saw Bernice downtown, I hugged her and said I was sorry, and that I know how difficult it is to see your child shot. Her reaction was weird. She said, 'No, no, no, I didn't see it. I wasn't there, I was outside.' I said, 'Oh, I'm sorry, Kayla said you were in the room.'"

The defense attorney objected and Perry overruled.

Lee continued. "I told her I was sorry. I thought she was in the room and had seen it. Then she said, 'All I did was see my baby drop, and I don't know who shot him.' Then I thought, if you weren't in the room, how did you see him drop?"

No further questions from either attorney.

Detective Rick Stanton presented evidence that he had obtained the Consent to Search prior to entering the apartment. He followed it with numerous exhibits (photos) of the Crenshaw Street crime scene, including a pool of blood, bullet holes and two assault rifles. He also identified Carr's Kevlar helmet, bulletproof vest, handguns, survival kits, machetes and ammunition.

When asked what he had overheard Carr saying to the detectives, Stanton gave the following testimony. "He was saying he and his wife were in the bathroom, and they heard a noise, and it ended up being the gun that fell. He went over and picked it up and must have bumped it against the wall and it went off."

"That was his explanation for how the child got shot?"

"Yes, ma'am."

When the prosecutor presented photos of the Floribraska Street crime scene, Stanton cleared his throat, visibly straining to maintain his composure.

"Can you identify exhibits 23 through 28?" Williams asked.

"Yes, ma'am."

Courtroom cameras focused away from the video screen when Williams displayed exhibits of the slain detectives. Detective Stanton said, "Exhibit number 26 is a photograph of the back of Detective Childers' head after it was cleaned and the bullet hole can be seen."

"State's exhibit number 27?"

"This is a photograph of Detective Bell showing the bullet wound to the left side of his forehead…"

After exhibit 28, the defense presented a brief cross-examination. He inferred the officers failed to recognize the danger and, in essence, Bowen did nothing wrong.

Williams asked one last question. "Detective Stanton, did you find any illegal weapons in the house?"

She said *illegal*. He answered honestly. "No, ma'am."

"You may step down," Judge Perry said, dismissing Stanton. "All right, call your next witness."

The State called Kenneth Kessler, a child abuse investigator with the Department of Children and Families. He began by saying he knew the defendant as 'Denise' Bowen, and her paramour gave the names Bo Bennett and Earl Reid.

"Was Miss Bowen present when he gave you those names?"

"Yes, ma'am."

"Did you ask Miss Bowen why she was evasive about names?"

"She stated that she was sort of in hiding from her ex-husband up north, that he was a very abusive person, and that was the reason they were being standoffish at first."

"Did she give any indication why neighbors had filed the abuse allegations?"

Kessler checked his notebook.

"She said they were having a feud with people in the neighborhood and the neighbors were making false allegations against them."

Defense asked one question before releasing Kessler. "Did you find any indications of abuse to Joey and Kayla?"

"No, sir."

Corporal Darlene Wilson, Detective Tindall and Detective Wolff connected the dots leading to the Gail Cox residence on East Paris Street, with Wolff recounting his telephone conversation with Carr. Steve Davenport, special agent with FDLE, took the stand next. He stated when he searched the cashier's area of the Shell Station he had found the Glocks stolen from Bell and Childers. One was empty, the other contained one bullet.

Corporal Mike Rossiter presented the court with evidence that Bernice Bowen lived at the residence of Gail Cox as late as March 28, 1998, leaving little doubt she knew Carr's real name on the day he killed Joey and the officers. He then offered proof Carr used the name James Earl Reid while managing the Crenshaw apartments. Two exhibits presented by the forgery expert came in the form of personal checks written to Hank Carr in 1995, with the authorizing signature clearly that of Bernice Bennett.

"And what do you find in exhibit number 68?"

"Books that describe how you can change your identification."

"And where did you find them?"

"In a brown cardboard box in the master bedroom."

Sergeant Mike O'Bryan of the Sturgis Police Department testified that in South Dakota in November 1995, Hank Carr spent time in jail for assault, and when he bonded out and failed to return for trial, a warrant was issued for his arrest.

Officer Harden provided compelling evidence to the court when he identified a jail booking card, whereas the prisoner named Hank Carr listed Bernice Bennett Bowen as his next of kin.

As incriminating evidence against Bowen continued to mount, Williams summoned Patricia Mercer to the witness chair, followed by FDLE agents Velboom, McDonald and John Wierzbowski.

After Wierzbowski, a forensics and ballistics expert, pointed to a diagram of Carr's apartment, Williams asked how many bullet holes he found in the doors and walls.

"Twenty-six."

The expert slipped into latex gloves to examine exhibit 43, the blood-stained dress worn by Bernice Bowen on the morning of May 19. He walked to the jury box and held up the dress so they could see the blood splatters.

Leroy Parker, another FDLE forensics specialist, next gave the court a detailed lesson on high-velocity blood splatter analysis.

"I'm a crime lab analyst supervisor," Parker began. "I supervise fifteen people. I do blood stain pattern analysis and I do crime scene reconstruction involving trajectory."

Parker donned latex gloves and verified exhibit 43 was the dress he had previously analyzed.

"Please describe for the jury what you saw upon examination of exhibit number 43."

"This dress had two types of stain. High-velocity stain, which are usually consistent with a gunshot. They were also contracted, which means transferred from a bloody object to a non-bloody object."

"Mister Parker, what is high-velocity blood splatter?"

After a comprehensive explanation—including use of the word *usually*—Parker concluded that eight stains on the front of Bowen's dress resulted from proximity to someone shot with a gun.

"Does your expertise give you any indication of how close this garment was to the person being shot?"

"A maximum of four feet. The person had to be within four feet of the impact site."

"Thank you. No further questions."

Judge Perry said, "Any questions, Mister Kromholz?"

"Yes, your Honor."

"Proceed."

The defense attempted to cast doubt by focusing on Parker's use of the term *usually*, making it synonymous with *possibly*. Parker said there are situations where *similar* conditions exist, but in this case, the stains were definitely high velocity.

Venus Taylor took the stand and testified that she had known Bowen for two years, but only knew her as "Denise"; she knew Hank Carr only as Boo or Earl.

"Did you see Earl with a gun?"

"Yes."

Williams asked when. "Just about every time he came over to the house. Big ones, small ones and little bitty ones. And these big things that had a bunch of bullets in it, that covered his arm."

Taylor testified she had witnessed Boo disassemble a gun, then give it to Joey and watch the boy skillfully reassemble it. The point well made: Joey knew how to handle guns.

Adrian Adams, a co-worker from Sturgis, identified the defendant as Denise. He testified knowing Carr only by the name of Eric, and witnessed him with a sawed-off shotgun and practicing Japanese sword techniques.

A second co-worker from the gas station in Sturgis testified that Bowen accused her of bumping Carr's Harley Davidson outside the gas station. "She told me I had to leave the property or she would make me leave," Shirley Salway told the prosecutor. "I said, 'You don't have the right to make me leave.' Then she hit me."

From across the street, Salway's brother Matt Merchant and his friend Chad Wallace saw the altercation and ran over to intervene. While Wallace looked on, Carr came from inside the station.

"He blindsided Chad and knocked him out."

At Bowen's urging, Carr jumped on the motorcycle and took off.

"Did anyone try to get help?"

"My brother tried to call on a payphone outside the station, but Bowen kept hanging up, telling him that he couldn't use that phone. So my brother ran down the street and found an officer."

"Did you hear what Bernice Bowen told the police?"

"No. They went inside and arrested her."

The defense declined to question the witness.

Williams also called Steve Adams, Dwight Hopkins and Andrea Wade, a representative of AT&T.

After asking Adams several pointed questions regarding guns, Williams said, "Did Bernice know Carr carried a handcuff key?"

"Objection," said Kromholz.

Judge Perry overruled, allowing Adams to answer.

"Yes."

The witness finished with confirmation that Bowen had stayed with him and his wife after the murders, and that she had called Gail Cox often without looking up the phone number.

Evelyn Sacks also provided damning testimony when recalling the visit to Pennsylvania in 1996.

"When you were in Belle Vernon, did you find out Bernice was there, too?"

"Yes."

"Did you have a conversation about the warrants in Ohio?"

"Yes."

"And what were the conversations about?'

"About how to keep him from getting caught and the things they were going to do to keep from getting caught."

"What was the plan to keep him from getting caught?"

"Obtain a false identification card for him."

"Did Bernice tell you how they were going to do that?"

Sacks explained how they obtained Joey's Social Security card and his birth certificate to obtain a non-driver's license identification in Joseph Lee Bennett's name but with Hank's picture on it.

"Did you ever see the ID?"

"Yes. It had the name Joseph Lee Bennett with the same hair color and eye color, and it said he was a non-driver."

The prosecutor called in Alisha Webb's aunt, Vivian Macar. She testified arriving at 709 ½ Crenshaw Street at approximately 9:30 and saw "Denise" Bowen sitting downstairs in front of the apartment with Alisha. By the time she parked and locked the car, Bowen had gone.

"I asked if Denise went upstairs," Macar said. "Alisha said she had. Then she said, 'Aunt Viv, stay here while I make some phone calls to make sure some ladies are in the office.'

"So I was sittin by myself facing the apartment and it was real quiet. The next thing I heard there was a big kabloom above me, and I looked up, and I don't know why, but I had a bad feeling. Dear God, no… Then it was real quiet. No screaming or anything. Then I heard somebody shuffling, vu, vu, vu." Macar gesticulated with her hands, like she was playing a piano.

"And I thought, okay, maybe an entertainment center fell over and they were picking it up. The next thing I knew, the door opened and they flew down the stairs, and it was Denise and Kayla. And she threw her hands up in the air and started screaming, 'My baby, my baby!' I started walking toward them, and Kayla was screaming and shaking. And then the guy was there, and he looked at Denise and said, 'Somebody help me!'

"Alisha came back at that time, and I looked, and there's the mother and the dad and the little girl, and I said, 'Someone go give him mouth to mouth, the baby's been shot and he's by himself.' I went back and made the 911 call. I came back out and Alisha had her arm around the little girl. I said, 'Alisha, where did they go?' She said, 'I don't know, Aunt Viv, they left. I guess the hospital.' I asked Alisha to take Kayla in and clean her up a little… They were gone."

"When they all came down, did they have Joey with them?"

"No."

"How long after you heard the shot was it before anybody came down the stairs?"

"I don't know. All I can remember is hearing the shuffling and shuffling, and… them coming down the stairs."

"When was the first time you heard any screaming?"

"When she was downstairs, she was probably in shock, and when she saw me she threw her hands in the air and started shouting."

"Did you hear anybody say anything prior to that? Did you hear anything other than shuffling up in the apartment?"

"No."

"Were you inside when they came down with Joey?"

"I was never inside. I was only inside on the phone when they had gone back up. I didn't see them carry him down or anything."

When Williams finished, Judge Perry took over. "Do you have any questions, Mister Kromholz?"

"Yes, your Honor."

Kromholz reaffirmed Bowen was downstairs when Macar arrived, then mentioned it was a frantic and stressful scene, suggesting she may have been a little confused regarding the timing of events. He asked her several other questions:

"Do you have any knowledge of this individual abusing Bernice?'

"I didn't know either one of them."

"You were never told about them?"

" My sister lived below their apartment, and other than just seeing them there, I knew nothing of them."

"Just one more quick question. Have you ever been convicted of a felony?"

"No, sir, I haven't."

"Any crime of dishonesty or false statement?"

"No."

"Thank you."

On the witness stand, neighbor Katherine Phillips told Williams she often heard gunfire coming from Carr's apartment, and had even seen a bullet hole in the floor.

"Did you know Hank Carr to have a handcuff key?"

"Yes."

"And where did he carry it?"

"Either around his neck or in his pocket."

"Did you ever see him practice getting out of handcuffs?"

"Not myself, but I heard—"

Kromholz objected: "Hearsay."

"Did you ever hear the two of them talking in gibberish?"

"They talked in it all the time."

Defense again objected and approached the bench. After a brief confab, the attorneys dismissed Phillips and the prosecutor called Iris Adams to the witness chair.

"Were you aware that he carried a handcuff key?"

"Yes. When he was at my house, he had it on a short chain."

"What did Miss Bowen say about the handcuff key?"

"I mentioned about the key being on his neck and she corrected me. She said no, he didn't have it around his neck, he had it in his little watch pocket."

At the end of the questioning, Williams asked, "What did she tell you about the conversation with the female detective?"

"She told me the detective had gotten to the ground on her knees and had said, 'Please, please tell us who he is.' And she said to the detective, 'I've given you all the information, bitch.'"

"Did she tell you what she was willing to do for Hank Carr?"

"She would do anything for her man."

"Is that how she said it?"

"Yes. She also said that she would always stand by her man no matter what."

In cross, Mister Kromholz said, "Are you saying she didn't have any remorse over the loss of her son?"

"She was more concerned about Boo."

Kromholz questioned why Bowen would confide such personal information to someone she had known such a short time. Adams had no answer. The attorney also got Adams to admit she never saw any beatings or heard of Bernice ever being beaten by Carr.

On the final day, Williams called Detective Melvin Henry Duran to the stand. "Can you identify state exhibit 89?" she asked, handing Duran a tape cassette.

"Yes I can. I've had a chance to listen to it, and it's an accurate reproduction of the interview with Bernice Bowen on the evening of May 19, conducted by myself and Detective Gene Black."

The jurors listened intently to the recording, and when it came to questions regarding taking the children swimming on the morning of the shooting, Bowen broke into tears.

When the tape ended, Williams queried the witness.

"Mister Duran, in addition to being a homicide detective, is there any other function you serve at the Tampa Police Department?"

"Yes, ma'am."

"Are you a hostage negotiator?"

"Correct. I'm assigned to a Tactical Response Team and Hostage Negotiation Team."

"Explain to the jury what is a Tactical Response Team."

"The Tactical Response Team slash Hostage Negotiation Team, of which I'm a team leader, responds to critical incidents, barricaded individuals. Anytime great danger is anticipated in the apprehension of an individual."

"And have you dealt with dangerous individuals before?"

"Many."

"Let me ask you this, Detective Duran, do you treat someone who is represented to you as a grieving father who accidentally shot his son differently than you would someone you knew to be a dangerous criminal who has vowed never to go back to prison—"

"Objection," the defense said. "That involves an opinion."

"I'll overrule the objection."

Duran answered. "Most definitely."

"If you know an individual's real name, what information does that open up to you?"

"Anytime you do not know the true identity of an individual, as a law enforcement officer you're at a great disadvantage. Because if you have the true identity, you can run what we call criminal history. Placing in the computer the possibility of obtaining a *hit*, which we refer to as a positive response if a person is wanted. It also relates to you an individual's propensity for violence, escape risk, his MO. And if you're not aware of what we refer to as the *special factors* of an individual, your officer's safety is greatly compromised."

"Detective Duran, when Bernice Bowen went home that night, were you aware that she had known Hank Earl Carr since 1993?"

"Absolutely not."

"Did you know that she knew he was a wanted fugitive?"

"Absolutely not."

"Did you know she had helped him in South Dakota by telling police officers there that she didn't know who he was?"

"Absolutely not."

"Did you know that she had gotten a fictitious Virginia ID for him in her ex-husband's name?"

"Absolutely not."

"No further questions."

Mister Kromholz stepped to the podium.

He began with questions about what Duran saw at the crime scene and the Shell Station in Hernando County. He switched to questions regarding Bowen's role in the hostage negotiation, then asked Duran if knowing Carr's real identity would have made any difference. His questions assumed law enforcement should have known the danger they were dealing with even not knowing Carr's true identity.

"With all those factors, don't you think law enforcement can put an opinion together without knowing what his name is?"

"Mere flight alone, no sir."

"All those factors? Everything you've just been asked? Of the dead child… the weapon... the flight."

The experienced detective understood the game. Long before the trial took place, everyone in the nation knew what a dangerous man Carr was, but no one knew it based on facts available prior to the murders—facts concealed by the defendant.

Before the third officer died, Duran knew only that "Joseph Lee Bennett" was a reckless, grieving father who owned legal guns and accidentally shot his son.

"You're detectives, though. You can look at scenes and events and put it together, correct?"

"That's correct."

"Talk about the propensity for violence… Assault rifle? Dead child? Weapons throughout the house? A propensity for violence?"

"At that time, we had an emotionally distraught father. I've seen people react in many different ways. I've seen accidental shootings with a firearm and a child. I've seen homicidal shootings with an adult and a child. You have to work it both ways. We don't go into a scene with tunnel vision."

"Well apparently then we disagree. On those factors, I'm arguing a propensity for violence. You're stating no?"

Duran countered, in essence, that an accidental shooting, panic, running from the scene does not automatically assume an individual has a propensity for violence. Moreover, such assumptions can lead to reactions similar to those of Carr. They may even lead to charges of over-reaction, unsubstantiated conclusion, profiling: charges that defense attorneys level at law enforcement with far less justification.

The detective reacted curiously to the remaining questions, which were too vague or convoluted to give a direct and proper response; Duran handled it well under the circumstances.

"You can't insist a dead man do anything, can you?" Kromholz finally said in closing. "Can you?"

"No sir."

"No further questions." Kromholz walked away.

"Call your next witness," the judge bellowed.

Williams faced the judge and said, "The state rests."

*

After a recess, the defense called Bernice Bowen to the stand, and when Kromholz asked how many children she had, the tears flowed effusively. At the attorney's probing, Bowen testified she had falsely given the name of Joseph Bennett when asked about Carr. He asked why she didn't tell the truth.

"Because I was afraid. My baby had just been killed. I didn't know what was going to happen."

"Why would you have been afraid of Mister Carr?"

"He was very abusive of me."

"What do you think would have happened if you told the officers who he was?"

"I don't know. I just know I was afraid."

"What had he done to you in the past to cause you to be afraid?"

Between sobs, she said, "He kicked me in my face. He kicked me in my ribs."

"Did he ever do any of this in front of your children?"

"No. If he did something like that to me, he sent my children to another room."

When asked what names she gave detectives when interviewed on Franklin Street, Bowen included the name Hank Carr. She seemed to recall most events quite well; however, she had apparently forgotten she only provided the name 'Hank' in a much-later interview.

From that point, the defense asked questions designed to convince the jury Bowen had cooperated from the very beginning. In closing, Kromholz pointed out to Bowen that many of the acquaintances who testified against her had criminal records. Bowen agreed, saying they were all lying. In the case of Evelyn Sacks: "She was jealousy of me for taking her boyfriend."

"To this date, do you believe that Hank Earl Carr committed a criminal act against Joey Bennett on May 19?"

"No, sir, I do not."

When prosecutor Williams confronted Bowen, the tears ended. She turned stoic and smug; her memory suddenly failed.

"Are you telling us today that you did not tell Detective Keene that you knew the shooting of your son was not an accident?"

"No, ma'am, I don't recall saying that."

"You don't recall? Is that something that you would recall?"

"Ma'am, at that point in time, I was really worried about what was going on with my son."

"Let me ask you something—you just told Mister Kromholz you don't recall if you were in the room or not when your son was shot?"

She nodded. "That's exactly what I said."

"You can't recall whether you saw your son shot in front of you?"

"No, ma'am, I don't recall."

"Do you recall telling Officer Lee you saw Joey drop?"

"I don't recall. I don't recall an Officer Lee."

"Were you asked to give anyone Gail Cox's telephone number?"

"I gave it of free will. I gave the address and phone number."

"And what number is that?"

"I believe it was 239-0049."

"Whose phone number is that?"

"At that time I thought it was Gail Cox," she said defiantly. "I made a mistake."

"And you had lived with Gail Cox prior to moving to Crenshaw, isn't that correct?"

"Yes, ma'am."

"And on the days that followed May 19, you called her numerous times, didn't you?"

"Yes, ma'am, I did."

"And you didn't reach her at that phone number, did you?"

"No, ma'am, at that time I was really upset. I'm only human. I make mistakes."

Williams reminded Bowen of the taped interviews she gave on May 19th. "In every one of those tapes you were asked if he was ever abusive to you or your children, and in every one you denied it."

"Yes, ma'am, I was very afraid of him."

"You were afraid of him at nine o'clock that night when he was dead at the Shell Station?"

"I believe I said in the interview that he over-turned furniture."

"And you said he had never struck you."

"Yes, ma'am, I did."

"Why?"

"I don't know why. I wasn't thinking clearly. It was a long day. It was a very long day."

"You were no longer afraid of a dead man, were you?"

"No, ma'am, I was not."

"Do you recall anyone asking you Carr's true name?"

"There were several people."

"And you never once gave them his true name, did you?"

"I did eventually, yes."

When confronted with information on the tape recently played in the courtroom, Bowen lost her memory.

"I don't know," she said, tears welling. "My mind is going in five million different directions. I've spent a year in jail. I haven't even seen my son's grave. I haven't seen my daughter, as a matter of fact."

Whenever Williams caught her in apparent lies, Bowen simply didn't know, didn't recall or blamed her actions on fear of Carr.

"I didn't know that he was a criminal at that time," she responded to questions regarding confiding in criminals. "I knew he had been in jail, but not in prison."

"Did you know that the newspaper in Marietta, Ohio published outstanding warrants on him for drug trafficking?"

"No, ma'am, I did not."

"Were you the woman who was with him in Spaulding County Georgia when he was stopped and deputies advised him there were outstanding warrants against him in Ohio for drug trafficking?"

"At that point in time, I believe the deputies said that they were checking things."

"And did you watch him run across four lanes of traffic to—"

Bowen interrupted her. "The deputy and him went off to use the restroom and the next thing I knew he did run."

"I have no further questions."

Kromholz strode purposefully to the podium, reminded Bowen those who testified against her were all criminals, and handed her a crime scene photo of her dead son.

"Sorry, Bernice, but this is what you saw that day. This is your son, correct?"

The defendant didn't touch the photo. She sobbed uncontrollably and had to be assisted from the courtroom. Once she recovered, she returned to hear final arguments.

"Members of the jury," Judge Perry announced, "I want to thank you for your attention during this trial. Please pay attention to these instructions I'm about to give you. Bernice Bowen, the defendant in this case, has been accused of three counts of accessory after the fact to murder in the first degree, accessory after the fact to escape, and accessory after the fact to manslaughter with a firearm. All of which were alleged to have been committed by Hank Earl Carr…"

The judge then read a myriad of legal definitions, terms, rules and requirements necessary for a conviction.

*

"Okay ladies and gentlemen, before I bring the jury in, let me instruct everybody we aren't going to have any outbursts in here. If we do, then you're gonna have a problem with me. Once this verdict has been taken and I have given the jury their final instructions, no one is to leave the courtroom until the jury has exited. Okay? All right, bring in the jury."

After three days of trial, the weary jurors returned to the packed courtroom. Judge Perry asked if they had reached a verdict.

"Yes, we have, your Honor."

A juror passed the verdict to the bailiff, who then handed it to the judge. A representative published the verdict aloud: "...The State of Florida versus Bernice Alane Bowen, Case number 98-10543.

"...We the jury find as follows to count 1 of the information, the defendant is guilty of accessory after the fact of first-degree murder as charged... We the jury find as follows to count 2 of the information, the defendant is guilty of accessory after the fact of first-degree murder as charged... We the jury find as follows to count 3 of the information, the defendant is guilty of accessory after the fact of first-degree murder as charged... We the jury find as follows to count 4 of the information, the defendant is guilty of accessory after the fact of escape as charged... We the jury find as follows to count 5 of the information, the defendant is guilty of accessory after the fact of manslaughter with a firearm as charged. So say we all, dated on the 20th of May, 1999..."

With smiles, tears and handshakes, the family members and law enforcement officers in attendance hugged each other tightly.

In the penalty phase, Bowen received a sentence of 264 months in the state prison system. But it did not end there. On several counts, the verdict was overturned in June of 2000.

Hillsborough County State Attorney Mark Ober ordered a retrial; private attorney Claude H. Tison Jr. represented Bowen before Judge Ron Ficarrotta. State Attorney Curt Allen prosecuted the case and successfully secured a second conviction and an automatic appeal followed. In an opinion filed on June 8, 2001, the Second District Court of Appeals affirmed the conviction. "The conviction withstood appeal," Allen said. "Her appeal was denied."

18

With a scheduled release date late in the year 2018, Bowen took up residence in the Homestead Correctional Institute in Florida, but she continued fighting the conviction, not only through legal wrangling but also in the court of public opinion. Montel Williams invited her to appear on his show, as did 20/20 and Court TV.

Detectives Julie Massucci and Rick Stanton also appeared in the 20/20 segment titled *Blaming Bernice*.

"Our featured story poses a question," John Quinones said. "What would it take for you to turn against the person that you love most? Tonight I'm gonna tell you about a women who continued to protect her boyfriend even after he had shot and killed her little boy."

Quinones told viewers he had the story of a women who "stood by her man."

A tearful Bowen talked about the shooting, repeating that it was an accident. She wasn't in the room and didn't see it happen.

"Bowen was sentenced to 21 years," said Quinones. "Not for what she did that day, but what she didn't do. Was she accessory to a heinous crime? Or was she a scapegoat, the target of a grief-stricken community seeking revenge?"

When asked how she would describe Hank Earl Carr, she said, "A cold-hearted monster. I can't stand him. I hate him. I hate him."

"But for some reason," Quinones said, after enumerating a partial list of crimes committed by Hank Carr, "Bowen would not—or could not—remove herself, Kayla and Joey from harm's way."

He introduced Massucci and asked about Joey. "A beautiful little blonde-headed boy. He was lying on the ground next to the fire truck, and he had a large caliber hole in the side of his face."

After exposing many lies and deception, Quinones said, "Police have no idea they're dealing with a violent felon. They treat him like a father who has lost his son."

They played the detective's recorded interview with Carr, where he claimed Bernice was in the bathroom when it happened. When Detective Stanton acknowledged that Carr was cuffed in front of his body, Quinones said, "Looking back, was that advisable?"

"They had been told they were dealing with the grieving father of a four-year-old boy who had been shot to death," Stanton stated frankly, looking him in the eye. "If we would have known all that up front, things would have been different."

"Ricky and Randy have numerous years of experience," Massucci added. "They knew what they were doing. I can't second guess what they did."

"Carr had something up his sleeve no one knew about," Quinones told the viewers. "No one but Bernice Bowen… Hank Carr carried a universal handcuff key."

Quinones led his audience through events preceding the deaths of the officers and suicide of Carr then asked several questions: "Was Bernice Bowen to blame? Could the truth about Hank Earl Carr have prevented all that bloodshed?"

Jane Turner, the mother of Ricky Childers, tearfully answered his question. "I can't sleep because I keep asking, 'what could somebody have done to change all this?' And every time, I just lay there and think it all comes around to Bernice Bowen."

"I know the pain they feel," Bowen told Quinones. "Better than anyone. But I did not pull the trigger. I did not kill those officers. I had nothing to do with it."

Bowen defended herself, laying blame on the fact that her four-year-old son had been shot and she was unable to think clearly.

"But why didn't you tell the officers that he was a wanted felon?"

"I didn't know at that time."

"But, Bernice," Quinones persisted, "this man had just shot your son. Why? Why in the world would you protect him?"

"I told you. That's the best I can do. I told you. My son had just been shot…" Bowen spoke of the abuse she endured from Carr. "He has kicked me in my face. Poked his finger in my eyeball. He kicked me in the ribs. One time I thought I was pregnant, he punched me in the stomach. I went through hell with Hank Carr."

Doctor Richard Carpenter testified that Bowen was a victim of child abuse. "She grew up in a home with a sadistic father," he said. "She was terrorized by Carr, and terrified of him."

"Why in the world would you stay with him?" Quinones asked.

"I had no where else to go," Bowen explained. "I wasn't allowed to have friends. We had no telephone in the house. When he beat me, he would lock me in the house."

"If she's a victim of domestic violence," Massucci pointed out, "here was a perfect opportunity for her to say he shot my son. He's violent. He's wanted." In explaining why she had no sympathy for Bowen, the detective said, "I sat and rubbed the back of her head with a washcloth while she was crying. I rubbed her face with a wet towel because I felt sorry for her at losing a son."

Bowen placed all the blame on the officers. "They handcuffed him in front. A man that has all these weapons in the house, okay? A man that just shot a child? They put him in an uncaged car. All he had to do was reach over the top of the seat, grab their gun and shoot 'em. You see what I'm saying?"

Quinones introduced video from the trial.

"He said he would never go to jail," Steve Adams testified. "And she'd stand by her man and go down in a blaze of glory. They'd stick together all the way."

When he questioned her about photos at the Starlite Lounge, with Bowen displaying an automatic weapon and a human skull, she blamed Carr. "That was something way before I had got my children back. That was something he wanted me to do. So I did it."

"But you helped him conceal his identity," Quinones said with a curious shrug.

"I'm not comfortable talking about that."

"But you did, though."

Bowen looked away. "Where's my lawyer at?"

She refused to answer the question.

"Had Bernice Bowen spoken up that day," Massucci said slowly and painfully, "the officers might still be alive. If they would have known that he used a fake name...or that he was wanted in another state...that she knew he had a handcuff key...that he said he'd never be taken alive...those send up signals that something is definitely wrong here."

"A Tampa jury agreed," Quinones concluded. "It took them only a few hours to find Bowen guilty of accessory after the fact. She was sentenced to the maximum of 21 years for failing to cooperate with authorities and 20 years to run concurrently for putting her children's lives at danger by exposing them to Hank Carr."

"Those two children had absolutely no choice," Judge Perry told Bowen during the sentencing. "And those two children, as a result of your choices, one is now dead and one will be affected for the rest of her life."

In another interview, with regard to the reported suicide of her boyfriend, Bowen exhibited anger. "I don't think he shot himself. He shot at those police officers to make them kill him. He didn't have the guts to take his own life."

She also claimed that officers entered immediately after Carr had released Kramer, giving him no opportunity to surrender. But the final minutes of hostage negotiations, recorded by Detective Duran, clearly indicated otherwise. In fact, from the time Carr released Kramer until the first gas canister hit the window, which covered five pages of negotiation dialogue, Bowen continued begging him not to shoot himself and to walk out of the station.

Carr refused and a single, audible gunshot followed. The SWAT team did not enter until well after the bomb blast, which occurred several minutes after deployment of the canister.

"One more lie," Julie Massucci lamented. "Just another lie."

PART V

AFTERWORD

19

Tampa, Florida
July 6, 2001; 1042 hours

Prior to summer of 2001, the Tampa Police Department had never lost a female officer in the line of duty.

On Tuesday, July 3, 25-year-old Nester DeJesus and his live-in girlfriend, Paula Gutierrez, committed armed robbery. For less than 100 dollars, the parents of a two-year old child stormed inside a south Tampa business and bound a woman at gunpoint.

Easy money, they thought. May as well do it again, only bigger.

At 1042 hours on July 6, they entered the Bank of America on Church Avenue. DeJesus, attired in military garb with a blue bandana covering his face, whipped out a MAC-11 compact machine gun and ordered everyone on the floor. As he ran to the teller stations, Paula Gutierrez, who was wearing a blue pair of cut-off shorts and a green camouflage T-shirt, waved a handgun and ordered everyone to keep their heads down.

Witnesses said they were very polite. According to customer John Silberman, they thanked everyone for cooperating.

With a cool nine grand and a dye pack inside the booty bag, the robbers jumped in a yellow Nissan SUV and drove south; a mortgage company employee next door observed the escape and called 911.

Again, relatively easy money. Not much to it. The unemployed air-conditioning repairman could now make the overdue payments on his Nissan, and Gutierrez could do some shopping.

A few minutes later, however, their luck changed when the dye pack exploded.

DeJesus tossed the money on Estrella Street and sped off to the intersection of Cleveland and Church Streets where the couple lived with DeJesus' mother in the Crossings Apartment complex. He left Gutierrez in the parking lot and drove to another apartment complex nearby. At approximately 11:05, DeJesus went back to the Crossings as a passenger in his mother's pickup.

Tampa PD responded to the robbery call, utilizing their helicopter to search for the yellow SUV. Once the pilot located the vehicle, he passed information to ground units. Officers Lois Marrero, Veronica "Ronnie" Hills, James Zipler, Cole Scudder and Gary Metzger began searching the area.

At 11:25, Mark Kokojan stepped out of his Crossings apartment and came face to face with DeJesus, who demanded the keys to his Oldsmobile. Kokojan reluctantly handed over the keys, but asked what the problem was and tried to calm DeJesus while following him to the parking lot where Paula Gutierrez waited.

Officer Marrero, an 18-year veteran, spotted the two men in the Crossings parking lot and parked her cruiser on the northeast corner of the complex. As she approached, DeJesus pulled the MAC-11and opened fire on the unsuspecting officer. Although wearing a bullet-proof vest, she took a round in the neck and another in the side.

"He just started shooting at the officer," a witness reported. "She fell to the ground and didn't move."

Responding to DeJesus' command, Gutierrez sprang forward and yanked the 9mm from Marrero's holster.

Terrified, Mark Kokojan scrambled to his upstairs apartment.

Forty-six-year-old Sherry Williams heard gunshots from inside her first-floor apartment. Then she heard someone yelling about an ambulance and suddenly someone was banging on her door, followed by more gunshots and bullets ripping through her door.

Several other panicked residents dashed inside their respective apartments, locked the doors and grabbed telephones.

When the first 911 call came in, dispatch issued a Signal-35, a *shooting*; police units and motorcycle officers rushed to the scene.

DeJesus grabbed Gutierrez and ran upstairs to find somewhere to hide. From the second floor landing, he saw Officer Cole Scudder come running around a corner.

"He started firing at me," Scudder said. "A bullet grazed my right thigh before I even saw him."

When the officer sought cover, DeJesus kicked at the door of an apartment belonging to Isaac Davis, a 20-year-old university student. This time, he broke through.

On the west end of the complex, Officer Metzger also heard the shooting. He ran around the building to find a body lying face down on the pavement.

"I thought it was a hostage trying to avoid the gunfire," Metzger said. "Then I saw the uniform and realized it was an officer."

Officer Hills ran to Marrero and found no pulse. She remained by Marrero's side, without cover, rubbing the officer's back and yelling for someone to get a blanket.

"It's no surprise that Ronnie risked her own safety to aid another officer," said Sergeant Rousseau, Hills' supervisor. "There's nothing she wouldn't do for other officers."

Tom Shindel, an automobile mechanic from the Lindell Honda Dealership next door, heard Hills' plea and offered a cloth fender cover, which the officer used to cover her fallen friend.

Isaac Davis missed school that day because of the flu, and while watching television, his door flew open. DeJesus and Gutierrez burst in, with DeJesus firing shots at officers closing in on ground level. Davis instinctively hightailed it for the bedroom, but DeJesus ordered him back into the living room, placed a chair against the busted door and forced Davis to sit on the floor.

DeJesus found a phone and called his mother.

Emergency rescue roared to the scene and took Officer Marrero to Tampa General Hospital. The news media converged as expected. Officers laid out the orange cones and crime scene tape; the hostage negotiations began as the SWAT team prepared for duty. While the media disseminated information, memories of the tragic events three years earlier flooded the minds of everyone living on the west coast of Florida. DeJesus and Gutierrez had agreed they would not go to jail, and with the officer reported dead—information they heard on the television—there was only one way out: a double suicide.

They made a pact to do it simultaneously on a count of three.

But first, DeJesus tried the Hank Carr strategy of calling a local TV station; Bay News 9 got the call. After several tries with nothing but a busy signal, DeJesus gave up.

"We'll pull the triggers on the count of three," he told Gutierrez.

With the TPD Tactical Response Team set up in an apartment next door, ready for forced entry, both suspects held guns to their own heads and began the count. At *two*, DeJesus squeezed the trigger and died instantly.

Davis made a dash for the door. He tripped and tumbled down the stairs toward awaiting SWAT members. Unsure of his role in the incident, the officers cautiously placed him in cuffs, behind his back.

Paula Gutierrez came out with her hands in the air, hoping she'd be perceived as a hostage rather than a participant; it didn't work.

While inside an interrogation room that memorialized Randy Bell and Ricky Childers, Gutierrez answered questions until the detectives charged her with numerous felonies, including the murder of Officer Lois Marrero. While Gutierrez chose to live and face the possibility of life in prison for her crimes, Officer Marrero received the death penalty simply for doing her job.

On July 10, the public again turned out en mass for the funeral of yet another law enforcement officer. In a symbolic final radio call on police frequency, the chilling words: "Radio to badge 327 . . . Calling badge 327 . . . Do we have Master Police Officer Lois M. Marrero on frequency?"

A river of tears followed the non-response.

"Our men and women never know what's awaiting them when they round those dark corners pursuing suspects," Joe Durkin said, referring to the inherent dangers. "Sometimes it's tragedy."

20

Bergen County, New Jersey
Thursday, April 17, 2003

The first female officer hired by the Fair Lawn Police Department earned respect from her male counterparts both as an officer and as a friend. Patrolman Mary Ann Collura eventually became know as "Mom" to the younger officers. She fit the role perfectly, exhibiting care and compassion not only for the welfare of her fellow officers, but also the citizens of New Jersey, the people she served.

Three days before Easter Sunday, Fair Lawn Patrolman Collura and Clifton Patrolman Steven Farrell responded to a call that led to a 23-year-old suspect named Omar Marti, a Hispanic/Black male. The officers took him to the ground prone, with his hands beneath his torso. While attempting to cuff Marti's hands, a struggle ensued.

The officers rolled the suspect to his side, looking for an opening to blast him in the eyes with a dose of mace. Just as Officer Farrell released the burning liquid, Marti pulled a handgun from under his shirt and fired wildly at both officers, wounding Farrell and killing Mary Ann Collura.

On April 18, 2003, Bergen County issued a warrant for Marti's arrest for the murder of Collura and attempted murder of Farrell. The investigation and manhunt began, and on the following day, at 2205 hours, a series of BOLO faxes reached Hernando County in Florida.

The Fair Lawn, New Jersey Police Department and the Bergen County Prosecutor's Office is currently seeking the below vehicle. The vehicle is wanted for the homicide of a Fair Lawn Police Officer and shooting of a Clifton, New Jersey Police Officer. Description is as follows: 1987 Oldsmobile Cutlass Supreme, 2 door gray. NJ registration KLM 81P. Use extreme caution. The party is considered armed and dangerous.

...Sustpect's name is Omar Marti...Any information regarding this incident or suspect please contact Fair Lawn Police...

...Alert to all patrol units and Florida police agencies...Wanted suspect in shooting death of police officer...Suspect Omar Marti DOB/01-31-1980 is wanted for the murder of police officer in New Jersey and may be traveling in the state of Florida...Suspect may be traveling with a second male party identified as Manuel Brignoni DOB/10-15-1976.

Photograph of suspect may be viewed at www.BCPO.net.For additional information, contact the Bergen County Prosecutor's Office Homicide Squad at 201-646-2518/3080...

Hernando County Deputy Bierwiler received a promotion to sergeant within months after the Hank Earl Carr incident in 1998, and on April 20, 2003, he answered Roll Call at 0500 hours.

"Easter Sunday and I hadn't even seen my kids yet," the sergeant said. "Lieutenant Blade handed me a BOLO in reference to a subject wanted for the murder of a police officer in New Jersey."

The information included a photograph of the suspect along with an address of relatives on Reynolds Street in Ridge Manor, a zone covered by Bierwiler.

"Keep an eye open for this guy," Blade said.

Bierwiler gave copies of the BOLO to Corporal Lawrence "Bo" Amann and Deputy John Melanson, requesting they meet at Highway 301 and State Road 50 to conduct a drive-by of the Reynolds Street address. The officers met outside a Circle K.

"I drove by the address," Bierwiler said, "where I saw the suspect sitting on the front porch of a double-wide mobile home."

Bierwiler proceeded past the residence and noticed a Cutlass matching the description provided by the BOLO. He advised Amann and Melanson to cover the only two exits from the area. Upon arrival at the intersection, Deputy Melanson observed the suspect's vehicle coming toward him.

"I followed the Oldsmobile at about 100 yards," Melanson said. "When he slowed to turn east on State Road 50, I read the tag number and determined it was the vehicle out of New Jersey."

The three officers took up pursuit, with Bierwiler giving the order to conduct a felony traffic stop. When Melanson activated his emergency lights, the suspect accelerated and fired several shots at the officer with a handgun. Melanson took evasive action, and Sergeant Bierwiler took the lead, pursuing the suspect at high speeds. When the suspect fired more rounds, Bierwiler ducked low and backed off, then pulled closer as the shooter reloaded his gun. When the chase entered Sumter County, the suspect fired at a Sumter County deputy approaching from the opposite direction. Then he turned north on County Road 469, where Sumter Deputies Thomas Williams and Daniel Button prepared to intercept with Stingers.

"The suspect obtained a rifle from the back seat," Bierwiler next reported. "He fired through the back window and used the barrel of the weapon to clear out the remaining shattered glass of the window that obstructed his view."

When Sumter deputies deployed their Stinger, the suspect veered onto the right shoulder, barely missed the spikes, and continued firing at pursuing officers.

Sergeant Lanny Corlew, another member of the 1998 Lockhart Gang, monitored the chase and heard Bierwiler say they went north toward Center Hill. "I was approaching 471 at that time," Corlew stated. "So I turned north to run parallel with the units."

From Center Hill, the suspect turned west on State Road 48, speeding directly toward the intersection of 471. Corlew and Deputy Claudio Alleyne parked on the shoulder and removed the Stinger from the sergeant's trunk.

While Alleyne held the pull rope, Corlew set up with his M-14. This time the suspect swerved toward the patrol unit.

"I had to back away," Corlew said. "But the suspect ran over the spikes and almost lost control of his vehicle. He continued westbound on 48."

Deputy Melanson said, "After traveling approximately one mile, the Oldsmobile came to a stop just north of County Road 561."

With both left tires flattened, the suspect abruptly stopped in the middle of the roadway and exited the driver's door holding a shotgun. Less than 100 yards back, Sergeant Bierwiler screeched to a stop and jumped out with his shotgun ready. Standing behind the door of his patrol unit, Bierwiler exchanged fire, and when the suspect reentered the Cutlass to retrieve another weapon, Bierwiler ran to the trunk of his cruiser and pulled out an M-14 rifle.

Other officers rushed to assist, including Deputies Tom Brooks, Joseph Montali, Kevin Smith, Amanda Pugh, Allyene, Melanson and Sergeant Corlew.

The deputies took cover behind their vehicles and exchanged shots with the suspect before he started running north, reloading his weapon as he darted back and forth. Sergeant Bierwiler entered his patrol unit and moved it forward, past the Cutlass, providing cover for the officers on foot.

When the suspect turned and resumed the shootout, Bierwiler fired back. Simultaneously, Deputy Bo Amann took a position on the left side of Bierwiler's vehicle and returned fire.

"At that point, the suspect fell to the ground."

"I heard shots discharge and several rounds flew over my head," Alleyne confirmed. "After the shots stopped, I saw the suspect lying on the ground bleeding."

Deputy Kevin Smith accompanied the incapacitated prisoner to Lakeland Regional Hospital in a Bayflight helicopter. None of the officers claimed credit for the fatal shot, a head wound. To them, the desirable ending resulted from a team effort, and credit went to both agencies and every individual involved.

At 1136 hours, Smith called dispatch. "Subject is Signal-7."

Another cop killer met a fitting end. Omar Marti would never again take the life of an innocent person, police officer or otherwise.

Deputy Carlos Douglas contacted detectives back in New Jersey, informing Russell Christiana and David Delucca of the death and continued manhunt for second suspect, Manuel Brignoni. Later that summer, an organization called the New Jersey Honor Legion invited the Sumter and Hernando officers to join them in honoring Mary Ann Collura. The Legion covered all expenses, including a stretch limo into New York to see the Statue of Liberty and a visit to the Atlantic City casinos. Over 300 men and women of law enforcement attended.

"The reception was overwhelming," Thomas Williams said.

"Hospitality out of this world," Button agreed.

Honor Legion Trustee Sgt. Peter Vilardi awarded Helen Collura, mother of Mary Ann, with an honorary plaque and presented medals to each officer. The NJHL held a 50-50 raffle, agreeing to donate its 50 percent split to the Mary Ann Collura Scholarship Fund. Sergeant Mike Koldij from the New Jersey Police Department won the raffle and promptly donated his $850 to the Fund.

"They treated us like royalty," Sergeant Bierwiler said humbly. "Heck, we were only doing our jobs."

Perhaps. But whenever someone—anyone—risks his own life to protect and serve the community, the folks in New Jersey believe that person deserves special recognition.

*

In memory of the slain detectives, Sergeant Grossi kept the June 1998 desk calendar on which he had marked the schedule changes required when Detective Bell moved to Internal Affairs. When Grossi retired, the revered calendar was passed to his successor, Jerry Clark. When Detective Clark transferred to the personnel department, he assigned the calendar to the protective care of Detective Bert Batista, where in now remains.

When Sheriff Mylander retired in the year 2000, Hernando County went to the polls in November, and on the first day of January 2001, Sheriff Richard Nugent took command.

In February 2003, Detective Henry Duran earned his first Super Bowl ring while providing personal security for Coach Jon Gruden of the Tampa Bay Buccaneers.

August 2003, newly elected Mayor of Tampa, Pam Iorio, appointed Stephen Hogue as Tampa Police Chief.

Vickie Childers remained with the Tampa Police Department; Donna Bell remarried and moved to Georgia.

In a 2004 video titled "Honoring the Fallen," produced by Captain Robert Guidara, Tampa Police Chief Steve Hogue paid tribute to all 25 officers of the Tampa Police Department who had lost their lives protecting the citizens of Tampa.

The svelte, gray-haired Chief strode proudly and purposefully to the gravesite of Officer John McCormick.

"Officer McCormick became the first officer to die in the line of duty," Hogue said, "in September, 1895, when he was shot and killed while investigating a disturbance."

The Chief then offered a solemn tribute to each officer, including a mention of how and where they died.

Officer JOHN McCORMICK; September 1895
Captain SAMUEL CARTER; June 1905
Officer JAMES RONCO; May 1916
Officer HENRY LETT; September 1922
Sergeant THOMAS CHEVIS; April 1938
Officer BRYAN REESE; August 1935
Detective JOE NANCE; October 1939
Vice Chief ARTHUR BERRY; January 1941
Detective LESTER HENLEY; April 1941
Officer RICHARD BOOTH; November 1943
Officer MORRIS LOPEZ; July 1949
Officer CARL CHASTAIN; February 1958
Officer ROLLA STANDAU; November 1963
Officer WILLIAM KRIKAVA; January 1965
Corporal JOHN COLLIER; December 1970
Detective KENNETH BERLIN, Jr.; September 1975
Sergeant RICHARD CLOUD; October 1975
Officer ANTHONY WILLIAMS; November 1975
Detective GERALD RAUFT; July 1981
Sergeant GARY PRICHER; November 1983
Officer PORFIRIO SOTO, Jr.; December 1988
Officer NORRIS EPPS, Jr.; January 1995
Detective RANDY BELL; May 1998
Detective RICKY CHILDERS; May 1998
Officer LOIS MARRERO; July 2001

Next on the video, from inside the Tampa Police Museum on 411 Franklin Street, where all 25 photos adorn the wall, Retired Chief Clayton Briggs announced the museum hours of operation. "Here," he then added, "you can pay tribute to Vice Chief Arthur Berry, who is memorialized on the Wall of Honor along with 24 other officers who have lost their lives in the line of duty."

Chief Hogue closed the video: "On behalf of the Tampa Police Department, may you and your family always be safe."

On April 20, 2004, Deputy David Abella tragically became the first officer at the Hillsborough County Sheriff's Office to die in the line of duty in over seventeen years. At age 26, the officer responded to an emergency call, swerved to avoid a slow moving semi, struck two utility poles and died at the hospital.

Let them never be forgotten

THE MONUMENT

I never dreamed it would be me,
my name for all eternity.
Recorded here at this hallowed place,
alas, my name, no more my face.
"In the Line of Duty" I hear them say,
my family now the price to pay.
My folded flag stained with their tears,
we only had those few short years.
The badge no longer on my chest,
I sleep now in eternal rest.
My sword I pass to those behind,
and pray they keep this thought in mind.
I never dreamed it would be me,
and on my heavy heart and bended knee,
I ask from all those here from the past:
Dear God, let my name be the last.

George Hahn, L.A.P.D., Retired

MISS ME BUT LET ME GO

When I come to the end of the road,
and the sun has set for me,
I want no rites in a gloom-filled room,
why cry for a soul set free?
Miss me a little, but not too long,
and not with your head bowed low.
Remember the love that once was shared,
and miss me, but let me go.
For this is a journey we all must take,
and each must go alone.
It's all part of the Master's plan,
a step on the road to home.
When you are lonely and sick of heart,
go to the friends we know,
and bury your sorrows in good deeds,
and miss me, but let me go.

Author unknown

NOTE TO THE READER

A percentage of *Signal-7* royalties will be donated to the National Law Enforcement Officers Memorial Fund and the Gold Shield Foundation, Inc. When promoted at events by any other organization or agency, the full donation from books sold at each event will go to the organization sponsoring that event.

For information on the above mentioned non-profit and benevolent organizations, please read the following pages.

THE GOLD SHIELD FOUNDATION, INC.

A foundation to provide immediate financial assistance and a college education or vocational training for the families of law enforcement officers and firefighters of Hillsborough, Pinellas, Citrus, Hernando, Pasco and Marion Counties killed in the line of duty.

A Non-Profit Foundation comprised of concerned, civic-minded citizens.

History of the Gold Shield Foundation, Inc.

In 1981, two firefighters and one police officer were killed in Hillsborough County in the line of duty, leaving behind widows and dependent children.

George M. Steinbrenner, principal owner of the New York Yankees, organized a group of concerned civic-minded citizens to insure that the families of these and subsequent fallen heroes receive early financial assistance and are guaranteed funds toward a college education.

Membership in the Foundation is select and is supported by dues, donations and special events.

Based on generous donations from the Steinbrenner family and the New York Yankees, the Foundation in 1989 was expanded to include local, state and federal law enforcement officers and firefighters in Pinellas County. Citrus County was included for coverage in 1997. Hernando and Pasco joined in 1999, and Marion County followed in 2004.

Purpose of The Gold Shield Foundation, Inc.

The Gold Shield Foundation was founded to provide immediate financial assistance and to insure a college education or vocational training for the spouse and dependent children of law enforcement officers and firefighters of Hillsborough, Hernando, Pinellas, Citrus, Pasco and Marion Counties killed in the line of duty.

Financial assistance in the form of $5,000 is provided to the slain hero's family to assist in their time of need.

Financial educational assistance is provided as scholarship to cover tuition, books and fees, as well as room and board (at State of Florida University rates). The foundation's policies are set by a Board of Directors whose members represent broad community interests with diversified business and professional backgrounds.

The Foundation is a 501(c)(3) organization supported by an initial membership fee of $300 and annual dues of $100, as well as contributions from concerned citizens and companies.

Contact Information:

The Gold Shield Foundation, Inc.
P.O. Box 271791
Tampa, Florida 33688-1791
Joe Voskerichian (813) 969-0417

NATIONAL LAW ENFORCEMENT OFFICERS MEMORIAL

National
Law Enforcement Officers
MEMORIAL FUND Inc.

"It is not how these officers died that made them heroes, it is how they lived."

The National Law Enforcement Officers Memorial was dedicated in 1991 by President George Bush. It honors all of America's federal, state and local law enforcers. Inscribed on the Memorial's blue-gray marble walls are the names of more than 15,000 officers who have been killed in the line of duty, dating back to the first known death in 1792.

Designed by Washington D.C. architect Davis Buckley, the memorial sits on three acres of federal land called Judiciary Square. The site has served for over 200 years as the seat of our nation's judicial branch of government. A glance around the space finds plush carpets of grass, nearly 60,000 plants and 128 trees decorating the Memorial grounds. Each year, around the first of April, some 14,000 daffodils make the Memorial one of Washington's most spectacular attractions.

Bordering the Memorial's beautifully landscaped park are two tree-lined *pathways of remembrance* where the names of the fallen officers are engraved. Each of the pathway entrances are adorned with a powerful statuary grouping of a lion protecting its cubs. The bronze statues were sculpted by Raymond Kaskey. They symbolize the protective role of law officers and convey the strength, courage and valor that are hallmarks of those who serve the law enforcement profession. An inscription on the Memorial wall explains the uplifting spirit that is felt by every visitor: "In valor, there is hope."

The Memorial includes a Visitors Center, with plans currently underway to establish the National Law Enforcement Museum scheduled for opening in 2009.

400 7th Street, N.W., Suite 300
Washington, D.C. 20004
(202) 737-3400

www.nleomf.com
info@nleomf.com

(Logo on back cover provided by the National Law Enforcement Officers Memorial Fund.)

A PART OF AMERICA DIED

Somebody killed a policeman today,
and a part of America died.
A piece of our country he swore to protect,
will be buried with him at his side.
The suspect who shot him will stand up in court,
with counsel demanding his rights,
while a young widowed mother must work for her kids,
and spend alone many nights.
The beat that he walked was a battlefield, too,
just as he'd gone off to war.
Though the flag of our nation won't fly at half mast,
to his name they will add a gold star.
Yes, somebody killed a policeman today.
It happened in your town or mine.
While we slept in comfort behind locked doors,
a cop put his life on the line.
Now his ghost walks a beat on a dark city street,
and he stands at each rookie's side.
He answered the call and gave us his all,
and a part of America died.

Author unknown

Detective Henry Duran
Tampa Police Memorial
411 Franklin Street

Deputies Stephen and Marisabel Kelly
K-9 Unit and Hostage negotiator
Hernando County Sheriff's Office

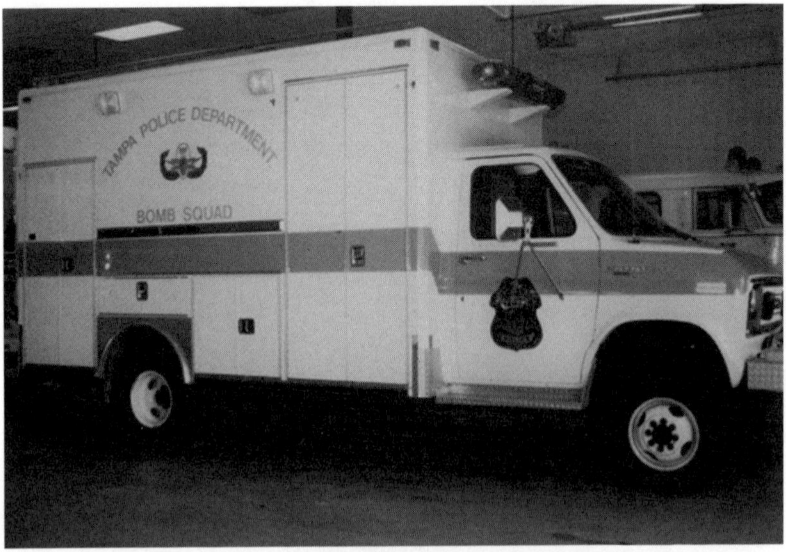

Tampa Police Department SWAT
Bomb Disposal Truck

Hernando County SWAT in training
Deputy Bert Stockton
"I'm taking no chances with a possum."

Pinellas County Sheriff's Office
Lieutenant Wayne Morris & "Peacekeeper"

Florida Highway Patrol Memorial
Tampa, Florida

—Other published work by the author—

IT'S ONLY A MOUNTAIN

Dick and Rick Hoyt: Men of Iron

In Dick Hoyt's world, the difference between a hill and a mountain is something called attitude. Along with their courage and determination, the Hoyt family conquered many mountains over the past forty years, literally and figuratively. They were devastated when their first son was born with cerebral palsy, a non-vocal quadriplegic, but they accepted the challenge. Rather than put Rick in an institution and forget him—as recommended by the doctors—they gave him a life unlike any other.

ESPN, ABC and NBC brought national attention to Team Hoyt when they conquered Ironman Hawaii and again when they traversed the Rocky Mountains on a bicycle. Dick tethers himself to a rubber dinghy and tows his adult son 2.4 miles in the Pacific Ocean. He then straps him to a seat on the front of a custom-built bicycle and pedals 112 miles. Next, they complete the Ironman events by running 26 miles, a marathon, with Rick seated in a *running chair*. Tremendous accomplishment, but they represent only a couple of rungs on Team Hoyt's inspirational ladder.

If you expect a simple sports biography, or a story about a man competing in triathlons and marathons, you are in for a pleasant surprise; it's not what you will find between the covers of this book. Instead, prepare for an emotional saga about the accomplishments of a handicapped person surrounded by a family motivated by love for one another as well as for humanity in general.

RIDING THE ROCK

Love and Murder in Morro Bay

On a typical workday, Nick Veldhouse escorts tourists from Morro Bay to Hearst Castle. Susan Martin frequently visits the Central Coast, usually alone, and occasionally takes one of the tours offered at the Castle. During one of her trips, she meets Nick, her tour guide, who introduces her to a lifestyle that she finds more favorable than the one she has in San Diego.

While Susan struggles to resolve the immediate problems in her personal and social life, a fatal and fiery explosion rocks Morro Bay. It appears to be an accident.

Nick and Susan share an emotional and eventful weekend together, but not everyone approves of their romantic merger. In fact, several individuals take rather drastic measures to sever the budding relationship before the initial spark has a chance to become a roaring fire.

The challenge for Susan and Nick, therefore, is to stay alive and healthy long enough to enjoy the rest of their lives together. In order to achieve that lofty goal, however, Nick finds himself taking an unscheduled scamper up the south side of Morro Rock, the historical landmark of Morro Bay.

For Nick and Susan, events and dialogue regarding the Rock prove to be a double entendre. On one hand, it represents moments of unbridled bliss between two lovers; while on the other, it refers to the illegal—and potentially fatal—activity the local residents call *Riding the Rock.*

MANNING TURNPIKE

From the screenplay, **NEVER A TOUCHDOWN**

Following the DUI-related death of a JV quarterback at Central High School in downtown Bakersfield, California, the court sentences the drunken driver to probation and his employer suspends him from duty—with pay.

Russell Manning, the boy's distraught father, soon becomes the primary suspect in the subsequent murders of two people who were involved in the "justice" process. In fact, even Manning's closest friend and jogging partner—the assistant D.A. who unsuccessfully prosecuted the drunken driver—is not completely convinced of Russell's innocence.

EIKO

A Romance Novel

A Midwestern farmboy stumbles naively into the unforgiving world of sex, romance, fatherhood, matrimony and love, but not necessarily in that order.

About the author

In 1961, Sam Nall left his hometown of Corwith, Iowa to join the United States Air Force. After completing four years of active duty, including two years in Japan, he lived most of the next 30 years in California and moved to Florida in 1996.

Sam is married to Marie Nall, father of Scott and Shelly Nall, father-in-law to Laura Nall, and the grandfather of Madelyn "Maddie" Grace Nall. When not writing books, screenplays or plays, Sam swims, bikes, and runs, competing regularly in triathlons. Based on 2003 accomplishments, he is currently an Age-Group All-American triathlete, ranked by USA Triathlon #1 in Florida and #7 in the USA.

Sam and Marie currently live in St. Petersburg, Florida, but will soon move to the lovely village of Homosassa.

Sam Nall
Ready to race: 2004

—Books in progress—

THE SKYWAY IS DOWN!

Based on the true story about the 1980 Skyway Bridge disaster in Tampa Bay, Florida. Thirty-five people died, including the bus driver and all 23 passengers aboard a Greyhound Bus, when a 20,000-ton freighter crashed into an unprotected piling that supported the Skyway Bridge. Genesis for the book title is the chilling (actual) Mayday call to the Coast Guard.

BLOOD RIVER

A collegiate swimmer seeks revenge and closure after his wife is swept to her death by the mighty Blood (Kern) River.

For book-signing events contact:

Sam Nall
samnall@juno.com

For additional copies contact Southern Heritage Press:

1-800-282-2823
soherpress@aol.com